*To my wonderful and competent wife, Norma,
who has continued with me on my route,
and to Amy and Ellie,
our delightful daughters, who have made the route
altogether worthwhile,
and to Michael and José, our sons-in-law,
and to our granddaughters,
Rachel, Emily, and Allison—
I give this to all of you as my gift, and wish for you
a most successful route.*

P.J.'s Route
A MEMOIR

Paul Johnson

SUNBELT EAKIN   Austin, Texas

For CIP
information,
please access:
www.loc.gov

FIRST EDITION
Copyright © 2002
By Paul Johnson
Published in the U.S.A.
By Sunbelt Eakin Press
A Division of Sunbelt Media, Inc.
P.O. Drawer 90159
Austin, Texas 78709-0159
email: sales@eakinpress.com
website: www.eakinpress.com
ALL RIGHTS RESERVED.
1 2 3 4 5 6 7 8 9
1-57168-748-3

Contents

Preface	vii
Acknowledgments	xi
Introduction	xiii
1/The Message	1
2/The Tools	9
3/Building, Moving, and Learning	15
4/Adventuring in My Town	27
5/Pre-Sub Days	38
6/Subbing	52
7/Learning More about My Route	71
8/Route 7	80
9/The Family Picture	93
10/Fall of '41	100
11/The Months After	112
12/Dog Days	125
13/Which Way Is Up?	134
14/Energized	141

15/Worms, Donuts, and Nose Pickers	152
16/As Time Goes By	165
17/The Friday Double-Hitter	179
18/What's Money, Anyway?	190
19/The Route Continues	198
20/Understanding Dad	212
21/The Ending and the Beginning	219
Epilogue	227

Preface

This seventy-one-year-old author had a very pleasant few months collecting information, poring over the microfilm of *The Durant Daily Democrat* for the years 1939-1945, and working diligently in order to recall names, events, and experiences. While writing this memoir, I seemed to be in a time warp, almost reliving the events as I wrote.

Upon completing the first draft, I read the manuscript again carefully to determine whether I had portrayed the events as they had occurred. I attempted to describe as honestly as I could, knowing that there were many unwritten episodes, as well as some dates, which may not be accurately remembered.

The review caused me to be aware of how I described P.J. as naïve, innocent, and almost too good to be true. Disbelief was one of my many feelings upon a second reading. Was I really like that? In adult life, as a licensed professional counselor, I have spent many professional hours assisting others in their pursuit of reviewing their past, working through their anger and hurt, figuring out their irrational thoughts and behaviors, and finding new directions for their lives.

Again, I asked, "Was I for real as described, or have I fictionalized myself too much?" Missing was any incidence of anger or pain, which would be normal responses to my dilemmas. Therefore, to discover more about thoughts and feelings of that era, I interviewed numbers of people who were born between 1930 and 1936 and asked them to recall, as best they could, any feelings of anger, resentment, hurt, emotional pain, and/or acting out behaviors resulting from any of these emotions. Those interviewed certainly would not qualify as a scientific sample, but represented, perhaps, the time, the mood, and the respect for adult authority in southern Oklahoma during those years. They recalled that adults, for the most part, were to be trusted; their voices were to be heard and obeyed, even if minor disobedience (e.g., chewing gum in class) occurred. Being young in that era was mostly an easygoing, idyllic time, even though World War II was an event which seemed to organize lives.

None of those interviewed remembered rebellion, major anti-authority acts, or resentment toward being corporally punished. A typical response, even though not unanimous, was "I got what I deserved," indicating, rightly or wrongly, that each family or institution had its standards and the offspring understood the consequences for deviating from these. After these interviews, I concluded that I was not an anomaly. I really was as I portrayed myself. While I had a most inquiring mind, I turned any potential rebellion or trouble-making into productive activities to contribute to my development, as my peers seemed to do. Was I slow in social development? Yes, in many social skills that my peers learned and became proficient in—dancing, for example—I was delayed. Do I now look back and regret that my church and mother may have prevented these skills from being learned? The definite answer is *yes*!

An anecdote from my recent experience will help explain. While attempting to dance with a good friend, I was told by her, "You really don't know how to dance, do you?" Instantly, the "old message" replayed, which is typical for the brain's process. But after years of maturing, my response was something like, "I guess you're right, but I do enjoy being with you on the dance floor."

It still remains my responsibility to learn to dance, as it is my responsibility to learn any social skills, or anything else, that I may have been made to feel guilty about in my development.

But anger in my youth just wasn't there. Anton Chekhov wrote, "One must not put a loaded rifle on the stage if no one is thinking of firing it." I refer to the quotation as a way of saying that no loaded rifle was ever on my "stage of life." There was no necessity for ever "firing the rifle."

Albert Camus wrote, "The rebel in me is that which causes us all to exist." P.J. had no real anger or hurt, and therefore had no need to rebel in anti-social ways. But "rebellion" did occur for me in adult life—not by quixotically fighting old windmills, but by working toward righting injustices, offering citizens opportunities to achieve their constitutional rights, and providing accurate information devoid of superstition, propaganda, and/or religious dogma. These activities, which I hope have been socially productive, came about through growth resulting from formal education, good mentoring, wise choices, and a good marriage, along with some serendipity.

The reader is not asked to look at P.J. as an adequate model of how a life should be, but as a young life that did, in fact, happen. If the reader recalls similar or related experiences and smiles as a result, I will be delighted. If the reader finds my young life inexplicably naïve, or disbelieves that a mother and/or father could treat a son as religiously or economically as is revealed in the book, then at least the reader will acquire a new appreciation for young people's different developmental experiences.

It is my hope that *P.J.'s Route* will not only be enjoyable to the reader but also will serve as a stimulus for discussion about families' values as we begin a new century. If neither, please enjoy the story of a part of my young life. I continue to look for men who will carefully and appropriately initiate and mentor young males. Using Robert Bly's words, "Only a man can bless a boy." As the father of two daughters and the grandfather of three granddaughters, I obviously wish for adequate mentoring and healthy growth-related experiences for young women, too.

Acknowledgments

There are numerous people who have inspired, encouraged, and befriended me as I did research and wrote. I want to thank them all.

Norma, my wife, in her quiet and supportive style always was willing to listen as I talked about my issues with writing. Her thoughtful suggestions were most helpful. I vow that I will love her forever.

Fred Tarpley was my friend, encourager, reader, critic, typist, and agent. He has made all our deadlines, never missed a meeting, and continually had convinced me to "keep the faith" that a good outcome would occur.

Sharon Russo, a psychologist, read the manuscript and offered helpful suggestions about the psychosocial development of P.J. Thanks, Sharon.

My lifelong friends Mack McElreath, George Boyet, and John Shaw have always just "been there." Even though we rarely see each other nowadays, I want to thank them for their friendship. Their lasting impression on me assisted me all my life. And to classmates and other friends, thanks for your friendship and support as we all grew up.

Pat Love, thanks for a zillion e-mails of encouragement.

The *Durant Daily Democrat* staff made it easy for me to research old issues of the newspaper. Their friendliness and cooperation are appreciated, as well as that of Mr. Bob Peterson, a former co-owner of the *Democrat*.

And I'd like to thank all men who are mentors to young boys, like Skip Bunn, Mr. Harrell Garrison, and, in a different way, my father.

Here's to everyone who ever had a paper route!

To my warm, caring, and supportive daughters, Amy and Ellie, I vow my love forever. And to their husbands, Michael Savage and José Domínguez, thanks for being those special men in my daughters' lives. Granddaughters—Rachel, Emily, and Allison—you're fortunate to have super parents.

To Durant, Oklahoma, thanks for helping to raise, protect, and educate me.

Finally, I was fortunate to have read Robert Bly's *Iron John*. A telephone conversation with him encouraged me to continue to study the route of young boys' initiations.

Introduction

This memoir was written to allow me to revisit my formative years in a small southeast Oklahoma town, Durant. Ellie, our younger daughter, has always been amazed at my long-term memory and my love for events in my childhood. *Amazed* may not be the right word; perhaps *bored* by "olden day" stories might better describe her reaction at times! Nevertheless, it became almost essential for me to write and record for posterity what it was like for me between the ages of seven and fourteen. While I continued a reasonably healthy development all of my teenage, young adult, and adult life, I chose these years, 1937-1945, on which to focus in order to gain a sense of the influences by adults and peers and the events of World War II, which created a different time than might have otherwise been.

Carefully considering a writing style, I chose to use the voice and language which was age-appropriate to my development. This decision was not an easy task. Dr. Fred Tarpley, my reader, reviewer, and agent, would remind me that a sophisticated adult word would not have been in my vocabulary at, say, age eight. I hope the reader will be sensitive to my language as I develop and enjoy my evolving love for words.

As a professional mental health teacher and licensed mental health care provider for all of my adult life, it was most tempting to analyze, evaluate, and create a "case study" of P.J.'s life. Obviously,

I have done this in my own way, but I chose not to do so in writing this memoir. I would rather readers come to their own analysis of P.J. Early readers of the manuscript were curious about my lack of major anger over the loan of money to my father, money that was largely never repaid. One conclusion that a reader might reach is that the act of lending the money was a giant step in P.J.'s classic struggle with the mythical adult male (my father) in his pursuit of initiation into manhood. The power transferred from the father to the boy may have been much more important than the money itself. But the boy, P.J., was not fully aware, at a conscious level anyway, of the symbolic process occurring, even though I remember being pleased that I had the money to lend to my father.

I mention this incident only as a way to ask readers to be sensitively aware of the multiple events in P.J.'s development. It may be trite to mention, but please be aware that all children have the same developmental needs but different life experiences, which, along with genetic structure, assist them with their maturation processes. I hope this memoir causes readers to review the many influences in their own development.

I also want to emphasize that I have not written about many games and activities which brought happiness, satisfaction, and "rule" and "structure" to my development. I have counted more than eighty of these games (and there are more) that I played outdoors, either with others or alone. A list of more than forty indoor games and fun activities was also remembered.

I have lived a busy, mostly happy, focused life around family, friends, school, work, play, and church.

I hope my memoir motivates readers to recall and write their own.

CHAPTER 1
The Message

Granny Johnson died in November 1938. Dad was her only remaining child. Shortly after her death, it surprised me to hear Dad say he wanted to drive around and talk to me about family things. Since I was only seven, the seriousness of his request didn't register.

But I was ready. The smell of our brand new '39 maroon Mercury was always welcome. And to be with Dad was even more welcome. After all, he was so frequently away from home, working, or I was so often away at school or at play that I didn't get to be alone with him much.

With a lot of curiosity, I started with him on our adventure in Durant, Oklahoma, our hometown.

Dad soon began to talk, even though he was slow and filled with emotion. "Son," he said, while driving slowly toward Main Street, "I want you to learn about the Johnson background and what it's been like for me to take care of your Granny Johnson and all of her personal and business affairs for the last few years." He paused for a while. I was being a good listener, trying to understand what he wanted me to hear, but puzzled as any seven-year-old would be. I knew I was saddened by Granny's death, but family stuff wasn't in my daily life yet. I sensed it was about to be.

Dad made a left turn off of Fourth Street east onto Main and drove slowly for a block and a half over a street I'd been over repeatedly. But this time, it seemed to be different. Dad's mood was entirely new to me. Quietly and almost reverently, he gently parked the Mercury and said to come with him. After walking across Main to the north side, he stopped and pointed to a building where a bookstore was located. I usually bought my school books and supplies there.

"This building was where my dad—your grandfather—opened and managed a successful grocery and feed store from the mid-1890s until his death in 1912." From a folder he carried, he produced a photograph of the store with the Johnson name on the sign high on the front of the building. The picture was old and faded, but certainly interesting to me, particularly the Johnson sign on top of the building.

"I'm not totally sure what happened to the business," he said, "because I was thirteen when he died. I've been told that the store and building were sold and that your Granny used the profits for other investments."

I felt like I was on sacred ground. Dad put his arm gently around my shoulder, something I wasn't accustomed to. I glanced at him, seeing a strong man with a long, narrow, handsome face. It felt good to have his arm on my shoulder, however brief it was. "My father was a good businessman," he continued, "who accumulated a good bit of money during his lifetime." Once again, I felt pride and respect for a man I'd never seen, except for the stiff and formally posed portraits of Granny and him. I had been told repeatedly that Annie Laura Wolfe and Hugh Landis Johnson had eloped, married in Bonham, Texas, and crossed the Red River into Indian Territory, later to become Oklahoma, to live for the rest of their lives. I also knew that my dad was the fifth born in a family of one sister, who died in infancy, and three brothers—Barney, Weaver, and Chester—who all died from TB in their late twenties and early thirties. Dad was born in 1899 in Durant, Indian Territory, in a house at Sixth and Main. Granddad died of TB in 1912.

I had a great fear welling up in my chest as Dad and I stood looking at the store. *What's he saying to me?* My feet didn't seem to want to make contact with the sidewalk from my need to run away. I expected to hear Dad say that he, too, now had TB. After all, he coughed a lot. Maybe it was from the two packs of Camels he smoked every day. I wasn't sure.

But then Dad seemed to switch moods. A smile crossed his face, one of appreciation. I felt warm and secure again. "Let's walk east on down Main Street," he said. As we walked, he pointed out the Durant National Bank and mentioned how one of his brothers, my Uncle Barney, was instrumental in establishing and working in that bank. I vowed at that moment that if I ever had any money to put in a bank that Uncle Barney's bank was going to be mine, too. We crossed Second Street, and after walking past several stores, we came to two buildings at the end of the block. Dad asked, with pride in his voice, "Well, Son, what do you think about these two?"

Not knowing how to respond, I shrugged and smiled. He continued, "I own these two buildings now. Mother left them to me in her will, and our family will get the monthly rent."

I liked the sound of money coming to our family because I had heard Mom and Dad talk about the depression and hard times. I ate a lot of food that Mom said "stuck to my ribs" because we lacked money to buy other food. With the rent money, I was beginning to see better food, new clothes, and a bike in my future. But I asked Dad how much rent we'd get monthly.

"About $75 total," he responded. That seemed like a lot to me. "Now, Son, let's drive around a bit."

I was enjoying the trip thus far, so I was ready for more. We drove west to Sixth and Main, where he pointed out the house of his birth, but he wanted mostly to show me the block south of Main between Sixth and Seventh streets. The Steakley Chevrolet agency was located in one building, and a Magnolia filling station was just west of Steakley's across a small creek.

"Your granddad owned this block before he died, and your grandmother sold it and used the money to invest in the stock market. I'll show you some of those worthless certificates when we get back to the house," he said disappointedly. "The stock market crash wiped her out."

"So, the money is all gone from selling this land?" I asked.

"Yes, and that's just a part of what I want you to know from our trip today. There's more."

This family stuff was of interest to me, but buildings, sales, certificates, and losing money—what did it all mean? Why was Dad doing this to me, his only son? And at seven years of age? Why not to Earleen, my sister, who was four years older? *Maybe*, I thought, *he's already been on this trip with her.* I asked him about any trip with Earleen. He responded that this was between him and me.

Back in the Mercury, we rode for several more miles so he could show me all the houses we had rented during my life. First was the house at 306 West Elm, where I'd been born, then a house on West Locust, then a house in the small community of Mead eight miles west of Durant on Highway 70, and then to West Beech to the house across from the Durant Hospital.

I remembered this house well. That's where we lived when I turned five. When he asked me how I liked living there, I told him how much I enjoyed the chinaberry tree, and the hens we owned, and the flowers in the vacant lot next door to us, and my friend next door, Gordon Wright. I recalled that Granddad Tate, Mom's dad, visited us there.

He asked me if I recalled the first money I made selling flowers. "Sure do," I replied. "Just like yesterday. A man walked across the street from the hospital and gave me a nickel to buy several larkspurs and poppies that I'd staked out and cared for. He was going to take the flowers to his sick wife. I was so excited that I showed the nickel to Mom, and she had me save it as the first money I'd ever earned. Guess I still have it in my lock box."

"Well," said Dad, "that was an important event. There'll be a lot more opportunities for you to make bigger sales and earn more money."

Sounded good to me. But I was still curious as to what was going on—what this trip was all about.

We got back in the Mercury and drove over to West Walnut, where we recently had lived. We lived there when Mom and Dad's last child, Linda, my sister, was born. He reminded me of that. Then he revealed a big surprise. Their first-born, Billy, had died when he was only two weeks old. It seemed important for Dad to tell me this. A tear seemed to trickle down his cheek, but as soon as it did, it was brushed away. I never had seen Dad cry before.

"Well, Paul, we've covered a lot of ground and family history today. But we're not through yet. Get back in the Mercury and let's go home." That suited me fine. While it was good to be with him for a couple of hours, I was ready to get the adventure over. But he had said it wasn't over yet. As Mom always said, I needed patience. I'd been told over and over I was short on that.

We had moved, after Granny's death, into her very large two-story house at 603 North Fourth. Dad had told me how he spent most of his growing-up years in an earlier version of this house. After it had been renovated, Granny rented four apartments—three upstairs and one downstairs—to keep her occupied and to make some money. I liked the big, rambling house with the outside staircase and strange water well in the large back washroom. And several trees on the lawn were just made for kids to climb. One large maple had a perfect limb on which Dad had hung a swing.

As we sat in the car, looking at the house, Dad continued his story. "When I was kicked out of high school for throwing an ink bottle at a guy, which he ducked, and it broke out a window, I decided I'd join the Oklahoma National Guard, even though I was only seventeen. Your Granny didn't approve. The First Oklahoma Guard United was soon mobilized and sent to San Benito, Texas, to guard against Mexican bandits. After returning, I went to Oklahoma City for a few years to learn to be an electrician. When I came back to Durant, I met your mother, Allie Lee Tate, while she was here attending Southeastern Normal School, getting her teacher's training. You remember that she is from Wapanucka in Johnston County, the one just north of our Bryan County?"

"Dad," I interrupted, "are we about through?"

"Not quite yet," he responded. "There are a couple other things I want you to know. Get out of the car and come with me."

Granny's large house, now Dad's, sat on a quarter-block lot. We walked the lot east to west, along Liveoak Street, north to the alley, and back east to Fourth Street.

"Now," he said, "I'll tell you what your mother and I plan to do. We're going to build a rent house on the west side of the lot facing Liveoak, move the family into it, then tear down the big old house and build a new house to live in for the rest of our lives. Also, we'll build a rent house on the north side of our house."

The news was pleasing. Even as a kid, I'd grown tired of living in different houses and making new neighborhood friends. But to get into the new house, we'd have to move again to the future rent house and then back to our new house. *Oh, well,* I said to myself, *this will be the last time.* I felt warm and good.

"What do you think?" Dad asked.

"When do we begin?" I replied. I wished I hadn't asked, because Dad went on for a while about how the new house would look. I listened carefully, fearing that I'd miss something important. After all, this was a totally different experience I was having with him. Here I was, a seven-year-old, being treated as if I were an adult. Part of me really liked that, but another part kept being curious and partly bored.

"Let's go inside and I'll show you those certificates of stock and explain some things to you." When we were in the room where he kept his papers, he got out the certificates. I told him that I didn't understand certificates, but he said he'd explain.

Telling me more than I could understand—and much more than I was interested in about the stock market crash—he proceeded to show me the names. They looked official and interesting, even to me—a kid—although I couldn't pronounce all the words on the certificates.

In large print, I saw SONORA BONANZA MINING CO., 400 shares issued to H. L. Johnson at $1 per share, dated August 19, 1904. The second was JARBRIDGE BUSTER MINING COMPANY of the State of Nevada, 1,000 shares issued to H. L. Johnson, at $1 per share, dated March 8, 1911.

The next was the purchase by Mrs. H. L. Johnson of 10 shares of DU ARD OIL CO. at $25 a share. Obviously, Granny kept investing after Granddad's death in 1911. She bought four more shares of DU ARD OIL CO. at $25 each on May 13, 1914.

The next certificate Dad asked me to look at was bought by Granny from the CLARKSON PETROLEUM CO. NO. 3 of Wichita Falls, Texas. This certificate was for 200 shares at $1 each.

And finally, CHOCTAW CHIEF LEAD & ZINC MINING CO. of Durant, Oklahoma. Granny had bought 200 shares of this company at $1 per share.

Dad took his pencil and a sheet of paper and began to do figures. When he was through, he showed me his results. A total of $2,150 of worthless paper. He said something negative about former President Hoover, which made no sense to me. While he seemed sad, he also seemed pleased about what he'd told me.

In a louder voice, he asked, "And how many other worthless certificates like these do you think we threw away?"

"I guess a few more," I responded.

"More than a few more. A rough estimate was more than $160,000 worth—and that's a lot of money! And it's gone forever! Most of what my father and mother worked a lifetime for!"

The way he said it caused me to think it was at least one-half of all the money in the world. *If only Dad had it now*, I thought. It was pleasant to think about the amount they had earned and saved, but it frightened me to hear Dad's excited tone of voice. I wanted to leave, but sensed he wasn't finished with me. As a kid I'd gone on many neighborhood and town adventures, but never an adventure like this. *Where is this going?* I asked myself in the best seven-year-old way I could.

I thought I'd try to end it. "Dad, may I go now?"

"Not quite yet. There's something else I want you to know," he said. "It's been important to me for you to do this today. You know that I've got your mother and your two sisters to support, as well as you. Your mother and I want to spend nearly all the money that I inherited from your Granny to get our family set up. We have a new Mercury, two business rental properties, soon a new house, and two rent houses. And you know that I earn money from my vanilla business, selling to grocery stores. So the way I've got it figured, with your help, we can make it financially."

I heard it. It leapt out from his words—WITH YOUR HELP. "Sure, I'll help, Dad. What do you want me to do?"

He replied, "If you'll work at odd jobs that young boys can get and earn your own spending money, that'll help me out. Also, I want you to take care of our lawn and the garden, help your mother with the house chores, and help me with my vanilla business."

Seemed OK to me, but I was surprised at how serious it all seemed coming from him. I guess I'd have to think about it for a while. But for now, I just said I'd do all that he asked.

"Do you understand that I'm asking you to be a strong young man?"

"Yes, sir," was about all I knew to say, not knowing what all that meant.

He then suggested that I go along and play. I looked at him for meaning as any son might do with his father, but I didn't get much help. He'd finished and turned away.

I went to my favorite maple tree in the backyard where Granny had let me nail boards to make a ladder to climb high into my rough-built tree house, where my make-believe friends lived, even though I didn't need them much anymore. I invited John, my smartest friend, to visit with me again. He listened and told me that my dad had told me not to ever be a financial burden to him. "But why me? Why not my older sister?" I asked. His response was simple. "The message is that you're the boy/man."

So that day in 1938 I heard, received, and began to live with the MESSAGE. I vowed to my make-believe friends and to myself that I'd never take even a dime from Dad the rest of my life. I used my pocketknife to cut my little finger slightly on my left hand until I got enough blood to leave a smear on one of the boards in my tree house as a reminder of my vow.

I even thought that I would run away from home so I would never be a burden. But John, my make-believe friend, argued with me about my weird thought of doing this. His reason won out when he convinced me that I could live in the house, eat the food Dad paid for, and get other benefits of family life just as long as I didn't take money directly from him. The bank at Second and Main came back into my thoughts, but how could I earn some money?

Dad did a good job on me that day, and now I had a new message with its challenge. I hoped I could keep my vow.

CHAPTER 2
The Tools

It was strange to see part of Granny's house, now our house, being taken apart board by board while we lived in one of the house's apartments. Construction on the west rent house had also begun. So in the spring of '39, I stayed around as much as school attendance would permit to watch and learn what the carpenters did. Since I vowed not to take money from Dad, I looked for a way to earn money helping them.

On a Saturday early in April, I priced a brand new lawn mower at Babcock's. Spring was arriving, and lawns would need mowing. I had saved $4.75, and the mower was $9.95. If I could get a new mower, I could be on my way to financial independence. Even though Dad had an old mower, which I used to mow our large lawn, it wasn't mine, and it was mostly worn out. I needed a new one that I could take care of and guarantee to any customer that it would mow closely and evenly. I always wanted any task I did to be done well. When people complimented me, I really wanted it to be for excellent work. Only then did I feel worthy of the compliment.

Later that day, as I was trying to stay out of the way of the construction men, the contractor asked me if I wanted to work pulling nails from the old lumber.

"How much will you pay me?" I asked.

"You think about it for a few minutes and make me your best deal," he responded.

Wow, what an opportunity, for me to decide and bargain with him! I got a hammer and a two-by-four with several 16-penny nails in it and pulled a few. Hard work. Those nails were really set in that old wood.

"Wait a minute," the contractor said, with a large grin on his face. "Let me show you something before you make me an offer that I couldn't accept."

He was gone a minute or so and returned with a crowbar and a small piece of board. He carried the two-by-four to sawhorses and placed it in such a way he didn't have to bend over to work. He used the hammer to knock all the nails back through the board so that they were ready to pull. Then, with the piece of board between the two-by-four and the head of the nail, he applied pressure with the crowbar, and the nail squeakingly released.

"Now, try this on the rest of the two-by and then give me your price," he said with an understanding smile. He seemed to enjoy teaching me.

So I gave it a go. It wasn't too hard, even though it took a lot of pressure to get the nail to release. There was an old empty coffee can nearby to hold the nails. The can gave me an idea for measuring the number of nails I'd pull for a price.

It seemed reasonable that I could fill ten cans with nails in an hour. And I wondered if he'd pay me a quarter for ten full cans. So, I began my contracting.

"Mister, I'd like to receive 25 cents for ten of these coffee cans full," I offered.

"Well, I guess that's a bit too expensive. But before I can reuse these pulled nails, they're going to have to be straightened. I'll give you the quarter for those ten full cans if you'll straighten the nails, too. Do you want to straighten out a few first? I'll show you how best to do it."

I tried a few and decided that he'd outdone me. But I wanted the money badly. The new mower was only $5.20 away. I went to my older sister, Earleen, with my arithmetic problem. She soon told me that I would have to have 210 cans full to earn $5.25. Seemed impossible! But I agreed, and he told me to go to work.

Soon I had a method and a rhythm. The nails became my enemy, and I had to defeat them. I got three different blood blisters and a few splinters. I wondered whether or not the enemy had won.

Mom was sympathetic and helped me by putting iodine on my wounds, but, wow, how it burned! I thought that the injuries were a small price to pay to get my lawn mower.

I got some surprise help when Mack McElreath, my best friend, rode up on his bike to play. He brought his repeat-shot air rifle, which his dad had bought for him. I had wanted one for a long time, but the one I had my eye on cost less: a single-shot Daisy Red Ryder. Mack's dad owned a large filling station and car repair shop at Fourth and Main, and it seemed to me that Mack always had more money to buy things than I had.

When I convinced Mack I had work to do, he decided to help. "Let me pull for a while and you straighten," Mack said.

"OK with me, but make sure you do it right." So we talked about our school year and what fun our experiences had been. The coffee cans began to fill. Oh, how I hoped he wouldn't ask me if I were making money for my job, because then he'd want some of my hard-earned money. And since I viewed Mack as already ahead of me when it came to family money, I wasn't eager to share. I felt a little guilty for withholding the information from my best friend, but he happily continued pulling while we visited and laughed together.

I asked him about his recently acquired bike. "Dad bought it for me," he answered. "Sure is fun to hop on it and ride anywhere I want to go. I've figured it out that I'll have more play time at school because I can get there quicker."

My heart sank a bit with envy. That meant he would be ahead of me in the work-up softball game we always played before school and at noontime. I needed a bike to keep up with Mack.

"Mack, I'm going to buy a bike soon," I bragged. "Babcock's has several I'm looking at."

It was mostly a true statement. I had looked at new bikes, but I knew they cost much more than I could afford. *Next time I'm in there*, I thought, *I'll look at the second-hand ones. Maybe I'll find one that I can eventually afford.*

Mack seemed pleased that I'd soon have my own bike so we could go places together. Since he lived close by, he suggested that we could ride to school together.

I liked his friendliness and support. I thought about how good it was to have Mack as a friend. I vowed to myself that I'd repay him by helping him learn to read better. While I was a good reader, Mack had difficulty with his *thats* and *whats* and *thens* and *whens* and knowing how to sound out new words. That would be my payback to him for helping me with the nails. My guilt for not telling him I was earning money immediately left. I made plans to ask my sister Earleen how best to teach him. After all, she'd been double-promoted twice and was in the eighth grade at only twelve years old. I thought she must know everything. But when I did ask, she wasn't much help, so I'd have to teach him the best way I knew.

After two weeks of work after school and on Saturdays, I had earned and saved $5.50. I was very pleased that the contractor bragged on my work and paid me regularly.

"Paul," he said with a smile, "you've done such a good job that I can use every nail when I'm building these houses."

I liked his compliment. I reminded myself of my vow that I would always try to do a good job at anything I did. It had paid off this time, and perhaps it would pay off in the future.

My total savings of $4.75 plus the $5.50 gave me $10.25. I took $10 in $1 bills and some change, and was ready to buy my mower. I was a bit unsure about my purchase, so I found Dad downtown selling vanilla to the manager at Piggly Wiggly. When he had completed his sale, I asked him to listen to my proposal. He agreed to listen, and as we sat in the Mercury on North Third Street, I asked for his advice. I showed him the money, told him my plan to buy the mower, and awaited his response.

He remained silent for what seemed to me forever. But he spoke gently. "Son, you've worked hard earning the money. Sam, the construction contractor, talked to me about your good work. Let's go home and get the old mower, and we'll drive together to Babcock's to see if the manager will give you any trade-in on the new one."

That pleased me because Dad was cooperating to help me achieve my goal. Soon we were at Babcock's, talking to the manager. Dad and he joked around in ways I didn't understand. But I did understand when I was told to pay only $8.45 for the new one. That meant I'd saved $1.50, which I could begin to apply toward my bike fund.

To my surprise and shock, Dad asked for the $1.50 for the old mower. I got upset for a moment, but then I reasoned it was his mower, and therefore he was entitled to the trade-in value. I gave him the $1.50. While the manager was putting the brand new mower into the trunk of the Mercury, I walked back to the repair area, where several used bikes were parked. Seven or eight stood there; kickstands supported them in an upright position. One immediately caught my attention. A Monarch brand, all black, with both tires inflated, good tread, seat in good condition, and a good chain guard. The grips on the handlebars were white and clean, but the kickstand was wobbly. Maybe I could get a new one. I'd also want a new basket to put in front of the handlebars.

Dad called. He was ready to go. "Just a minute, Dad." I asked the manager how much the Monarch bike was, and he said he wanted $7 for it.

"If I come back in a few minutes, may I ride it for a while?" I asked.

"Sure, be glad for you to try it out."

I was quiet about my bike plans as I rode home with Dad. I thought he'd approve, but I needed more planning and more money before I asked his permission to buy it.

As soon as the new mower was in the garage and Dad was gone again in the Mercury, I got Mom's permission to go to town. I didn't walk but *ran* the six blocks, fearful that the bike would be gone.

The manager showed me the bike, told me about its advantages, and tried to convince me what a bargain it was for only $7. "Go ride it for a few minutes. Give it a good try. See what good brakes it has," he said with a voice that convinced me I had to have it.

Riding it seemed to convince me even more that this one was right for me. It wasn't new like Mack's, but what difference did that make? We could both have wheels and more freedom, and we could be everywhere more quickly.

But I didn't have the money in my savings. I wondered how long it would take to earn the money mowing lawns. Would it be sold before I had the $7? A lot of pressure was on me.

When I rode back and told the Babcock's manager I wanted to buy it, but I didn't yet have the money, he gave me a look that clearly indicated I would never get the bike of my dreams.

"Paul," he said, "I can tell you like it, and it's a wonderful bike to go adventuring around Durant, but business is business. If someone comes in with the money, I'll have to sell it."

I walked home determined that I'd have the $7 pronto. I liked his word "adventuring." I immediately referred to the bike in my mind as *The Adventurer.* I tried *The Monarch Adventurer,* too, but I liked *The Adventurer* better. It was perfect for what I needed.

The new mower was great! I immediately found six lawns to mow and trim for 50 cents each. The mower glided over the grass like roller skates over smooth concrete. In three days, I'd earned $3. And each day I went by Babcock's and checked on my *Adventurer.* It was still there. The manager said he hadn't had any serious customers, so I was greatly relieved.

The next three days I walked the streets, pushing my new mower and knocking on doors where the lawns needed mowing. I earned $3 more. My feet seemed tired, my body sore, but my spirits were high. Six dollars saved and one to go, so I told Dad my plans. He seemed less pleased than when I told him about wanting to buy the new mower.

Why? I wondered. It seemed as if he'd like for me to have a bike. I continued to make my argument with him about why I needed the bike, and he finally said that it would be OK as long as Mom approved.

Mother agreed with my plans as long as I promised to ride carefully and keep her informed about where I'd be and that I'd always be home when we agreed. I eagerly promised.

When I took the $6 to the manager six days after I bought the mower, he agreed to let me have the bike if I'd pay the other dollar within a week. We had a deal.

I proudly pedaled my *Adventurer* home. Another of my great adventures in Durant, Oklahoma, was about to begin.

I earned three more dollars within a week, paid the dollar to Babcock's, and had a new mower and a used bike. I felt my chest sticking out a bit more. Just a few weeks earlier, Dad had laid out my future. Now I thought I had the tools necessary to be successful. And I had $2 in savings left over. I mowed, rode my bike, played, and watched the building of our new house.

And I was ready for school to be out.

CHAPTER 3
Building, Moving, and Learning

The west rent house was soon built, and we began moving into it in late September 1939. It was then that I discovered why God had created boys. Mother discovered that I had legs, arms, and some muscle. I carried boxes from one house to the other and helped move furniture until I was exhausted.

Mother was appreciative. She promised me my favorite pie—butterscotch. It seemed as if I always tasted Dad's good vanilla in it. Whether I really did or not, I imagined I did, and that made it better. When I put a bite of her butterscotch pie with the meringue topping in my mouth, I was ready to carry another bunch of boxes. Did Mom ever know how to reward me! But I already knew that Mom loved to please me, at least most of the time.

The move was accomplished in four days. I had worked after school each day to help us move and get things straightened up.

Granny Johnson's house was almost completely torn down. The one exception was that the large concrete front porch was left, and Dad proudly told people that we were building a new house that would attach to a large old porch.

I loved that big porch with its green swing where I'd swung on many occasions. As I looked at the porch, I was reminded of one of my life's real challenges. I recalled that one day, when I was six, Granny was irritable with my fidgeting. I think that she wanted me to prove to her I was worthy of being her grandson by being still and well behaved.

"Paul," she said rather sternly, "I'll give you five cents if you'll sit in the swing and be totally quiet and still for five minutes."

I recalled my thought, "What an easy nickel to earn." Little did I know how long five minutes of quiet and stillness were. I earned it, though.

Granny had said, "Well, Grandson, you've proved something to me and to yourself. You are able to be still, and you are motivated to earn. You'll go a long way in this world."

I hadn't liked being still, but I had liked the five pennies she gave to me. I had put them in my lock box with the nickel I'd earned selling flowers when I had lived across the street from the hospital.

Now when our new house turned into my new home, I'd have the large porch and wonderful swing to remind me of Granny.

In early December 1939, we moved into the new house. Again, my legs were in constant motion. I kept wondering why Earleen didn't seem to have to do much. "She's studying," was always the reply Mom gave. I had some homework, but I always did it quickly. Too quickly, I sometimes thought.

And to keep my pledge to help Mack, I would tell Mom that I had to go study with him. She'd let me go, with my promise that I'd be back before supper, and help move more things.

Mack lived a block east at Third and Liveoak, where we would sit on his porch of the big two-story red brick house and read from our school reading book. We went over and over the reading book until he seemed to have learned all of the words. He even got to where he could tell the difference in the *whats* and *thats* and the *whens* and *thens*. I liked the smile that would cross his face when he was successful. I thought that maybe I could be a good teacher someday.

We were such good friends that he convinced me to spend $1.29 to buy the BB gun I wanted, the Daisy Red Ryder single shot. We cemented our everlasting friendship in mid-December by trying to light a match held in our teeth with a shot from the BB gun from ten steps away. We each got two shots. Talk about fear! But it was a double-dare, and a real guy didn't ordinarily back away from a double-dare.

We were both greatly relieved when that event was over. Neither of us hit the match, and, fortunately, neither of us got hit. But the trust we had in each other was great. It was as if we had become brothers, and that was good since neither of us had a brother.

I was glad when we were completely moved in, because I wanted to show Mack my new room. I felt very good knowing that Dad had said we'd live here for the rest of our lives and that my best friend lived just a whistle away. My room was large, had lots of windows, was next to the one bathroom in the house, and overlooked the large lawn between our house and the north rent house. Mack liked it, too. We decided we could play lots of Monopoly and other games in the room when the weather was too bad for us to be outside, and lots of football on the wide lawn during good weather.

I fixed a special place in one drawer in my chest of drawers for my lock box. I had four special pocketknives, three four-leaf clovers in a special press, a rabbit's foot on a chain, my Grandfather Tate's political campaign card, the five pennies from my Granny Johnson, the nickel from the sale of the flowers, and a used billfold Dad had given to me.

I read Grandfather Tate's campaign card frequently. It reminded me that he was the elected county tax assessor for Johnston County, with his office in Tishomingo, Oklahoma, and his creed was printed on the back of the card, which I liked:

MY CREED
The man who is clean inside and outside, who neither looks up to the rich nor down on the poor, who can lose without squealing and win without bragging, who is considerate of women, children and old people, who is too brave to lie, too generous to cheat, too sensible to loaf, who takes his share of the world's goods and lets others have theirs, is indeed, a true gentleman.

I barely knew my grandparents Tate. Grandmother Tate died when I was four and Grandfather Tate when I was five. Mother described them to me often as being good, hard-working, God-fearing people. I also liked to say the name of the town in Johnston County where my mother was born. It rolled off my tongue so easily—Wapanucka, Oklahoma, near Tishomingo, Oklahoma. Words were fun.

The four-leaf clovers and the rabbit foot were in the box for fun. I guess I really didn't believe in luck, but, if they helped, so be it. The knives were for trading and whittling.

I told Mom and Dad to stay away from my lock box. It was for my private stuff, I told them, and I had the only key to the lock, even though the lock box was only a cigar box. I'd cut a hole in the front panel and one in the lid so that the lock could fit through and, with a small push, lock.

Mom and Dad said that it was OK to have my lock box and that they would never interfere. Dad teased me about having my "sweetie's" picture there. I blushed a bit, and that seemed to cause him to push the tease more. While I didn't have a picture, I sure had a crush on that beautiful redheaded girl in my third-grade class named Jeanne Paul. Whenever I found her name written on her paper or on the blackboard, I'd put a "+" between Jeanne and Paul. It'd look like *Jeanne* + Paul. She didn't seem too impressed, but she never did discourage me. I thought that someday I'd have her picture to put in my lock box. Either hers or one of Steveanna Harrison, who sat by me and was always so pretty and nice.

The afternoon that school let out for Christmas holidays, Mack and I rode home and played for a while, but Dad called and said he wanted me to help him, so Mack left.

"OK, Dad, what's up?"

"I want to teach you how to help me with my vanilla business," he said.

"That's great! I'd like to help you and learn about what you do."

Dad had built a special room at the back of our new house that we named the "Vanilla Room." It had a large gas stove on which to set the fifteen-gallon vat containing the ingredients to become vanilla, a sizeable, tall work table, and a set-up on that table to place the five-gallon bottle so that gravity would feed the vanilla through a line into the bottles.

Dad told me about the formula, which was rather technical to my ears, but I watched and listened.

"See these chemicals?" he said. "These are ordered from Monsanto Company in Kansas City." He carefully measured and then weighed them to be exact and emptied them into the vat.

"Now for the sugar," he said as he continued to teach me. Next came the caramel color, then lots of water, and it was ready to cook.

"Most vanilla extract contains some alcohol," he said, "but mine is an artificial brand." Because of all I had heard about alcohol, I was glad there wasn't any in the vanilla.

"Look at the labels," he said, holding one up. "They are printed in a shop in Sherman, Texas." In red and blue on a white background was printed:

> TRI-PURE Brand Vanilla Extract
> an artificial flavoring that will neither freeze out
> nor bake out
> Manufactured in Durant, Oklahoma
> Satisfaction Guaranteed or Money Back

Dad placed the large vat on the stove for cooking. Then he told me that he ordered all the bottles and their caps from a glass factory in St. Louis, Missouri.

"Ahh, where my favorite baseball team, the Cardinals, play," I said with pride in my team.

"Yes, the bottles are stored over here." He ignored my reference to the Cardinals.

He reached into two boxes and took out a four-ounce bottle from one and an eight-ounce from the other. Each had a small inset in which to glue the label.

"I have several different runs, as I call them, that make up a full day calling on owners or managers of grocery stores. I drive through southeastern Oklahoma and parts of northeast Texas on my runs. I sell a dozen four-ounce bottles of vanilla for $2 and a dozen eight-ounce for $3.75. I usually mark the grocer's price on the bottle, place them on the shelf designated for my vanilla, write up the bill, receive the pay, and after some friendly talk and perhaps buying a Coke and a snack, drive to my next customer. The grocer usually sells the four-ounce bottle for 25 cents each and the eight-ounce for 40 cents each, so he will sell the dozen four-ounce bottles for $3, a $1 profit, and the eight-ounce bottles for $4.80, a $1.05 profit."

I was impressed with all the information, pleased that he was so open and willing to share it with me, and proud that he was my dad. He seemed to feel good as he informed and shared with me. But he then told me he didn't make much profit. His costs were about 85 cents per dozen, leaving only $1.15 profit for a dozen four-ounce bottles. I could sort of understand why the money he made selling vanilla plus the money from the rentals didn't add up to much. I was still pleased that I'd vowed to never take money from him.

Soon he asked me to help him put caps on the bottles as he managed the line which filled each bottle. After all were filled and capped, he put the labels on, and I put each bottle into a small space reserved for them in the large box. It was easy to do, and seemed to please Dad, and we had lots of time together.

I was glad when he said I could have as many bottles of vanilla as I could sell to friends or new customers by calling directly on them at their houses. He added that I should first ask if they already bought TRI-PURE brand at the store. If so, I wasn't to sell. So I needed new customers. A new challenge and a new way to make money.

Mom was my next source for information.

"Tell me what vanilla is used for," I said.

She went into more detail than I wanted, but it seemed that vanilla was added to the recipe for pies, cakes, ice cream, and some other sweet desserts. Not much was used. I could see that a bottle might last a long time, so I left knowing that I'd not sell very many bottles. At least it was another way to earn and save.

Mack and I continued to play and enjoy each other's company. But I needed to go try to sell vanilla.

"Mack, would your grandmother buy a bottle of vanilla from me?" I asked.

"What's vanilla?" he responded.

I tried to explain, but didn't do very well. Finally, I just told him that that's what my dad sold. Trying to explain vanilla wasn't easy.

Mack lived with his father and Mimmie, his grandmother. I never did know for sure, but I thought that his mother had died. Mack also had an older sister, Mary Lou, who was so very pretty. I always liked it when she'd sit on the porch with us and listen to us read. Sometimes she'd hug me when I read every word perfectly. It seemed as if my fiery red hair would turn ever redder and the hundreds of freckles on my face would stand out an inch from my skin when I was blushing. My big ears would burn, too. But the hug from a twelve-year-old pretty girl seemed to make the embarrassment tolerable. It was another reason to do a good job. The hug gave me a good feeling, one that was different from my mother's hug.

Mack said it would be OK to try to sell a bottle to his Mimmie. Since I had a box with three each of the four-ounce and eight-ounce bottles in my bike basket, I went immediately to ask her to buy one.

"My, Paul, where in this wide world did you get bottles of vanilla to sell?"

I went into my explanation and sales pitch. *Not bad,* I thought, *for a third-grader.*

Then I asked if she bought this brand at her grocery store. Relieved when she said no, I hoped for my first customer.

"How much for this big bottle?" she asked.

"Only 40 cents," I eagerly responded.

Mack stood by supporting me.

"Mimmie, Paul told me it makes pies and cakes even better than the great ones you bake for me now," he said with some urgency in his voice.

She left and soon brought me a quarter and fifteen pennies. My first sale. I politely thanked her and asked if I could have a piece of the first pie or cake she baked using this vanilla. I said I knew it would be the best one she ever made.

Laughingly, she said I should quit school and be a door-to door salesman. Mack, taking her more seriously than I did, said that I should stay in school so we could study and learn together.

Telling Mimmie and Mack goodbye, I pedaled rapidly home to tell Dad about my sale. He seemed pleased. Mom, overhearing us, cautioned me not to ruin my appetite by eating too much of Mimmie's desserts.

"Yeah, I know you think I'll like her dessert better than I like yours," I teased. She laughed lovingly. I knew she'd soon bake me a butterscotch pie. She did.

Back in school again in January 1940, Mack and I rode to the neighborhood grocery store where the kindly Mrs. Montgomery sold me five pieces of bubble gum for a nickel. I thought I owed Mack for helping me make the sale of vanilla recently to Mimmie, so I gave him four pieces of gum. I popped the other piece in my mouth, and he carefully unwrapped one of his. Soon we were seeing who could blow the biggest bubble. We laughed as they exploded and stuck all over our noses and faces. We knew it couldn't get much better than this.

Mack put the other three pieces in his pocket, and we soon

went to our own houses. It was a good feeling to give Mack the gum, and he liked it, too.

The next day was an especially cold January day for Durant, but Mack rode by to get me on our way to Washington Irving Elementary School, where we both were in Miss Hughey's room. Mack blew bubbles with his new piece of gum on the way to school. Unfortunately, he forgot to spit it out before class.

Miss Hughey, a great teacher and seemingly our friend, temporarily became our enemy when she caught Mack with a blown bubble and marched him immediately to Principal Garrison's office. She returned and lectured all of us about school rules.

I thought I'd die. My gift of gum and Mack's forgetting to spit it out had gotten him in trouble. While it wasn't my fault altogether, I wanted to ask permission to go to Mr. Garrison and tell him it was my fault that Mack had the gum in the first place. But I didn't know what to say or how to ask. I figured Miss Hughey would say no to my request anyway.

In about twenty minutes, Mack returned. He seemed fine. We talked with our hand signals while the teacher's back was turned, and he told me that everything was OK. No licks. At recess he told several of his concerned friends what Mr. Garrison had done.

Mack said, "Mr. Garrison asked me why I was sent. I told him. He asked me if I had another piece of gum. I reached in my pocket and showed him the pieces I had left. He asked for a piece and said we'd go for a walk on the playground. It was cold outside, but he treated me kindly. He unwrapped the piece of gum, put it in his mouth, much to my surprise, and began chewing and blowing bubbles. He didn't bust any on his face, though. He asked me where we were. I told him we were on the playground. Then he asked me if school rules permitted chewing gum on the playground. I said yes. Then he said how cold it was and let's go back in. As we did, we both put our gum in the outside wastebasket. He reminded me that I had made a small mistake, not a large one, put his arm on my shoulder, patted it, and with a giant smile on his face asked me if I was ready to return to class. I said yes. He reminded me to obey the rules of the school and to do my very best. I returned to class."

"Weren't you scared?" I asked. "I would have been."

"Just for a minute. But Mr. Garrison, I could tell, wasn't going to punish me. He was very kind."

I decided then and there that I wanted to know Mr. Garrison better. I planned to go to his house and see if I could sell a bottle of vanilla. A little risky, but if he were that kind to Mack, maybe I would find out more about him.

The next Saturday morning I rode my bike around, knocking on doors and trying to make a sale. I had no luck, but soon I was purposefully in Mr. Garrison's neighborhood.

In a brief moment after I knocked, I was surprised and pleased that he opened the door. I could see Mrs. Garrison sitting across the room from the door.

"Well, Paul, it's nice to see you. Come in."

I did, and he introduced me by my full name to Mrs. Garrison. I fidgeted a bit and blushed some, too, standing there holding two bottles of vanilla, one in each hand.

I began my sales pitch. It was more difficult to say than usual, but I finished it.

Mrs. Garrison responded, "Paul, I didn't know that your dad made TRI-PURE. I've been using it since we moved here two years ago. It's a very good product."

Disappointed, I explained to them why I couldn't sell to her.

"Just a minute, before you continue," she said. "What's your telephone number?"

"416," I responded.

She reached for the phone. I was a bit scared as to what was going on. In a few seconds, I found out.

"Mrs. Johnson, this is Mrs. Harrell Garrison. Your son is here selling vanilla and has told us that he can't sell to customers who already buy his dad's vanilla at the grocery store. Well, I do, and I like it. Please give me permission to buy two bottles. I want one, and tomorrow we're driving to my mother's, and I want to take her a bottle. May I have your permission to break Paul's dad's rule? Good! Pleasant to have talked with you. Hope we can meet at the next PTA meeting. Goodbye."

What a fine woman married to a fine man, I thought. Made me want to be around them more. Maybe I could be the principal's helper when I got in the fourth grade.

"Paul," she asked, "do you have another large bottle with you?"

"Yes, ma'am, I'll go outside and get another." So she paid me 80 cents for the two bottles and thanked me for coming by. Mr.

Garrison put his arm on my shoulder, thanked me for being a good student, and made a statement about helping Mack improve his reading. I couldn't figure out how he knew, but I thought that maybe he just knew everything about his students.

As I rode away, I looked back, and he was still standing on the porch. He again waved. I decided I liked that man. Maybe, I thought, I could learn a lot from him.

Since it was still cold, and since I'd made 80 cents, and since I felt good, I decided to go home and warm up.

When I got home, I said, "Mom, thanks for telling Mrs. Garrison that it was OK for a regular customer of Dad's to buy from me. Do you think Dad will be upset?"

"No, I'll discuss it with him when he comes in. I think he'll be pleased because she called and asked permission."

When Dad came home, he said, "Mom told me that you sold a couple of eight-ounces today. The Garrisons seem like good people." He said that since the rule was broken with permission, it was OK.

"It seems as if I learned something today," I said to Dad. He nodded his agreement.

I walked into the living room, where Earleen was practicing the piano Dad had bought along with a lot of new furniture when we moved into our new house. She still wasn't playing very well after two months of lessons from Mrs. Hunsaker. Somehow that pleased me. It reminded me, once again, of how she had played last Christmas morning. It wasn't too successful. "Joy to the World" was more like "Pain in the World" as all five of us had gathered around the Christmas tree. I smiled as I remembered how she butchered a few notes. Why was it that she got a piano, which cost several hundred dollars, and I was told to go earn my own money? I had repeatedly asked myself that question.

And then, on that gift-giving day, I remembered acting surprised and happy to have been given clothes, a jigsaw puzzle, and a game called Chinese Checkers.

Mack had gotten numerous new toys and gadgets to play with. I was always glad for him, and for me, too, because he shared so well with me.

The rest of that spring went quickly by without any unusual events except for my new back account. I had sold enough vanilla and earned a bit by going on errands for neighbor women that I had saved $22. As I had promised myself I'd do, I went to my uncle's bank, the Durant National, and opened an account with $20. I did this in May of 1940, just after my ninth birthday. Somehow, as I walked out of the bank with the deposit slip in hand, I felt like a millionaire. Also, I thought that my uncle, even though I had never met him, would be pleased.

I told Mack and he liked it that I'd saved money. He said he'd do it, too, if he had to. Dad grunted his approval when I told him. I'd learned a lot in 1939 and in the first few months of 1940.

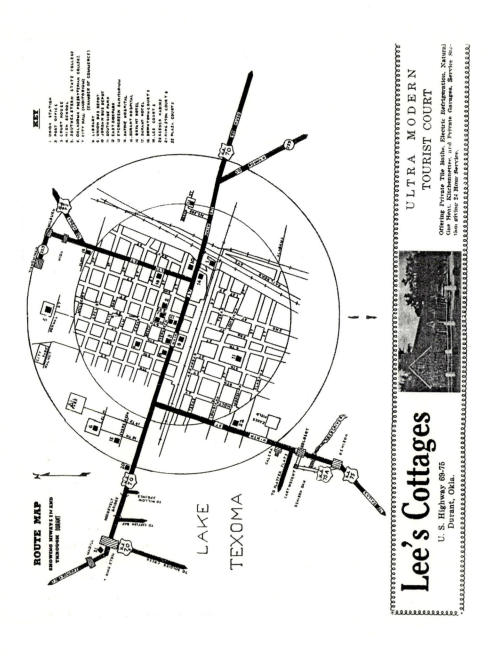

CHAPTER 4
Adventuring in My Town

Mack and his family moved about nine blocks away to West Cedar Street. While we saw each other frequently during the late spring and early summer, I also developed another close friendship with George Boyet, who lived on Ninth Street five blocks from me. He had a large stack of comic books, and I wanted to trade from my collection of about a dozen. George agreed, so he and I began to visit, play, and trade. George's dad owned Boyet Drug Store on Main Street next to the Ritz Theater. George was an only child and seemed to be very smart. We enjoyed each other's company and began to play a lot of Monopoly, which he usually won. I studied his game plan, but when I described it to Earleen, she told me that I'd have to do more thinking about how I spent my money on property. She said that I thought too small and was too fearful to risk my money on houses and hotels or on expensive property. She said that I'd rather save my money, while George always spent all of his to buy property and then he'd get all my money and win. She had a point, but I just put that into my "Will Figure Out Later" box of thoughts.

I was successful that summer mowing lawns, maybe because the mower did such a good job and the customers seemed pleased, and that kept me very busy. Mack joined me for a while, and we worked as a team. We hooked our mowers onto the backs of our bikes and looked for lawns to mow. He never seemed to mow as much of the lawn as I, but I never complained. After all, he was my friend, and I just worked faster than he did.

Dad began to let me go with him on sales to grocery stores, not only in Durant but also on some of his runs. I liked that because it was new territory to explore. It was fun to hear the men talk and tease Dad about his vanilla being nothing more than muddy water. One owner said, "Well, Earl, I thought you'd be calling on me because it rained the other day. I knew you'd bottled some more muddy water."

Dad would respond with something that would counter the statement, like, "Sure, the only way I can make a profit from you is to cut way back on expenses. Muddy water isn't too expensive." And everyone would laugh. I did, too, not yet understanding all this "men's talk."

Dad called me his "swamper." I'd go to the Mercury and load a box with the order and proudly carry it to him. I especially liked being treated to a soda pop and peanuts after Dad had been paid because I thought I had earned the reward.

The summer wore on. After my work responsibilities were finished, I frequently went riding on my bike, *The Adventurer.* I had $60 in my bank account and three new pairs of jeans. Also, I had bought new school supplies.

Durant, with its 10,000 people, was an easy town to live in. Not too many cars, a great downtown area, many wide streets lined with magnolia, elm, sycamore, and maple trees, and wide sidewalks. The county seat of Bryan County, its three-story courthouse had a statue of the Confederate soldier standing guard on the front lawn. The public library was named the Robert L. Williams Library. I was proud that Mr. Williams was from my hometown and had been governor of Oklahoma. His large grave memorial stood out so that everyone could easily see it upon entering the main gate of Highland Cemetery, just south of town.

The Country Club, which I wasn't allowed to visit, was just south of the cemetery. The names of our streets were easy to know and remember. Main Street was an east-west street with businesses located from the Missouri, Kansas, and Texas (MKT) tracks just east of First Street westward to about Seventh Street, and then Main continued another fourteen or fifteen blocks. First Street was also U.S. Highways 69 and 75 going north toward Atoka and McAlester.

Highways 69 and 75 turned west off of First Street and proceeded on to Ninth, and then south toward the Red River about fifteen miles away and on into Texas. Highway 70 also ran along Main Street. It went directly west toward Madill and Ardmore and east toward Hugo and Idabel.

The north-south streets west of the MKT tracks were in numerical order, with the exception of Washington Street about where Twelfth Street should be. I never knew why that happened. I just accepted it.

The east-west streets north of Main were named for trees. Northward, they were Evergreen, Beech, Cedar, Elm, and so on. The exception was College Street, which was the southern boundary of Southeastern State College. The college was on top of a small hill, and the campus was mainly between First and Seventh streets at the very north edge of town. We kids affectionately called the college "Ignorant Hill." Many hours were spent by those of us who owned bikes in contests to see which bike and its rider could coast the farthest south down the hill on Fifth Street. We'd begin by Southeastern's gym and pedal as fast as we could until College Street, then never pedal again until the contest winner had been declared. No prizes were awarded—just the bragging rights for winning. I always wanted my tires to be well inflated.

The streets east of the MKT tracks were NE First and so on, and south of Main were SE First and so on. The Frisco tracks ran parallel to Main Street, about a block south of Main. East-west streets south of the Frisco tracks were named for states—Louisiana, Texas, Arkansas, and a few more.

The three public elementary schools were Washington Irving for the northside kids, George Washington for children east of the MKT tracks, and Robert E. Lee for students living south of the Frisco tracks. Also, Southeastern had Russell Training School, where each class had only ten to fifteen students. This school was housed on the Southeastern campus. So the streets and tracks helped me understand more about the town's families and their income. All elementary schools were grades one through six, and then the students entered Woodrow Wilson Junior High School for grades seven through nine. Durant High School, just across the street from the junior high on Cedar Street between North Fifth and Sixth, was home to grades ten through twelve.

It was always interesting to me that no black families lived in Durant. When I asked Dad this, I was told a story that I didn't like. It was very ugly and something that I didn't like about my town's history. We had numbers of Indians in Durant. Both my mother and dad had been born in Indian Territory. (Oklahoma became a state in 1907.) And Grandmother Tate was one-eighth Chickasaw, or so I was told by Mom. I enjoyed being a red-headed, freckled-faced Chickasaw. Durant residents who had Indian blood were mostly Choctaw. All of us kids got along great. We didn't know who was what, and we really didn't care.

The downtown area had wide sidewalks and wide streets, and on Saturday nights all parking places were filled early. Families visited while the kids and teenagers strolled the sidewalks of the business area and did whatever kids do. There were four movies—the Plaza, Ritz, Savage, and Metro—five drug stores, about twelve grocery stores, three five-and-dime stores, two banks, three hotels, several dry goods stores, shoe stores, hardware store, newsstand, book store, ice cream parlor, furniture stores, auto parts and appliance store, bakery, six cafes, flower shop, lawyers' offices, a photography studio, optometrist's office, dental office, two hospitals, ice houses, funeral homes, a pool hall, several places that sold beer, and the building that contained the local daily newspaper, the *Durant Daily Democrat*.

The new city hall had just been built on Evergreen Street north of the *Democrat* and west of the U.S. Post Office. West of the new city hall was the Bryan County Courthouse. Within three blocks north of downtown on North Third were the Methodist, First Christian, and Presbyterian churches. At North Second and Evergreen was the First Baptist Church. Numerous smaller churches were located elsewhere, such as the Church of Christ, Church of the Nazarene, Calvary Baptist, Wesley Methodist, and others. There was no Roman Catholic Church, and the Episcopal Church, located at Beech and Sixth, was mysterious to us kids. We often double-dared each other to open the door and look in. I guess I had too much respect or fear or something to take the double-dare.

At North Sixteenth and Elm was a small college named Oklahoma Presbyterian College for Indians. All I knew was that Indians lived in dormitories and attended college classes at Southeastern.

Several industries, some of which pertained to peanuts and cotton, were located in the eastern and southeastern parts of town. Some oil distributors had businesses just east of the MKT and Frisco tracks. There were two train depots, one which served the KO&G, and one which served the much busier MKT and Frisco. The father of my friend John Shaw was the station agent at the MKT depot. Also, there were two bus depots.

On West Main Street between Fourth and Seventh streets were the Ford, Oldsmobile, Buick, Dodge and Plymouth, and Chevrolet dealerships. Several drive-ins for hamburgers and Cokes were along Main Street, North First, South Ninth, and other places. While not a drive-in, the Little Onion on North Third was a place where I enjoyed buying chili buns. Mr. Spradlin made them so good!

Between the MKT tracks and North Second, bordered by Main and Evergreen, was the Farmer's Square. On many Saturdays I saw wagons pulled by teams of horses or mules roll into town. Some farmers brought vegetables to sell while others came to town to shop.

At the southeastern corner of the square was the mule barn, a place where mules and horses were traded. Was it ever a smelly place! When Dad was out of sorts with me, but not enough to spank me, he'd threaten to get me a job at the mule barn shoveling mule stuff. I always knew he was teasing, or at least I hoped he was.

I could hardly ride my bike eight blocks anywhere in town without seeing another neighborhood grocery store, and I had counted twenty-two gasoline filling stations in town. There were also several parks, baseball fields, and a large, privately owned swimming pool, the Natatorium, on North Sixth.

Businesses, churches, schools, parks, colleges, beautiful trees, wide streets and sidewalks, friendly people—all these and more caused me to love my town. I always felt safe, free to adventure and to use fully the playgrounds, parks, and swimming pools. And to have both a high school and college, with all their athletic events, doubled the time I spent attending football and basketball games, tennis matches, and track meets.

I had been told not to go inside the businesses that sold beer. Also, Mom said I couldn't see any movies or go into the pool hall. She said people who made movies wanted to influence me away from the teachings of the church she attended with my two sisters and me. It was the Church of the Nazarene on South Ninth Street, just a block south of the Frisco tracks. I was not happy leaving the Methodist church and hearing all the hellfire sermons at the Nazarene church, but Mom made me go.

Mom also warned me about the pool hall, where men gambled. She said I would learn things which were evil and sinful, but I was very curious about what went on in the back of the pool hall. And Dad told me never to go into Siegel's Dry Good Store. He never explained why, and when I asked why, he always responded, "Just do as you've been told. Don't question."

Obviously, as a curious kid, I asked Mom why I couldn't go into Siegel's. She patiently and cautiously explained that the two Siegel brothers who owned and managed the store were Jewish.

"What difference does that make?" I asked of her. Her explanation didn't make sense to me, so I made up my mind to go into the store. While there, I bought a pair of socks for me and a pretty, lacy Sunday handkerchief for Mom. I was glad she liked her handkerchief and was really glad when she didn't ask where I bought it.

I would continue to learn more about my parents and what they believed.

My town seemed to be a kid's heaven, although I spent a lot of time working and earning money. But I had enough time to adventure, too. That summer, I explored Chuckwa Creek, running west to east just behind Southeastern State College's property. Just east of Highways 69 and 75, there was the well-known Round Hole on Chuckwa Creek. That's where I learned to swim in my birthday suit, along with fifteen to twenty other guys who often swam there. Older guys who were there often stayed on the banks of the creek and walked around, showing off their bodies. I was told that they were "bank walkers" because of the size of a particular part of their body! We younger guys stayed in the water as much as possible and learned from the actions of the "walkers." My secret hope was that I'd grow to become a "bank walker." Mack and I sometimes discussed these matters and laughed.

The City Park on North Eighth was a good place to meet and try our bike-riding skills on the small, rocky hills. And at the northern boundary of the park was a small creek running west to east. Mack and I caught lots of small perch and crawdads and had many rubber gun fights and cowboy and Indian battles. There was a small walk-across bridge over the creek. On the underside of the bridge were many, many initials carved in the wood, as well as words that my mother had told me Jesus would not approve of. My vocabulary increased, but I didn't understand the meaning of all the words, even though I knew I couldn't use them around Mom. I did try to learn most of them, so I'd know what they meant when the older guys used them.

Before bedtime, Mom would make Earleen, Linda, and me listen to her read the Bible and then pray. She said that each of us was to pray silently while she prayed. I didn't like to pray, but when I listened to her prayer about my Dad needing to be saved and beginning to go to church, I wondered what he needed to be saved from. So I just said in my prayer, "God, help Dad and me get along well together." I really didn't want him to go to church where we went and hear all the stuff I heard. I knew he wouldn't be happy to hear it. Or, at least, I knew I wasn't.

One Sunday afternoon in late August 1940, after a good dinner which Mom had invited our preacher to share with us, I said I wanted to talk to her. She said I could after the preacher left.

After his departure at about 2:00, Mom called me. "What's on your mind, Son?"

"Well, Mom," I replied, "I don't like that dratted preacher, and I don't want to go to church anymore."

"Hush your mouth immediately. I don't like vulgar words, and you know I've told you not to use them ever," she strongly replied. "Now go get me a switch. Even though I don't like to switch you on Sundays, you've sinned and need to be punished. I must teach you to use only proper words. Go get me a switch."

I knew there was no reasoning with her. There never had been before. I'd had to go get the switches so often that the peach tree looked bare where I'd broken off small limbs. I didn't even know, until she told me after my switching, that the vulgar word I had used was *dratted*. She said it stood for the word *damned*.

Since I had brought her a very small switch off the young peach tree in our backyard, the switching hadn't hurt as much as the injustice I felt. It wasn't fair. What was a boy to do with his language? Maybe when I was out with friends and roaming around town, I'd just use *drat* anytime I wanted. I'd have to remember not to use it around Mom.

Later that Sunday afternoon, when Earleen saw me, she said, almost in a boastful way, "So you got some more peach tree tea, didn't you? You really get a lot. Why don't you behave yourself like I do, and then you won't get so much 'tea'?"

I felt my face flush and anger rise. I struck back at her with my newly discovered vulgar word.

"Drat it, Earleen, just leave my business alone. Go study, or play your piano, or mind your own dratted business. Leave me alone."

That felt good. Then I chuckled to myself when I thought that maybe I'd even use *damn* when I needed it. Probably soon. Mom would read from the Bible about not cussing, and then she'd pray aloud for God to deliver me from the temptation of strong words. I'd listen, but I promised myself I wouldn't obey. After all, my town needed to hear my language as I grew. I didn't want to be very different from my friends.

That week, Dad and I bottled vanilla and talked about fishing. He said he'd heard about my "peach tree tea." He said we probably needed to go fishing for some crappie.

"Paul, I've got the key to Mr. Wilson's wooden row boat that he keeps above the low water dam on Blue River. Let's go see if we can land a few crappie."

"That'd be great. I'll buy a couple dozen minnows for us. When can we go?"

"Friday morning. But you don't need to buy the minnows, because I've been selling quite a bit of vanilla lately and have a few dollars ahead."

The last Friday of August was clear and hot. I knew it'd be around 100 degrees just after lunch, so we probably would stop fishing before lunch and drive back through the community of Armstrong and stop for lunch. I knew he'd stop at a small grocery store where he sold vanilla. I'd been on a sales run once when we sold there.

When we stopped to buy minnows, Dad asked the bait man for two dozen. Then he said to me, "Son, you pay money for your dozen, and I'll buy my dozen."

I was surprised after what he'd told me earlier. But I dug into my jeans pocket and produced two dimes and three nickels. I had a dime left. I wondered to myself if it would always be this way. I was proud of myself for having the 35 cents but hurt that he had gone back on his promise. I wiggled my thoughts around to the place where I must have misheard what he had said the other day. Besides, going fishing in a boat on the Blue River was worth my 35 cents anyway.

Unlocking the boat, we rowed upriver against a gentle current until Dad said we'd reached a good crappie hole. We got our cane poles, put on the fishing line with the red and white cork, the lead weights, and the large hook. My minnow really looked ready for a large crappie.

Sure enough, in just about five minutes the cork disappeared, and I landed a large crappie.

Dad said, "That's one of the largest I've seen around this area of the river. Must be near two pounds."

I was very proud, especially to have him brag on my catch. And before we left at 11:30 A.M., I'd caught eleven more, and he had six rather small ones. I'd noticed that he kept putting his line nearer and nearer to where I was fishing, but my fish were larger than his.

I could hardly wait to get to the store in Armstrong to hear him describe the morning's catch. I bought an RC Cola and a Moon Pie with my dime. Dad bought a Coca Cola and some peanuts. That was our lunch.

The owner, a kindly sort of man, said, "Earl, did you catch them all today?"

"Well, we did have a good day," he responded. "I think we're taking seventeen home to clean. We'll have some good eating off those."

I waited for him to describe my catch, especially the largest of the day, but I was disappointed. They began to discuss the news from Europe, particularly Hitler, the man I'd read about in our local newspaper, the *Durant Daily Democrat*, and had heard about over our Atwater-Kent radio. I wanted to talk about my fish, but I knew it was Hitler that would be the topic.

Dad talked with the grocer about having read last month in the *Democrat* that in July thirty-six men from Durant had enlisted in the military.

"Yes," the owner added, "and I read that FDR has clamped down on shipments of oil and scrap iron to Japan."

"It's scary," said Dad. "You've noticed that the *Democrat* has a daily feature now called 'The War Picture,' and the U.S. Senate just authorized the mobilization of the National Guard, if needed."

"Yes, but I was pleased to read recently that family men won't be drafted in peacetime. That seems right. But the selective service is really busy getting everyone registered," the grocer added.

"Do you think we'll have to go to war in Europe?" Dad asked.

"More and more it's looking that way," the grocer responded.

By this time I'd finished my food and left for the car. Dad and the owner walked out on the porch of the store and talked for a few more minutes.

When Dad got into the Mercury, he seemed quite concerned about the battles going on in England and in Europe. He finished by saying, "Hitler should be killed."

I vowed then and there in Armstrong, Oklahoma, on the last Friday of August 1940 that I'd never like Adolph Hitler.

Arriving home, I got the stringer of fish to show to Mom. Earleen was in the kitchen and said that Dad had really caught some good fish and that she'd look forward to a good fish dinner.

I didn't say anything about the fish I'd caught. I just quietly thought that I'd pray that night for God to cause her piano to quit playing.

I told Mom that I'd caught the biggest fish, and she bragged on me. I beamed and blushed.

While Dad and I cleaned them, he promised me that he would take me catfish fishing on some Saturdays in the fall on both the Washita and Red rivers. He carefully explained how the federal government was building a dam on the Red River about a mile west of the bridge on Highways 69 and 75 and that the dam would cause a huge lake to be formed. He said the Red and Washita rivers would be forever changed after the lake filled.

"And I want you to know these rivers as I knew them when I was young," he said.

"I want to catch the largest catfish in both of them," I responded. And that night, I dreamed that I did and that Dad smiled and bragged on my catches to other men. In the morning, I vowed that I'd try to catch the biggest catfish.

A couple of weeks later, I was back in school and in the fourth grade. Miss Vaughan was my homeroom teacher. She was so pretty and kind and seemed to be a good teacher. I always had liked school, and I knew this would be a good school year. She, too, was redheaded, and I liked that. Maybe she'd take up for me when the guys teased me by calling me Red or Freckles.

One day, when she was reviewing the personal data cards of her homeroom students, she called me to her desk. "Paul, I see that your birthday is April 26. That's mine, too," she told me with a large smile on her face. Then she pulled me close and gave my waist a big squeeze. I liked that and liked her. I vowed I'd get her a present on her birthday.

The next Saturday, I knocked on the door of her house, and her mother came to the door.

"Oh, you're Paul, aren't you?"

Puzzled that she knew, I said, "Yes, ma'am."

"Come in. I see you have brought me some vanilla to buy. How much is the large-sized bottle?"

I again wondered how she knew I'd brought it for her to buy, but I had to ask her if she already bought TRI-PURE at the grocery store.

Relieved when she said she didn't, I told her the large size was 40 cents. She left to get the money, and my teacher, Miss Vaughan, brought the 40 cents back. I felt blushy around her, but she was kind and appreciative. She gave me a cookie from a plate on the table and the 40 cents. I hurried away after thanking her and asking her to thank Mrs. Vaughan, too.

Riding away on my *Adventurer*, I knew that all was right with my world in a great town named Durant. I wanted to live here the rest of my life. I prayed that night that everyone had as good a town as I had. And I remembered to tell God that I didn't like Hitler, and I prayed for more people, like Mack, George, John, Miss Vaughan, and Mr. Garrison.

CHAPTER 5
Pre-Sub Days

    Dad had screened in the north one-half of our large concrete porch, and Mom had made and hung privacy curtains that went two-thirds up the screened-in room. It became more my room than anyone else's, and I used it for my privacy and for being closer to the outdoors. Mom had moved a bed for my younger sister into my inside bedroom, much to my disgust. I asked why she didn't room with Earleen, but I was told that a teenage girl needed more privacy than I needed.
    It didn't make much sense to me, so I was happy that I had a new room, a small radio, a comfortable mattress on a steel cot, and a table for studying and playing board games. I could listen to the sounds of the night as well as use my radio to hear the St. Louis Cardinals on clear channel KMOX. I knew I'd want to move into the house when the weather was really cold, but I thought I'd tough it out as long as I could. And then I'd look forward to an early spring when I could return.
    After school in early October, I'd just walked out from the screened-in portion on my way into the house when I got hit in the back. Looking down to see what hit me, I saw the afternoon newspaper, the *Durant Daily Democrat*. I wasn't hurt—just surprised. Then I saw the carrier coming to the porch to see if he'd hurt me.
    I told him, "No, I'm not hurt." He apologized. I said, "It wasn't your fault... it just happened." And I introduced myself, "I'm Paul.

I've watched you ride your bike and throw your papers day after day. Sometimes I've paid you when you've collected on Fridays. Is being a carrier fun? And do you make a lot of money by throwing papers?"

"I'm Joe," he replied. "I guess I like the route, and I make about $4.50 a week. The two worst things are collecting and having to get up so early on Sundays to deliver the paper."

"You've had this route for several months, haven't you, Joe?" I asked.

"Yeah, about seven months. I know most everything there is to know about delivering papers," he bragged.

"May I get my bike and ride with you and throw some papers?" I asked, almost begging. After all, he must have been in the sixth or seventh grade, and I was scared I'd get in his way, or that he'd say no.

"Sure, come on," he answered in a friendly way.

After I got my bike from the side porch, I yelled to Mom that I would be back in about an hour. She didn't reply, but at least I had told her.

Joe gave me twelve papers, and as we rode he told me which houses needed a paper.

"Always put it on the porch when you throw. If you miss, park your bike and go put it on the porch. Always remember, as my boss, Mr. Bunn, told me, 'A paper off the porch is the same as not delivering it.'"

I had no problem with that rule, except I missed the porches on my first five throws. Joe patiently waited while I put them on the porches. He was grinning most of the time.

"Not as easy as it looks, huh, Paul?"

"No, but I'll learn. Maybe I'll have to ride through the yard so I can get closer to the porch," I replied, wanting to do a good job.

He nodded approval.

I hit the next seven porches, but I was aware that the houses were closer to the street and that they had larger porches. Nevertheless, I was pleased with my throwing accuracy from the sidewalk.

He was nearing the end of his route, so he let me throw the rest. And then we rode to Montgomery's grocery store, and he bought us each an RC Cola. We sat on the curb to drink our colas, and I talked with him about getting my own route.

Joe seemed helpful as he told me how to become a delivery boy.

"Well, I had to sub for quite some time and prove to Mr. Bunn that I was reliable. I was taught well by the guy I subbed for. And he also taught me about collecting, about keeping records, and about paying Mr. Bunn on time."

"Do you think I could become a sub?" I asked.

"Probably. Why don't you ride with me for a week or two and also help me collect? Then you'll be better prepared to become a sub."

I liked that proposal, and I liked his helpfulness and friendliness. I told him I'd get my mom's permission and asked him when and where to meet him the next day.

"Come on down to the *Democrat* as soon as you get out of school. Take any school books home and meet me no later than 3:45."

I said I'd do it, but I still had another question to ask.

"How much money does a sub make each week?" I inquired.

"Not much, Paul. It depends on how many customers are on the route. We carriers have our rule. For any route which has fewer than fifty customers, the sub is paid 50 cents each week. And that includes helping to fold papers, helping to insert on Sunday morning, and helping to collect each Friday as we deliver. And if the route is fifty or more, the going rate is 65 cents each week for all those responsibilities I've mentioned."

Shocked by the small pay, I asked, "Is there any way to get your own route without subbing?"

"No, not that I'm aware of, unless you're the son or nephew of the Storys, who own the *Democrat*," he laughingly responded.

"How long do I have to be a sub?"

"Until you work your way up. There will be six or eight subs ahead of you waiting for their own route. There are always more subs than that, but they quit often."

I thought that I could understand why anyone would quit. The pay was so small, and the route took quite a bit of playtime away after school.

Pressing more, since he seemed so cooperative, I asked, "Joe, how often do route carriers quit and routes become available?"

"There is always some turnover. I subbed on this route for Bill for about eight months before he finished the seventh grade and quit. I'm a seventh-grader now, and I'd like to quit when I enter the ninth. But, if I can afford to, I'll quit after the seventh grade."

As I took the last swig from the tasty RC, I told him I'd see him the next day at the *Democrat*. "I get out of school at 3:30 and can be there before 3:45."

He said, "Great," as he rode away.

On my short ride home, I did my money calculations. I had spent $27 for school clothes and school supplies in August. That had taken all my cash except for $2 from my lock box. I had $80 in the bank, having deposited $20 from lawn mowing in August and September. Now I'd be faced with fall and winter. Maybe I could rake leaves, but not for much money. And I just couldn't get out of the habit of earning. And, if I had a route, Saturdays would still be available for fishing with Dad, and, just maybe, I could convince Mom that I'd be too sleepy to go to Sunday school and church because I'd have to be at the *Democrat* by 5:00 A.M. each Sunday. And, if I had to sub that long to earn my own route, I'd be the best sub that the *Democrat* had ever had.

I shared my plans with Mom, and she said it was OK with her as long as my grades stayed high and if Dad approved.

The one plan I didn't share with her was about missing church. I knew at that point she wouldn't approve.

That evening Dad gave me approval. His only reservation was that I might have to help with his bottling of vanilla after the evening meal. I told him I'd be available. Then I asked him if he'd bottle on Wednesday nights.

"Why Wednesdays?" he asked.

"Oh, sometimes we don't have as much school homework on a Wednesday because so many of us have to go to church prayer meeting on Wednesday nights," I told him, hoping he'd understand and agree with my unspoken message.

It was the first time I could ever remember seeing Dad wink. "We'll see what we can do. Sometimes I think vanilla cooks better on Wednesday mornings than at any other time in the week."

It was pleasant to have an ally in trying to escape church, but I knew Mom too well to know this wasn't over yet.

I knew I could listen to several radio programs that I enjoyed if I could help Dad with vanilla. When I had begged off from church on Wednesday nights, I enjoyed hearing "Mr. District Attorney" and "Dr. Christian," and sometimes there were great boxing matches. The programs were easy to hear in our workroom because the Atwater-Kent was a good radio with lots of volume. Dad enjoyed these programs, too. I'd learned: "Mr. District Attorney, champion of the people, defender of our right to life, liberty and the pursuit of happiness... *Dum de dum-dum-dum-dum*... and our program opens tonight with Harrington...." Dr. Christian was so kind and good to everyone, the type of doctor I'd want to treat me if I were sick.

The next day I met Joe and all went well. He loaned me his extra newspaper bag with the padded shoulder strap to keep the loaded sack from cutting into my shoulder. Printed in big black letters was *Durant Daily Democrat*. What a proud moment. He showed me how to fold the six-page paper, and since we were both right-handed, it was easy to do it as he taught me.

"First," he said, "take the paper in your left hand, make two foldovers with your right hand, and then hold the end of the paper closer to you in your left hand. With your right hand, begin folding it over your left hand. Then tuck the end firmly into the hole as you remove your left hand. Be sure it's tight, because it'll throw better. Also, it won't come undone during the time in the air or after it hits the porch."

He was a good instructor, and with three or four of my folds he nodded approval. His route had sixty-two customers, so he guessed at one-half of his route's papers and gave them to me to put in my bag. Thirty folded, six-page newspapers weren't very heavy.

As we rode to the first house on his route at North Third and Beech, he told me that on Thursdays, when the paper was usually an eight-pager, it was harder to fold and that on Sundays, after the funnies and any other inserts were put together, we'd roll the paper lengthwise and hold it with a rubber band. He said he paid 19 cents to the *Democrat* for a box of one thousand. I wondered why the owners didn't furnish the paper route carriers with free rubber bands.

As we rode and threw papers, he told me to always stay out of Mr. Price's way when he was operating the printing press. If the paper broke and the press had to be stopped to be rethreaded, he'd get out of sorts, even to the point of blaming any news carrier within twenty to thirty feet.

"There's a story he tells about how years ago a carrier kept throwing something onto the paper as it was moving through the printing press. The carrier was fired. I doubt that it was true, but he seems to like to keep us clear of his work, and he likes to threaten us with his story."

"I'll remember to stay away," I responded.

As we departed, he said, "And another advantage of being a sub or having your own route is that your family gets the paper free."

I knew Dad would like that.

A couple of weeks later, nearing the end of October, Joe told me that Gene, a carrier, needed a sub for his route 27.

"Are you interested?" he asked. "If so, I will introduce you to him today. You two can talk as you fold papers."

"Sure, I'm very interested," I replied.

So Joe called to Gene to come over. We met and he told me that his route was small, with only thirty-seven customers, and that it didn't begin until far North Washington, then turned eastward on Chuckwa Drive, eventually including houses north of the college, and finished on First Street, very close to Round Hole.

"Only thirty-seven customers?" I asked. "They are really spread out, aren't they?"

"Yeah, and that's why I need a sub. Joe says you're very good, and that's what I need. I'll be gone some, and you'll deliver the entire route while I'm away," he said.

"How much do you pay?" I asked.

"Going rate for a sub on a short route is 50 cents a week," he responded.

I looked to Joe to see if he would give me the "go" sign. He nodded and smiled.

"Yeah, Gene, when do I begin?"

"Well, this is Thursday. How about next Monday?"

"OK with me. I'll be ready for route 27," I agreed with eagerness.

On our delivery that day, Joe told me he'd sell me the paper bag he'd been letting me use for $1. Since it was in good shape, I accepted. I promised to pay him Friday.

As we continued the route that day, Joe surprised me by inviting me to go to the carnival with him the next night, a Friday. "You know that it's being set up at the very end of South Second Street in a large pasture. It comes here every fall, and I've always gone," Joe said with a sense of satisfaction. "You oughta go with me."

The preacher of the Nazarene church had always said that we should not go into places "of the devil," like movies, pool halls, beer joints, circuses, and carnivals, and, as I thought about it, lots of other places. I momentarily wondered how the devil got around so much.

But Joe was waiting for my answer. I hesitated because I wanted to go, but I was sure I couldn't get Mom's permission. And then there was the question of money. I thought I might be able to say no to Joe if it cost too much.

"How much does it all cost?" I asked.

"Since you've helped me for several weeks, I want to pay your 25-cent entrance fee and buy you fifteen tickets for a dollar. If you bought each ticket separately, it'd be $1.50 for fifteen. But you get a bargain by buying fifteen at one time. What do you think? Want to go?"

How could I turn down that kind of a deal? Without much more thought about Mom's reaction, I excitedly accepted.

"Ride your bike to the end of South Second and meet me there at 7:00 P.M.," he said, pleased that I'd agreed to join him.

I was anxious all the next day. It didn't seem as if I could keep my mind on my lessons. One time Miss Vaughan had to remind me to pay attention. But I kept wondering about the carnival and whether I should go. And if I went, how could I keep Mom from finding out? If she did find out, I knew I'd get a good dose of peach tree tea. And if she didn't, how could I live with the fact I'd deceived her?

Classes went by slowly, and the paper delivery and collection were not fun. But Joe kept talking about all the fun we'd have at the carnival.

His enthusiasm for the night wore through my other thoughts about consequences. When we were finished with our final time to work together, I thanked him for all he'd taught me and for helping me get a sub's position. I told him I'd see him at 7:00.

Arriving at home, I just blurted out to Mom that I had been invited to Mack's house to play Monopoly at 7:00. First out-and-out lie that I'd ever remembered telling, and I didn't feel good inside.

Mom said, "That's fine, Son. Be sure and take your game spinner along with you because Mack probably uses dice with his game."

The guys had always kidded me about having to use a spinner that Mom had made for my Monopoly game, but they seemed to respect me for my religious belief—well, Mom's belief.

So I quickly got the spinner and showed it to Mom and told her I'd take it to Mack's. The deception was somewhat lessened by this act, but not altogether.

After supper, I got a few coins and put them in my pocket, mounted my bike, and rode off in the direction of Mack's house. Then at Fifth and Evergreen, I cut over to Second Street and headed south. While riding, I recalled how Mom and Dad had permitted Earleen to go with a group to the Texas Centennial celebration in 1936 in Dallas. I had listened to her talk about the ferris wheel and other rides, along with the fun she said she had on the midway. And those things didn't seem much different from what Joe said about the carnival I was about to attend. I now had an argument to justify going, but none for the lie.

Joe was waiting. He paid my way in and bought me fifteen tickets. We walked around, enjoying all we saw. His laughter and fun seemed to cause me to relax and get caught up in the excitement.

We rode the ferris wheel twice, bought some cotton candy, and enjoyed listening to the men trying to get people to come into the tent to see the fat lady. This didn't appeal to either of us. We did spend a ticket to see the snake handler, though. We bought a cola for one ticket and a hot dog for two tickets. I spent two tickets to try to knock the milk bottles off the small platform but was unsuccessful. We rode three other rides, one which made me dizzy. I knew that my early childhood bout with car sickness had revisited me, but at least I wasn't throwing up. Still, the hot dog taste was right at the bottom of my mouth.

Wanting to recover a bit, I told Joe that I was dizzy, and I thought I'd better just walk around for a while. I gave him my remaining three tickets and told him I'd be at the front gate when he was through.

While I was waiting, I heard someone speak to me. "Well, Paul, I'm surprised to see you here. Did your mother give you permission?" Mrs. Russell asked with a strange expression on her face. Mr. Russell just nodded.

"No," I replied, "I'm just here waiting for a friend."

While it was true I was waiting, I figured she'd know that I wouldn't be inside the gate of the carnival unless I'd been at the carnival. I felt trapped.

Mr. and Mrs. Russell walked out the gates. Then I collected my wits enough to remind myself that Mrs. Russell was my Sunday school teacher. "What was *she* doing here?" I asked myself. I didn't have a good answer, only more confusion. My thought was that I hoped Mrs. Russell, who was a good friend of Mom's, would never tell her about seeing me there.

Joe showed up, and we rode together to Second and Elm, where he left me to go to his house. "I enjoyed the carnival, Paul, and hope you did, too. I'll see you Monday at the *Democrat*. Hope you like working for Gene."

And he rode away, leaving me very alone. When I got home, I retrieved the Monopoly spinner that I had hidden in the garage, went inside, and made sure that Mom saw it as I went toward my room.

"Son, I need to talk with you," she said harshly. "Just come here right now." From her tone, I knew that Mrs. Russell had already called. Well, I'd just have to be truthful and argue my side.

"Were you at the carnival tonight?"

"Yes, ma'am," I responded with fear in my belly.

"So you lied to me."

"Yes, ma'am, I guess I did. But I—"

She cut off my intended argument. I thought it was time to go get a peach tree switch, so I just headed that way, saying, "I'll go get a switch."

"No," she said sternly, "go get one of your daddy's belts. Lying deserves a good belting." Having never had the belt before, I didn't know exactly what to expect. But after it was over, I knew I didn't want the belt again. She told me it hurt her more to do it than it hurt me. I wanted to argue that with her, but I was in no condition to do it.

I asked her if I could go on to bed, and she pointed her finger toward my room.

As I was walking away, she told me to put Dad's belt away. "And be certain to ask the Lord to forgive you for your lie when you say your prayer tonight, and don't you ever lie to anyone again," she said with a strong emphasis on the word *lie*.

My backside hurt, really hurt. Just as I found a comfortable position in bed, Dad knocked and came in. Linda was soundly sleeping in her bed, so he quietly asked me if I'd like to go fishing at the Washita River in the morning.

"Yes, sir, I'll be ready," not asking him how early we'd leave. With that, he left me to think and to sleep. I needed more sleep than I thought, because my behind throbbed with pain. I had a troubled sleep, probably waking up three or four times to turn to my side so the pain would be lessened.

At 6:00 A.M., Dad told me it was time to get up. It was cold in my room, and I quietly dressed so I wouldn't wake Linda. She looked so warm and innocent from the beam of light reflecting off of her from the closet light I'd turned on. I wondered if she, too, would get some kind of privileges that I thought Earleen had gotten. But I didn't linger on those thoughts long because Dad said it was time to go.

Dad had already put the two very long and heavy cane poles into the "Y" he'd had built onto the front bumper of our Mercury. He got in on the driver's side, and I tied the poles to his door handle. Then I entered on the passenger side. I didn't have breakfast because Dad didn't believe fish would bite, especially catfish, if you dawdled around eating breakfast. I hurt when my backside came to rest against the car seat.

We went to the bait shop, where the keeper already had three customers ahead of us, and when our time came, Dad bought a pint of stinkbait for 60 cents. Then we headed west on Main Street and onto Highway 70, past Mead, past several side roads, until Dad turned north on an old dirt road.

"We'll have our bait in the Washita in a few minutes," he said.

"What's stinkbait?" I asked.

He laughed as he told me, "You'll know why it's called stinkbait when I take the lid off the pint jar. It really stinks. It's made from dead minnows and flour; it's all mixed together to make a paste-like bait. We'll use a three-pronged hook with a sponge over the three sharp hooks, put them all down into the bait jar with a stick, and then we'll catch the big channel cats," he bragged.

He hadn't mentioned my belting. I knew he knew about it. But it seemed that he wanted me to enjoy fishing.

We soon parked the Mercury, and, after I untied the poles from his side, we walked briskly toward the Washita River. On the way there, Dad explained to me that the river got its name from the Choctaw words *owa* and *chito,* which together mean "big hunt." So we were on our big fish hunt, I thought. I could hear the current of the river as we got nearer. When we could see it, I was impressed with how murky red the water was. As we looked for a good place to fish, I became fearful and cautious of the river and its steep banks.

Dad and I kept walking until we found a place where the current was slower. Drifts of logs had lodged together to form what Dad described as a good place to catch the catfish.

The lid of the bait jar came off, and I thought I'd pass out from the odor. I could now understand why the bait was called "stinkbait." Dad submerged my sponge with the triple hooks into the smelly paste and suggested I toss my line into a quiet-looking spot near a big log. This I did. He put his line with the big brown cork, like mine, into the water about twenty or thirty feet downstream from where I was fishing.

Then he said, "Son, we'll have to be very quiet. If we disturb the fish, only the small cats will bite. And we want the big cats."

This information was new to me. I thought he wanted to be quiet so we didn't have to talk about my belting. I'd have to wait and see. But it was good to be with him in the early morning light. It was a very cool late October morning, and I wasn't dressed too warmly, but I'd have to show Dad how tough I was by not mentioning that I was cold.

I tried sitting on the bank by my fishing pole, but it was too painful. So I stood and propped the other end of my pole on an overlapping tree limb and held the end of my pole in my hands. Dad was quietly sitting and watching his cork while he smoked a Camel cigarette.

I tried to talk to him, but he said to be quiet. After a seemingly long silence, I saw him set the hook and land a large catfish. He said it'd be about five pounds, a good eating size, and I was pleased because I liked to eat catfish. Dad caught four more within an hour. He baited my sponge again and suggested I throw my line closer to his.

"There must be a school of these cats right around where I'm fishing. Maybe you'll catch a good one, too."

So I put mine five feet from his, and again I became silent. But even standing up, my behind still hurt. Cold and hurting, but enjoying being with Dad, I thought about lots of things. But I knew I had to be quiet.

I caught a small catfish, and Dad bragged on my catch while putting it on the stringer with the other fish he'd caught.

"Well, Son, you've at least caught your ride back home," he kidded. "The old saying among fishermen is that you must catch at least one, or you have to walk home."

He seemed to be very approving of his nine-year-old son. I felt warmer inside but still cold outside. We fished until about 11:30 A.M., and he'd caught eight good cats. I caught one other small one.

"Time for us to go now. The cats have quit biting for the day," he said.

Getting our fish and our poles, we returned to the Mercury, loaded up, and drove to Cunningham's grocery store, one of Dad's vanilla customers just west of Mead. He bought me a Nehi orange soda and a Moon Pie. He got his Coca Cola and peanuts. Mr. Cunningham walked out to the Mercury to look at the mess of fish we'd caught. Dad bragged how he'd caught all the big ones. They both laughed when Dad pointed to the two small ones I'd caught. I wondered to myself why he hadn't bragged about the big crappie I'd caught in Blue River when we'd been at Armstrong. But life hadn't been very good to me in the last few hours, so I didn't think about it anymore.

Driving the eight miles or so home, Dad finally asked me about what happened the night before. I told him everything in great detail. He just drove and listened, never even glancing my way.

When my story was all told, the silence remained. I was curious, but fearful of interrupting the silence. Entering the city limits, at just about the Foote Nursery, he put his right hand on my left knee, patted me gently, and said he hoped I learned something from it all.

"Dad," I asked, "did you ever lie like I did?"

He was silent for a few seconds. Then he turned toward me and said, "Yes, I did, Son, several times. A big one got me in trouble in high school and got me kicked out of school when I threw the ink bottle. Then a lie about my age to enlist in the Oklahoma National Guard caused me to be sent to San Benito, Texas, in 1916, to guard our nation against Mexican bandits. And I told a woman that I loved her when I really didn't, and we got married, had a child, who died shortly after birth, and got divorced before I ever met your mother. I know I've told other lies, but those are the biggest ones I remember right now."

I was very upset about this information. I just sat there, not knowing what to say. I wasn't quite ready to hear all this.

He talked about his experience in the U.S. Army until we arrived home. He said he'd show me pictures of his army camp. I untied the cord holding the poles against his car door handles, and we unloaded all our fishing gear. Inside, Mom was pleased to see the fish. She liked fried catfish, too, especially the way Dad fried them.

I was tired, still hurting, and hungry. Dad cleaned the fish while I sat soaking in hot water in the bathtub. Mom knocked on the bathroom door and asked if I was all right.

"Sure," I again lied. I wouldn't dare let her know what pain I was in. She left and I soaked. When I was in my room after the soaking, I backed up to my big mirror and saw ugly bruises. I got dressed, got some food, and went outside to be alone. I just couldn't sort it all out no matter how hard I tried.

Sunday morning when I woke up, it dawned on me that from now on I'd have to get up around 5:00 A.M. to get to the *Democrat* by 5:15 or so. It wasn't a pleasant thought, but there was a part of it that still excited me.

After I delivered and was back home, Mom fixed pancakes and sausage for my breakfast. Dad even bought a copy of the *Daily Oklahoman* with its statewide news and great comics. He slid the comics over to me. I read and laughed at the "Katzenjammer Kids," as well as other comics that I didn't get in the *Democrat*. Then he showed me the army camp pictures and talked about his experiences in San Benito, Texas.

When Mom, Earleen, Linda, and I got out of the Mercury at the Church of the Nazarene at South Ninth and Texas, I felt physically better, even though I didn't want to see Mrs. Russell, my Sunday school teacher. I was really surprised to see another person in our classroom who introduced herself as our new teacher. She just said that Mrs. Russell wanted to quit teaching for a while.

So she got herself into trouble, too, I thought. I grinned about that.

In church I always sat on the west side of the building near the windows with my church friend Dan, who was two years older than I. There we could see Highways 69 and 75 when the window was raised. We filled in time with unimportant things like betting a dime on whether twenty Chevys would pass down the highway before twenty Fords did. I bet on Fords. Dan won 20 cents.

During the altar call after the preacher's sermon, I saw Mom nod her head in a way that said I should go to the altar and be saved. I thought it might help me to get back on her good side, so I went down and knelt at the altar, or what many people in the church called the "moaner's bench." Two other people came to be saved. The preacher told the saints of the church to come and kneel and pray for these sinners who needed God's help. I got saved. Or at least, I told those who were still in church that I did.

As we left, Dan cornered me. "What did you do to get saved?" he asked.

"I'm not sure. I just said, 'Jesus, save me,' and waited until everyone else who was kneeling around me prayed loudly and hit me on my back a few times and urged the devil to leave my soul."

"Well, are you saved?" was Dan's next question.

"I don't feel a bit different, but maybe in time I'll feel saved," was the only honest response I knew to give my friend.

"Do you want to continue our dime bets on cars now that you're saved?" he asked.

"I'll have to wait and see," I told him.

As our family drove home from church, Dad hit the bumpy Frisco railroad tracks especially hard. I knew he was irritated, as he nearly always was when we didn't get out of church on time. But I was used to his irritation on Sundays.

Mom looked back at me and smiled. When we got home about 12:45, the pot roast she had left cooking when we went to church was burned to a crisp. Dad got really irritated, but he simmered down after a while and fried us some really great catfish.

In less than forty-eight hours, I'd told a big lie, been to the carnival, had my former Sunday school teacher tattle on me, gotten a real belting, gone fishing, heard Dad tell me more than I wanted to hear, been saved, and tackled a new problem of deciding whether I'd bet a dime in the future with Dan in our Ford-Chevrolet game while we sat in church. Whew!

All these events made my head dizzy and stomach queasy. And my behind was still bruised and sore.

CHAPTER 6
Subbing

After school on Monday, I rode my bike as fast as I could so I'd be on time to meet Gene at the *Democrat*. He was already there, so we got the thrity-seven newspapers, folded them, and rode for about a mile before the first house. I rode standing up because my behind was still tender. The route was easy to learn since nearly every house received the *Democrat*. It took us about thirty-five minutes to throw the route, so we had finished shortly before 5:00 P.M.

Gene suggested we stop at Lee's Auto Park and Skelly-S station and grocery to get a drink. He bought me a Dr Pepper.

"Paul," he began, "I liked the way you helped me today, and I can tell you'll be a great sub. But I want to let you in on a secret. If you're going to work for me, I don't want to call you Paul because I have an older brother named Paul I just don't get along with. So I've decided that if it's OK with you, I'll call you by your initials, P.J. How are you with that?"

"That's fine with me," I responded, thinking of the various nicknames of Red, Freck, Ears, Waxy, and others I had not liked.

"P.J. it'll be, then," responded Gene. He seemed to be pleased that I'd agreed to the new name. We finished, rode four blocks together, and departed.

The rest of the ride home, I repeatedly went over my new name, P.J. Then I added, "P.J. has a route." I knew that I was only a sub, but to me it was like my very own route.

Two days later, on Halloween, Gene called me early before I left for school and asked if I thought I could deliver the route by myself. Feeling very confident that I'd learned all the customers' houses, I assured him that I could.

All that school day, while we did Halloween-type stuff, the idea that I would deliver by myself kept spinning through my head. I rode rapidly to the *Democrat*, told Mr. Bunn that I'd be delivering that day in case there was a kick, gave him my phone number, and began folding papers.

The carriers kidded me about so much responsibility in so quick a time. They began to say that I'd probably miss several houses and that Mr. Bunn would chew me out for missing houses. Several carriers crowded around me to tease me even more. It seemed strange to me, but I'd been teased all my life. Dad had taught me that if a boy wasn't being teased, it meant he didn't have friends. At that moment, I thought I must have a lot of friends, even though there was something fishy about all this.

Having folded my papers, I left. I knew the route and felt proud of my ability to have learned it so quickly.

About halfway through the route, I became aware of an almost flat back tire. It wasn't an unusual event because I'd had lots of flats, but as I was looking at it, I noticed the valve cap was missing. Upon closer inspection, I could tell that the valve stem had been loosened. Now I knew why I'd gotten such close attention as I was folding my papers. Someone had played a dirty trick on me. I was upset, but I didn't have anyone specific to blame. Was it because of Halloween? Was it part of an initiation? Was it because I wasn't liked? I just didn't know. I vowed that I'd never mention it to anyone.

I quickly found a solution to my nearly flat tire. My valve stem on the front tire had a cap with the stem-tightening tool on its top, which I used to tighten the loose stem on the back tire. After I did this, I rode with low air pressure, finished my delivery, and aired the tire at Lee's. Tire problem solved. People problem unsolved. When I got home, I waited around to see if a call would come from Mr. Bunn about a kick. I was relieved that no more came.

The next day at school, Miss Vaughan called me to her desk. Since she was smiling, I figured everything was hunky-dory. She took me out in the hall and talked to me about what a good student

I was and about how Mr. Garrison, the principal, liked to reward good students by letting them help him in his office.

Needless to say, I was thrilled. Miss Vaughan said I could take twenty minutes of her class time to work as long as I kept my assignments up to standards. Then she asked me to go to his office.

After Mack's experience with Mr. Garrison the year before, and my experience selling vanilla to Mr. and Mrs. Garrison, and then another bottle a few months later, I entered his office feeling good. I wasn't disappointed. Soon I was delivering notes to teachers from him, as well as collecting the absent and tardy slips teachers were to provide his office. I thought that I, again, was a deliverer and collector, and this thought caused me to walk down the hallway with a happy quickness in my steps.

After I had done his chores, he called me into his office. "Paul, please be seated," he said. "I want you to know how pleased I am you're in my school and that you are not only a good student, but you also have excellent conduct."

Suddenly, my tongue was almost tied. I didn't know how to respond, so I just blurted out, "Thanks, but Miss Wheat said my art isn't very good."

"You know, mine isn't either," he reassured me.

Trying to keep my embarrassment under control and knowing that I liked and trusted him, I asked, "Mr. Garrison, do you go to church?"

"Well, yes, I do. Why do you ask, Paul?"

For an instant I felt that I shouldn't have asked him that question. But it seemed important to me, and it could sidetrack his praise, which I desperately wanted but was embarrassed to receive.

"Mrs. Garrison and I belong to and attend regularly the Methodist church. We enjoy being there and like the good people who attend. Do you attend a church, Paul?"

"Yes, Mother takes my two sisters and me to the Nazarene church. Dad doesn't go to any church," I told him, somewhat hesitantly.

"That's interesting, Paul. I grew up attending that church and graduated from a Nazarene college in Bethany, Oklahoma. But when I married Mrs. Garrison, who was a Methodist, I joined her church. I've been most satisfied with my decision."

I sat there a minute, letting all that sink in. It knew that it was about time to go back to class, but I'd just gotten new information from a man I liked very much. As I walked the few yards down the hallway to my classroom, I vowed to marry a woman who was a Methodist. As I grinned, I thought, *After all, Jeanne Paul is a Methodist.* Jeanne still didn't pay much attention to me, but was she ever smart and pretty! Her long red hair deserved the attention of another redhead.

I won the contest that day in our music class by placing notes on the lines and spaces for e-g-b-d-f and f-a-c-e when the teacher would call out words. My winning word was *bead*, which quickly defeated my friend John in the finals, and John already played the cornet. I guess I just wrote the notes more quickly, because John knew music very well. The e-g-b-d-f was easy. "Every good boy does fine" and "face" I knew well, and quickly could figure out where to place the notes from the word the teacher would call out.

Strange, I thought, *that I can win but can't sing well at all. Music and art just aren't my subjects. Maybe I can be a Methodist and not sing or have to do artwork. At least I hope so.*

When I arrived at the *Democrat* that afternoon, I was curious as to what the carriers might ask about my tire, or whether they'd say anything at all. While I was folding my share of Gene's papers, Joe, who had gotten me involved by inviting me to help him, told me to come over to where he was folding. When I got there, he was silent for a moment while he looked around.

"P.J.—that's what I hear you've been named by Gene," he quietly said as he continued to look around.

"Yeah, I like that name. Call me that lots of times so other people will catch on," I replied.

"All right, P.J., but let me tell you something. And don't you dare tell anyone I told you. Swear to it?"

"I swear," I said, knowing that if I ever did really swear and Mom found out, I'd have more troubles.

"OK, now listen. If someone gives you a piece of gum, take it, thank him, but don't chew it. You hear me, don't you?"

"Sure do. But why?" I asked.

"Go on back and fold papers and remember you swore not to tell anyone," he said quickly and quietly.

I did as he suggested. Shortly afterwards, one of the older carriers came by.

"Here is some gum, P.J. Today I've been giving subs pieces that I got trick-or-treating last night."

"Thanks," I replied, as I suspiciously looked at the Fleer's Double Bubble gum he gave me. He left, and I reached into my pocket and got out my own Double Bubble and left his piece in my pocket. After beginning to chew it and blow my bubbles, I noticed that several experienced carriers a few yards away were laughing and having a good time.

Gene and I had our papers folded when one of the carriers, while leaving on his route, said, "P.J., I hope you have enough toilet paper with you today because if you don't, your bottom will get ink all over it from using pages from the *Democrat*. You'd better go ask Mr. Bunn for some extra papers." Now I knew. Joe had saved me from more troubles.

As I got close to home after delivering, I could smell the sweet odor of Dad's vanilla. If the wind was in my favor, I could smell it as far as a block away. That evening I helped Dad bottle vanilla, and I shared with him the two events of the low tire and the gum.

"Son," he said with an understanding voice, "you've just been through initiation. Regardless of what it is, men have to be initiated, and it really never stops. Sometimes I think I'm still being initiated. I could tell you lots of stories from my youth, but for now you'll just have to accept what I say. Tomorrow I'd suggest that when the subject of gum comes up, you just laugh and say you got two kicks from using the *Democrat* for toilet paper. They'll laugh, too, knowing that they caused you trouble."

"But wouldn't that not be telling the truth, Dad?" I asked, knowing that a recent lie had gotten me the belting of my life.

"Well, let's say it's just the way we men talk," he responded knowingly.

I was confused but pleased that Dad seemed to know what he was talking about. I'd try it tomorrow. I vowed then I'd never be cruel or mean and would not participate in initiations that hurt and caused people pain.

Three carriers crowded around me the next day. One asked how I was.

"Fine," I said.

"How long did it take for you to throw your route?" another asked.

"Longer than usual," I said, looking disgusted.

"Your health OK today?" another asked.

"Just barely. It was a tough go, and I had to stop in the woods a couple of times. Got a couple of kicks because I didn't have enough newspapers." I said, knowing I was misrepresenting the truth. They all grinned and left, saying something like, "P.J., we welcome you to the group."

Maybe I had passed. Maybe no more bad stuff would occur. Maybe I was now an official sub. Time would tell. But then I remembered that Dad said men get initiated all their lives.

Gene and I delivered, collected, had a good time together, and had our Dr Peppers at the end of our route. He told me the stuff I'd been through was usual. I didn't tell him that I'd switched the gum.

My money was not adding up very quickly because I'd had to buy a warm mackinaw coat at Perkins Brothers for $8.95, which had taken all but a dollar of my money in the lock box. Making 50 cents per week plus vanilla sales in the winter just didn't add up very fast.

Christmas came and went. There weren't many presents, but the clothes I got were nice. I had written a check for $10 to buy presents for Mom, Dad, Earleen, and Linda. Dad gave me a kickstand and two fender reflectors for my bike. I needed those, so I was glad. Dad continued to talk about Europe and Hitler and the fact that he had registered for selective service. A new daily column had appeared in the *Democrat* for the wives of drafted men.

When he'd had our house built, Dad decided it would be cheaper to heat with coal than natural gas. While we had natural gas for the hot water heater, the kitchen stove, and a small heater in the bathroom, he decided that he'd build a small storage house on the northwest corner of our lot to hold the coal and kindling—either corn cobs or small wood—which he had delivered from some man who sold this stuff. He bought a huge coal-burning stove, which went into the room we used in the summer as our dining room. When the weather began to cool in late October, he and I would put up the coal stove and hook the exhaust vents into the flu to the brick chimney he'd had built with our new house.

I had expected to get the chore, and I did. I had to bring in two large buckets of coal and one of kindling every evening. Also, when the stove had to be cleaned, I had to remove and dispose of the clinkers and the ashes left from the burned coal. Dad did build the fire early each morning. We all stayed in the warm room during the evening and at night. Dad had the radio, Earleen and I studied, Linda played dolls, and Mom darned socks, mended clothes, or whatever needed doing. The cigarette smoke from Dad's Camels filled the room, but we had mostly gotten used to it.

On a February morning in 1941, after Dad had built the fire and gone to town for his early coffee, I smelled smoke. Mom said it was just smoke blowing out of the stove, but I wasn't sure. While dressing for school, I kept checking because it smelled like pine wood burning. About the third time I looked at the ceiling near the chimney, the flames were just appearing, and I screamed, "Fire, fire!"

Mom called the fire department, Earleen got Linda and went outside, and I filled several buckets with water and threw them on the flames with little result. Since the firetruck had only four blocks to drive, the firemen were there very quickly. They efficiently put out the fire, but what a mess they made. Dad arrived and took charge after the firemen left, and he told Earleen and me to go on to school.

Friends asked me about the fire. They'd either seen the firetruck at our house or had heard about it from others. I didn't enjoy school that day. Not only would it be messy with more work when I got home from my route, but also it would be cold in the house. And the big problem would be where Dad would get the money to repair the damage. He had told me there was no insurance.

Fortunately for me, Dad and Mom had the house mostly cleaned by the time I got home, but the smoke smell remained.

"Dad," I asked after supper, "do you have enough money to repair our house?"

"Yes, I've already called a carpenter, and he looked at it and said he'd fix it for $200. I'll use what little savings I have plus the rent money and we'll get by."

I was saddened but relieved. I was ready to use my money in the bank to help pay for it, but now I wouldn't have to. I vowed that I'd try to earn more money.

A couple of days later, while I was helping in the principal's office, Mr. Garrison asked me about the fire. I told him, and he said, "You must have been a hero," with his usual smile.

"I don't think I was. I just did what I had to do."

"It seems to me that you're a hero," he emphasized. "I'll have it mentioned in my principal's note to all my teachers."

I was taken aback because I didn't think I'd done anything special, yet he said I had and that he'd even announce it to all the teachers. I changed the subject.

"Mr. Garrison, I'd like to work all five days for you like I used to when I began," I said.

"And it would be nice to have you every day, Paul, but I try to let a boy and a girl both work for me."

I didn't like his response, but it seemed fair. At least I got the three days a week. Continuing, I asked, "Mr. Garrison, why don't you hire men teachers who are like you? Seems as if all our teachers are women."

"Well, next year you'll have Mr. Sharp for geography and playground activities. Then, too, we have a nice man, Mr. Threlkeld, who is our custodian. But, yes, Paul, I'd like to hire more teachers who are men, but not many apply."

"But I enjoy your friendliness and willingness to spend so much time during our lunch hour watching us play ball and teaching us," I said. "And last March when you made the big box kite and let us all have turns flying it was really fun. I'm not saying my women teachers are not good, or anything like that, but I still would like to have some men teachers, especially ones who'd accept my artwork."

He laughed as he said, "Paul, your artwork will improve, just like all your other work will. You'd better go on to class, and, before you leave, Mrs. Garrison asked me to remind you to bring her two large bottles of vanilla. Her mother needs one, as well as Mrs. Garrison."

I'd see to it that she got them soon. As I left, I wondered if someday I would become a teacher in the elementary grades.

On February 13 a carrier named Jerry Anderson approached me and asked if I'd become his sub. He told me he had a sixty-customer paper route on South First, Second, and Third. That meant I'd make 65 cents a week, I'd have a route that wasn't so far out at the edge of town, and I'd be closer to having worked my way up the waiting list for my own route.

I agreed that I'd like to be his sub, but I told him I'd need to talk to Gene. Gene agreed that it'd be a good move for me, and he thanked me for helping him. I said that I was the one who should thank him, which I did by asking him to go with me the half-block to the Durant Drug Store, where I bought him a fifteen-cent Malt-O-Plenty. The Durant Drug was the kids' hangout. They treated us kids great.

As I folded the papers that day, I noticed an article on the front page. The headline was "Revival of KKK to Combat 5th Column Is Revealed." I had always heard such bad things about the KKK. I wondered if Hitler or the KKK was worse. But I had my papers to deliver and my new job to think about, so I soon forgot the headlines. I changed bosses and routes the next day. My new one was route 11. I excitedly told Mom and Dad about my new responsibility that night. They seemed pleased and happy for me.

I reminded Mom to pack my lunch the next day. I had met Mr. Threlkeld, our school custodian, and he had invited me to have lunch with him in the basement-like room where the school furnace, electrical controls, and his supplies were. He seemed nice, and since Mr. Garrison had suggested that I meet him, I agreed. So on Valentine's Day, we were to eat our lunch together.

He had brought a lunch, but his was in a rather long, black lunchbox. Mine was in a paper sack, which was from the Piggly Wiggly grocery store. We ate and talked. Since it was cold outside, I wasn't missing the games on the outside. He mostly told me about himself. I asked if he'd ever wanted to be a teacher. He said that he'd quit school after the sixth grade and was never a good student. He'd worked on his dad's farm for years before he married, moved to Durant, and had three kids. He'd been at Washington Irving school for nearly three years and thought he'd remain as long as they liked his work. He then told me a bit about his work. I appreciated him sharing with me.

We finished lunch, and it was time for me to go to class. I thanked him and left. I had made a new friend on Valentine's Day and I liked that. Mr. Garrison was in the hallway, and I told him about having lunch with Mr. Threlkeld.

"That's fine, Paul. I'm glad you visited with him. But remember that there's a lunchroom students are to go to when they bring their lunch from home. It's OK this time, but I must be consistent. Please remember next time."

Feeling a bit flushed, I agreed to do that. "Mr. Garrison, I guess I didn't think it'd hurt anything," I added. Even though he was kind, he had rules and was consistent, I thought. I walked on to class, where Miss Vaughan announced that we'd write Valentine poems. I had to write what thoughts I had about Valentine's Day.

After a few tries, I finished my poem:

> When I see roses, I want to say
> That I just love Valentine's Day.
> And when I see a girl with hair so red,
> Her smile knocks me almost dead.
> So while violets are blue
> I always think of her, not you.

After she collected the poems, Miss Vaughan handed them out so that no one got his or her own poem. And then, one by one, we stood and read the poem she'd given to us. It wasn't easy to recognize who'd written the poem, even though Miss Vaughan asked us to guess. Everyone laughed and had fun when we guessed. But when Gwen Enochs read mine, I was aware that I was really blushing. Miss Vaughan didn't even ask who wrote it because all the class was yelling out my name. I wanted to disappear through the floor. Miss Vaughan defended me by telling others how well I'd rhymed my poem. No one ever knew that I was writing my Valentine poem to my favorite teacher, Miss Vaughan. They all thought I meant Jeanne Paul. Well, I did think of her, too, when I wrote it. I survived the teasing at that afternoon's recess and was ready for my new route with Jerry.

Jerry seemed pleased with my skills. He showed me that some of the porches were old and rotten and that I'd have to be careful to keep the paper from falling through the old rotting boards of a few of the houses. But most were well kept, even though it was obvious to me that the families who lived in these houses had less money than my family—maybe a lot less.

Jerry taught me who paid regularly the 10 cents every Friday and those who seemed to put him off. He'd have to try two or three times to collect. And some moved away owing him for one, two, or three weeks of papers. He said that he lost money because he still had to pay Mr. Bunn for his papers. I hoped I'd get a route where everyone paid. It didn't seem fair for me to lose money if I couldn't collect from customers.

That Friday I found out for myself what Jerry meant. I collected from only five of the first nine customers. Two said they'd pay me Monday, two weren't at home, and one woman just said she didn't have any money and quit her subscription. Jerry said that she'd probably start up again in a couple of weeks.

At the end of the route, at the intersection of the MKT and Frisco tracks were two old three-story frame hotels. Each had a large front porch with a swing. Three young women sat in one swing. Two sat in the other hotel's porch swing.

Jerry grinned at me and told me to go collect. When I got on the porch at the first hotel, I told one of the women I would like to collect 10 cents for the *Democrat*.

She responded, "How about taking it out in trade? I like young boys," she said with her red lips parting into a wide smile. The others laughed.

I knew I was uncomfortable, but I didn't know why. I looked to Jerry, sitting astraddle his bike seat while balancing himself with both feet on the ground. He just laughed and yelled, "Get the money and let's go."

An older woman opened the front screen door and paid me the dime. "Now, run along, young man. Pay no mind to my girls."

I said, "My name is P.J., and I'm Jerry's new sub."

"Well, it's good to know you, P.J. Now, get along." I thought she liked my new name, P.J., by the way she said it.

The young women in the swing on the next hotel's porch were all laughing when I went to collect. One, who said she was cold, asked me to come and sit on her lap, and we'd both stay warm. They laughed even more.

Again, I said, "My name is P.J., and I'm Jerry's new sub."

Another said, "Well, P.J., we're glad you're new because we always are looking for new customers." They were jabbing their elbows into each other's ribs gently and laughing.

One reached into a pocket and paid me the 10 cents. "Now, you come back, P.J."

Innocently, I gave the 20 cents to Jerry, feeling that whatever had just happened to me, I didn't understand.

Jerry asked, "P.J, do you know what a whore is?"

"No."

As we were riding back to the *Democrat* to pay Mr. Bunn, I got surprising information from Jerry.

I continued to enjoy the route in spite of the hotels. Jerry was especially helpful and nice, and the extra 15 cents a week wasn't much, but every cent helped.

On February 25 one of the headlines on the front of the *Democrat* read, "Food Stamp Plan Given to Grocers." In my own nine-year-old world, I was becoming increasingly concerned. Several articles each day focused on how the U.S. was preparing to help our friends in Europe. We also discussed some of these topics in class at school. I didn't understand it all, but I was worried, and Dad listened more and more to the war-related news on our Atwater-Kent.

Mother hadn't bought my argument about being too sleepy to go to Sunday morning church, so I had to go. I hadn't forgotten about my bet, but the church windows had been closed all winter. I needed to keep my friendship with Dan, the one that I liked in church, so we kept our dime bet going when the weather started warming a bit in March. We'd open the windows by our pew and begin our game. Since we had a Ford Motor product, a Mercury, and since Dan's parents had a Chevrolet, we continued our bet on Fords vs. Chevys. Only cars could be counted—no trucks, not even pickups. For every Ford or Chevy that passed by the window, we'd make a tally mark on a sheet of paper, and the winner was the first to get to twenty. It was always a close call. Dan and I thought we'd about broken even over the many months we'd entertained ourselves. But we surely had to be careful and keep our activity secret.

It sure seemed a better way of filling in time than listening to Brother White and his hellfire and damnation stories. These were sort of interesting but scary. When I did listen and watch him, he'd move from behind the pulpit carrying an open Bible on one hand and use the other to point toward the congregation, toward the ceiling (which I guessed must have been toward heaven), toward the floor (the other place), and in a booming voice which sometimes began to r-o-l-l out G-o-d and J-e-s-u-s, he would tell us to repent and be saved. And then he'd shout, "Glory hallelujah, praise God! Now you all praise Him with me." And most of the congregation would echo his words.

Nearly always two or three babies would begin to cry. The mothers would try to hush them, but usually they couldn't, so

Brother White would get louder to overcome his competition from the babies. Dan and I rooted for the babies.

We watched and heard this week after week after week. Thank God for Fords and Chevys and babies.

It was late March before I knew it. The green weeds appearing in lawns thrilled me, except for those in our own lawn. Dad helped me clean, oil, and sharpen the blades of the lawn mower. Money began coming in a bit more regularly. I kept very busy with school, paper route, mowing, helping Dad bottle vanilla, selling vanilla, playing, and going to church.

Playing was important, and I used as much time to play as possible. After throwing my half of Jerry's route, I stopped nearly every day at the playground at the junior high school, where there would be some kind of ballgame. My favorite was football. I was good at catching passes and, in a choose-sides game, was usually chosen early. I was OK in softball and basketball, too. After we played football, I usually went home with something bruised or bloody. Mom would always caution me not to get hurt. She never did say directly, but I sensed that she thought that football was a tool of the devil. I thought that I'd have to teach her more about football so maybe she'd know why I liked it so much.

On Sunday afternoons, I continued to play checkers, Monopoly, or other games with Mack, George, or John Shaw. And sometimes we'd go to the MKT depot, where John's father was the station agent, and watch the trains rumble by. Other times we'd go to the basement of the Methodist church and play ping pong. We really had great times together. These three guys were my best friends. We'd discuss school, girls, the war in Europe, how we got along with our parents, and other stuff. I was the only one of the four who worked for money, so they didn't seem very interested in my work activities. But Mack did say he might be interested in mowing with me after school was out.

I just kept busy. No new surprises, no new initiations, no new switchings, or beltings. Things just went smoothly for a change.

For my tenth birthday on April 26, 1941, Mom surprised me with a birthday party at our house. Lots of my school friends, both boys and girls, came. I really got lots of gifts, which I was unaccustomed to receiving. I really blushed when "Happy Birthday" was sung, and I was completely red after blowing out the candles on the angel food cake Mom had baked. Patsy Ruth surprised me—no, I guess a better word is *upset* me—when she planted a big, juicy kiss on my cheek.

The *Democrat* even had a nice write-up in the society section the next day about the party. I cut it out and put it in my lock box.

I gave Miss Vaughan a pretty Sunday handkerchief that I'd bought at Siegel's for her birthday, the same day as mine. She gave me a big hug and wished me happy birthday. I knew she couldn't give me a present because she'd have to give all her students a present on their birthdays. Her hug was a good present. Now that I was ten, I decided I was old enough to talk to Mom about some of my thoughts I'd been having for a long time. As soon as the timing was right, and I'd gotten up enough courage, I asked her to sit in our living room and talk with me. It was on a Saturday night, May 10, after all the chores were completed and before Bible reading and prayers.

"What's on your mind, Son?" she asked.

"Mom, it's hard for me to talk about these things, but I want you to hear me out and try to understand," I said with as much authority in my voice as I could muster.

"Go on," was her only response, said quite coldly.

With fear, I continued. "Do you remember that you let Earleen see *Gone With the Wind* when it came to the Plaza in 1939?" I knew the date because I'd recently asked Earleen.

"Yes, we let her go because it was supposed to be such a great epic. Her teachers wanted everyone to see it," she responded quietly.

"And didn't you let her go to the Texas Centennial in Dallas in 1936?" I asked, gaining some more courage, yet still fearful.

"Yes, we did. And she had a good time except when the ferris wheel stopped working, and she had to stay near the top of it for about an hour."

That was news to me, but I didn't want to focus on that.

"Well, Mom, do you think she sinned by going to those two things?" I wanted to know.

"With God as my witness, I'd rather she not have gone," she said.

I did a quick glance and noticed a tear in her eye, but I needed to continue.

"Mom, I want to go to a picture show, too, and I just don't think it's sinful or that I'll be a sinner for going."

She was quiet for a few moments. But I sat looking her straight in the face, which was difficult to do under the circumstances.

"Do you have a good show in mind?" she asked with some emotion.

"I just want to go to a Saturday afternoon show at the Plaza, see a western, the cartoon, and the serial."

"Has someone asked you to go?"

"No, I just want to."

"I'll talk with Dad about it, and then I'll tell you," was her last statement before she left the living room.

I sat there for a few minutes, going over my chances. I left the room, feeling that Dad would say it was OK. And Mom, I thought, to be fair with me, would let me go. Soon we read the Bible and prayed. I was surprised that Mom didn't mention to God my request to go to a show.

After church the next day, while I was drying dishes as she washed, Mom told me that I could go one time to discover how Hollywood deceived us with the moviemakers' sinful ways.

I was thrilled, but I kept my face straight. I kept drying and wondering how I'd learn about the deception. Soon I told her that I'd probably go by myself to the Plaza the next Saturday. I knew that there was always a western playing on Saturday afternoon and that they changed movies for the 10:00 P.M. preview, which also showed Sunday and Monday.

So the next Saturday afternoon, I went. I paid my 10 cents, and no one saw me go in. I enjoyed all that I saw, while trying to figure out the deception. I decided that Hollywood tricked me in two ways. First, the good guys don't always defeat bad guys, but I was still having fun enjoying the story. I knew it was only make-believe. And, second, as I grinned thinking about it, Hollywood fooled me by not ever letting the good guy lose his white hat in the horse chase while the bad guy always did. Not bad deception, I thought. I laughed at the cartoon and was sad that I wouldn't get to see the next episode of the serial.

It was over too soon. I walked out of the Plaza and was instantly blinded. My thought was that God had taken my eyesight for sinning. Then my eyes readjusted from the dark of the movie auditorium to the beautiful sunlit May day, and I grinned at myself. I knew better, but still Mom's message was powerful.

As I pedaled home on my *Adventurer*, I knew that what I had done was not wrong, had not hurt anyone except Mom, and that she'd have to rethink her thoughts.

That night, she prayed for me in our family Bible reading and prayer time. She asked God to forgive me for having sinned again.

When we were all through, I said, "Mom, I didn't sin, and I'm not a sinner." She didn't agree, but she remained quiet. I felt a bit stronger.

School would soon be out, and was I ever ready! I'd made all Satisfactories (S) except in art, in which I'd gotten an I, meaning "Improvement Needed." I still hadn't forgotten how Miss Wheat during art class looked at the picture I was drawing with crayons on a large sheet of manila paper. I had a house with a chimney, a door and windows, flowers, green grass, a tree, and a sun up in the left corner of the page with sun rays coming from it. I liked it. But Miss Wheat said, "Paul, you can do better than that. Now throw this one away and start over." I decided right then that I didn't like drawing pictures. She'd said mine wasn't good. I may need improvement, but I would never let Miss Wheat help me improve. Just stubborn, I guess. Or at least that was a word used before to describe me.

I'd had a great fourth-grade year. And I'd been told that Miss Vaughan would be my fifth-grade homeroom teacher, which pleased me very much.

In late May, as I was just finishing folding my papers while reading the *Democrat* comic strips, which were limited in number (only "Red Ryder," "Freckles and His Friends," and "Alley Oop"), Jerry told me that Mr. Bunn wanted to talk to me. I went in immediately to his desk in the front part of the *Democrat* building.

"You asked to see me, Mr. Bunn?" I inquired.

"Well, yes, P.J. I want you to have your own route. I need you to take over route 7. Can you do this for me?" he asked.

Thrilled to the point I was almost speechless, I did manage, "Yes, sir, Mr. Bunn. When do I begin?"

"I'm glad you can. And you'll begin tomorrow, Friday, to ride with Jack to learn the route. I've found out that you learn a route quickly, and that's what I need. Friday is Jack's last day. I'm unhappy that it's happened so quickly, but that's the situation. So

Sunday morning you'll be on your own. At least on Friday when you collect, you'll find out the various places you have to go to collect. Several collections are done downtown where your customers work," he added.

"I'm ready and I'll learn," I responded eagerly.

"And on Sunday morning you'll have the route book with names and addresses, so if you're in doubt you can check your book. And I'll give you fifteen extra Sunday papers, so if you still aren't sure, just throw a paper," he said, trying to reassure me. "Let me tell you about route 7. It has between eighty-five and ninety-five customers, one of our largest routes. It begins at Fourth and Main and has the houses and businesses between Main and the Frisco tracks, a block south, all the way west to Fifteenth. Do you think you can manage this by yourself?"

A large route. My own route, which I'd worked toward for so long. And a good boost in money. All these thoughts raced through my head. I heard Mr. Bunn, but just barely, because I was so thrilled with my new job.

"Yes, sir, Mr. Bunn. I'll do you a good job. Gene and Jerry have been good teachers, so I know how to deliver well, collect, and pay you what the paper costs me. And I'm responsible."

"I know that, P.J., or I wouldn't have offered you this route. You'll be our youngest carrier. And the route is a big responsibility. I called Mr. Garrison, your principal. He told me you'd do a good job."

"Thank you. When do I meet Jack?" I asked.

"I've already talked to Jerry, so he knows that this is your last day with him. As Jack was leaving on his route today, he told me that tomorrow is his last day. That surprised me, so I had to act fast. I thought of you, called Mr. Garrison, talked to Jerry, and called you in. You'll meet Jack tomorrow. And, by the way, I give all new carriers two *Democrat* route bags."

He went to a large box and took out two brand new bags with extra padded shoulder straps. They were so nice and clean without all the dirty ink black on them.

And the timing, I thought, was great. When school was out in a week, I'd have time to get everything on my route up to my standards.

I told Jerry I'd miss him and his route, and I thanked him for teaching me. As we left, we stopped by the Durant Drug Store, and

I bought him a Malt-O-Plenty. I even teasingly asked him if he knew whether there were any hotels on my new route with lipsticked women sitting in swings on the front porches. We laughed together.

Then he said, "No, but P.J., that route will be all you can manage. You'll take care of it, though."

I trusted what he said. "I'll do my best," I replied. And we left to throw our papers.

My parents were thrilled, even though Dad was concerned about how little time I had to learn the route. "I'll just do it, Dad," I said to end our conversation.

The next day I told several of my friends at school about my new route. Also, I told Miss Vaughan and thanked Mr. Garrison. The school day went by rapidly, and soon I was meeting Jack at the *Democrat*.

We collected from eight customers at their downtown businesses even before we got our papers. Then, since we didn't fold papers on collection day, we got our ninety papers and left. Jack asked me to carry all the papers in my two new bags to get used to the weight. I knew he just didn't want to carry his, but that was all right. After all, I'd be carrying all of them Sunday morning.

It took us until 5:30 to finish. Collecting from that many, plus going to businesses downtown, consumed time. Jack gave me the money he owed Skip and told me to go to the *Democrat* Saturday morning and pay him. That was OK with me.

I asked, "How much is your weekly payment to Mr. Bunn and how much do you make weekly?"

"I pay $4.50 weekly to Skip Bunn, and I made around $4.50. But if I can get a few extra papers every day, especially on Sundays, I sell about $1 worth. The route is good for selling because West Main is Highway 70, and Highway 69 and 75 intersect at Ninth and Main and people stop me to buy a paper."

"How do you get extras?" I asked.

"Just snoop around the press. There'll always be a few imperfect papers that they'll put in an unusable stack. They're perfectly good except maybe they've been miscut or misfolded. I keep them separate to sell. Never had a complaint," he added.

Tired but pleased, I got home just before supper. The next morning I paid Mr. Bunn.

He smiled and said, "P.J., all my carriers call me Skip. You may do that, too, now that you are a carrier."

It seemed awkward for me, but I said, "Thank you, Skip. I'm going to go ride my route this morning with the route book so I'll be ready in the morning. I also need to finish collecting."

I finally had my own route I'd so long wanted.

CHAPTER 7
Learning More about My Route

I didn't sleep well that Saturday night. And since I didn't have an alarm clock, I was constantly using my flashlight to look at my wristwatch, which Dad gave me from Granny Johnson's stuff after she died, to see if it was 5:00 A.M. yet. When it was time, I was wide awake. Quickly putting on my clothes, drinking a glass of milk, and grabbing my two new paper bags, I was soon inserting the comics and rolling my Sunday *Durant Daily Democrat*. The two boxes of rubber bands, which Skip had given me in addition to the two paper bags, were rewards for being a new carrier. I rolled the papers tightly. Skip had given me fifteen extra papers, which I hoped I didn't need to throw so I could sell them.

As a result of Saturday's review of the route, while I was finishing collecting from the unpaid customers, I was sure I wouldn't need any extras, but it was nice to have them. I had asked Skip if it would be all right to sell any extras, and he said it'd be fine. Sunday papers sold more easily than weekday editions.

I had no trouble throwing the route that morning. And I had sixteen papers left. One for our family, and fifteen to sell. So, after finishing, I rode to Ninth and Main, where Highways 69, 75, and 70 all went by, and I held a paper up to people going by in cars. Within thirty minutes or so, I'd sold fourteen, with a good profit of 70 cents plus, and much to my surprise, 40 cents in tips. And I'd traded one paper for the *Daily Oklahoman* with a friend who delivered that paper. So I went home with a *Democrat*, an *Oklahoman*, and $1.10. I thought I'd struck a gold mine. I put a dollar in my lock box and left the dime for spending.

At breakfast, Mom asked me if I had been tithing regularly. "You know, Son, God blesses those who give back to Him His ten percent."

I had thought that tithing was for persons who made more money than I, so I asked Mom, "Do you tithe?"

"I try. But your father doesn't earn much, so he doesn't give me money to tithe. But I try to save money that I can to give back to the Lord."

"If you don't, why should I? I just don't make much, and most of what I make, I save," I replied.

"Well, the Lord provided for you to have your own route, so you need to give back to Him for opening the way for you to be successful."

"I thought it was through my hard work I got the route," I replied, knowing that it wasn't the correct thing to say.

"Don't be disrespectful to the Lord, Son. He's given you so much. Don't disappoint Him now."

That morning in church I put $2 in a tithe envelope and placed it in the collection plate. Dan noticed. "Do you always give your money away?" he asked.

"Only when my mother makes me," I said.

And that afternoon I set up a bookkeeping system that insured that I would give 10 percent to the church. I didn't need Mom putting more God on me. And that afternoon I wondered whether what I got was a result of God's blessings. And I decided it was what I did, not some divine gift.

It was the last week of my fourth grade. Book learning was over, and we were coasting in. The teachers were in a good mood, for which we were all thankful. The class had a great picnic outing on Chuckwa Creek, and Miss Vaughan said good things to us. I liked that, and I liked her for being so kind to all of us.

And on Friday, the very last day, while I was working in Mr. Garrison's outer office, he called me into his office.

"Please sit, Paul, I want to talk to you," he said as he motioned to a chair near his desk. "You've been a great deal of help to me this year, and I want to thank you. I've already thanked Jeanne Paul, who also was my office helper. I've checked your attendance record and have seen that you've had two years of perfect attendance. I like that, and I hope you'll always be as responsible as you've been. Now I want to share with you some things I've learned about boys as they grow up. Are you ready to listen and learn?" he asked.

"Yes, sir, I think I'm always ready to learn from you," I said respectfully.

"Some things I've learned from books, some from observing boys, and some from having been a boy, but what I'm about to tell you I think you can understand. Boys play many, many games that have rules, boundaries, and procedures. If you foul, there's a whistle, if you're off-sides, there's a whistle, if you strike out, you sit down, and there's always a consequence to the team and to you. So as boys grow up, they learn that there are lots of rewards by not fouling, by staying on-sides, and by putting the ball in play. You may not always win, but you hear a lot fewer whistles. Do you understand, Paul?"

"Yes, I guess I do," I responded, nodding my head up and down. I hoped I did understand, but I wasn't too sure.

"I thought you would," he said. "I've not called a foul on you this year. As a matter of fact, not since you've been in Washington Irving school. I want you to continue being a successful student and learn much as you grow. Promise me you will," he urged.

"I'll always try," I promised.

With that he gave me some errands to run. I liked Mr. Garrison even more. I vowed that there wouldn't be many whistles blown on me if I could possibly keep from it. And that I'd stay on-sides, too.

Fourth grade was over, and summer activities began. The freedom from school was a good feeling. I knew I had to find lawns to mow, and I had the route to throw, vanilla to sell, errands to run, and chores to do around the house, but there always was some time for swimming in Round Hole, firing my Red Ryder BB gun, playing with friends, and listening to my Cardinals on KMOX, St. Louis. The first week of summer I moved back into my screened-in porch room.

Dad put the mower into the trunk of the Mercury and drove me to a $2 lawn far out on West Elm. It took me all morning to mow because it was a large lawn, and the grass was unusually high. But I finished, got my $2, and, feeling pleased, began my walk home. A woman called out to me and asked if I'd like to mow her lawn.

"Sure," I responded, even though I was starving for lunch.

"Well, look it over. I also want you to trim the grass away from the house."

It was a small lawn, and trimming would be easy. "Ma'am, I'll do it for 50 cents."

"How do I know you'll do a good job?" she asked.

"I try to be responsible, I have a good mower, and I've been mowing for some time now," I assured her.

"OK, go to it."

I worked rapidly, as I always did. In fifteen minutes I'd completed everything, so I knocked and asked to be paid.

"You can't be through," she said in an abrupt voice.

"Unless there is some part of the lawn I didn't know about, I am," I replied, not understanding why she was so upset.

She and I walked the yard and looked at my trim job. She inquired, "Did anyone help you?"

"No, ma'am, I did it by myself."

"But you've been here just over fifteen minutes."

"I work rapidly."

"Regardless, I can't pay 50 cents for fifteen minutes of work. Why, that'd be like paying you $2 an hour, and grown men don't make that much."

Confused, I hardly knew what to say, but I managed, "Our agreement was for 50 cents. And I work fast—always do."

She went into her house and returned with a quarter. "This is all I'm paying you."

"Is there something I've done wrong mowing or trimming?" I asked.

"No, you've done an excellent job. But it's not worth 50 cents."

So I took the quarter and left.

Later, after my route was delivered, I told Dad about the incident.

"Let's drive out there," he said, getting up to go to the Mercury.

"Let's leave it alone," I begged, knowing that Dad might get angry with the woman.

"Get in the car. No one treats you like that."

I did. We drove, and he talked to her. She paid the other 25 cents. Dad was firm but nice.

Driving home, he said, "There are some things that are right and some that are wrong, and some we don't know about. But what she did was wrong. Be polite, but stand up for yourself."

I was proud of him. Maybe, I thought, this was one of those rules Mr. Garrison had talked about.

"Thanks, Dad," I said appreciatively.

The next day, around noon, I swam in Round Hole with about fifteen other guys. As we sunned on the sandy beach, stories about this and that were being told. I told my story about the woman cheating me and how my dad had defended me, and they all liked my dad for doing what he did, even suggesting that their dads might not have done as much.

That night I told Dad that it had meant a great deal to me.

He responded, "Thanks, but I just didn't want you to lose the quarter. After all, we'll need it someday if we go to war."

"What do you mean, Dad, if we go to war?" I asked.

"It increasingly looks like Hitler is waging such a war in Europe that our country will get involved. You read the paper. You know the events don't look good," he said with worry all over his face.

"Will you have to go into the army, Dad?"

"Probably. But I'll be drafted last because I have a wife and three children. And I'm already forty-two years old. But if I should have to, you'll really have to have jobs and money to support your mother and sisters. So the quarter I helped you collect is needed for you to save in case I'm gone to war, and she should have to pay you anyway."

I couldn't come to grips with all he'd told me. My thoughts whirled around about having to earn enough money to support Mom, Earleen, and Linda.

When Mom called us three for Bible reading and prayers, she asked me to pray. It was unusual because Earleen or she usually prayed aloud. But she asked me.

So I began, "Dear God, please cause Adolph Hitler to become sick and die and—"

She stopped me. "Son, you don't pray for someone to die. That's awful. Even if Hitler has done wrong, God will have a way to deal with him. Now go ahead with a proper prayer."

And so I finished a proper prayer. And I didn't tell Mom that I prayed that way because I was scared Dad might have to go to war and that I might have to make enough money for our family to live on. I thought it strange that others sometimes didn't understand what was really going on inside of me.

I worked extra hard to find lawns to mow and was successful. So my plans were to try to make $3 a day mowing and $5 a week from my route. And maybe I could sell $3 of vanilla each week. That would give me $26 each week. My tithe would be $2.60. That would leave me $3.40 for Cokes, peanuts, an occasional Malt-O-Plenty, and bike repairs. I'd have saved $20 each week—over $240 during the summer. I'd have money for fall clothes and other stuff. My goal, I planned, would be to use $50 for those things, which would leave $90. And then with the $70 I had in the bank, I'd have $260 when entering the fifth grade. I liked my plan.

After my second Friday to collect from my paper route, I went on Saturday morning to pay Skip Bunn my fees.

After he counted out the money, he asked about the route.

"Any difficulties?" he asked.

"No, I think everything is OK."

"I'm pleased, and I'm glad, too, that you haven't gotten a kick. Keep up the good work."

About that time, an older man came by and Skip asked him to stop and visit.

"P.J., I want you to meet 'Uncle Bob' Story. Mr. Story, this is Paul Johnson, our newest carrier. He has route 7. Mr. Story is senior owner of the *Democrat*."

"Uncle Bob" shook my hand and said he was glad I was a carrier. He said he'd known my dad for many years.

"Come with me," Uncle Bob said. And he took me into an office and introduced me to his son, Bennett Story. "Bennett is the real owner and manager. I just hang around and help in whatever way I can," he explained.

Bennett Story also shook my hand and told me he was glad I was a carrier. They both made me feel glad I worked for them.

I knew that Bennett Story lived across from Washington Irving Elementary School. He and his wife had a son, Bob, and a daughter, Betty, I knew, even though they were younger than I. Also, I had sold Mrs. Story a bottle of vanilla once when I was just going door to door. I vowed that I'd work hard not only for Skip, but also for the Storys.

I went back to Skip's desk. He asked me to be seated, saying he wanted to discuss how to save money.

"P.J., I always encourage my carriers to save most of what they earn. What are your plans regarding saving?" he asked.

When I outlined my plans for the summer, mentioned what Dad had told me about perhaps being drafted, and explained how I saved dollars, half-dollars, and quarters but spent dimes, nickels, and pennies, he began to laugh.

"I'm wasting your time and mine," he said. "Now go on and find lawns to mow." He seemed pleased, and I was also.

When I got home, I told Mom that Skip had introduced me to the Storys. "I'm glad that you met the owners because they are very influential people in our town. You get along with them well, hear?"

"I will, Mom. I try to do right," I replied. "I think I'll go finish mowing our back lawn because I just mowed the front yesterday."

"Son, it will already be mowed. You know how men come to our back door and knock and ask for food?" she continued, telling me something I already knew.

Mom couldn't say no to them. Ever since we'd been living in our new house, men that Dad called tramps had come by asking for food. Dad always got angry with Mom for feeding them; he argued that if Mom fed one, others would come. But Mom just seemed to have to feed anyone who asked.

She continued, "A man insisted that he do some work to earn the food. I told him that I'd give him a sandwich and an orange and that he didn't have to work. He kept insisting, so I showed him your mower and showed him where to mow. And since I had a sandwich already fixed, I gave it to him so he wouldn't be hungry as he mowed. So the lawn will all be mowed."

Seemed OK with me. So I said, "I'll have more time to mow for money. I'll get the mower and be on my way. See you before supper."

When I looked for the mower in its customary spot in the garage, it wasn't there. Thinking it had been left in the yard, I looked. No mower. I told Mom, and she came outside and we looked everywhere. Still no mower.

Upset by my loss, I asked Mom to call the police. Instead, she called around until she located Dad and told him the story. I could tell by Mom's face that Dad was upset with her.

Dad went by the police station and reported the theft, but when he came home, he told me to get enough of my money to buy a new mower from Babcock's. And so I began mowing in mid-June of 1941 with a new mower and almost eleven fewer dollars. But this mower seemed even better built and mowed very smoothly.

Mom didn't feed any more men who knocked on the door. And I vowed I never wanted to live in any time period when there was a depression, which caused so many men to leave their homes and have to ask for food. It seemed as if there were so many situations in my life that caused me to vow a lot.

A couple of weeks later, I was folding my papers when four of the older carriers grouped around me and told me it was time for me to be initiated into the world of full-time carriers. I'd heard about this initiation, and since I knew it happened to all new carriers, I went with them.

On the west side of the *Democrat* building was a brick-paved alley, and on the west side of the alley was a thorn bush hedge shielding the lawn of the Evergreen Sanitarium, one of Durant's three hospitals. So in this alley, I was to be initiated. "P.J.," an older carrier said, "you know that we carriers line up on either side and make a lane for you to run through. As you do, we hit you with the shoulder straps of our news bags. You're lucky, though, because you have route 7, and you only have to go through seven times. Get ready."

And so I got initiated again. The licks hurt. About ten guys on either side of the lane laughed and yelled and struck as hard as they could. Even though I ran as fast as I could, it seemed as if I'd never finish. But I was still standing when it was all over.

Several comments were made to me and about me, but I was in so much pain that I couldn't hear them. I was just glad it was over.

While I stood to finish folding my papers, I once again vowed that I'd not participate when another new carrier was initiated. I didn't sit on my bicycle seat much that day as I threw the papers.

The next day I had on my swimsuit while watering Mom's flowers. She came out to recommend how to do my job, as she nearly always did, and noticed that below my swimsuit my legs were bruised.

"How did that happen?" she inquired.

Feeling trapped and not wanting her to know what happened, I just lied. "Yesterday a dog ran at me on my paper route, and I hit a curb. I had a bad fall and my bike came down on my legs. Guess that's how it happened."

"Well, Son, be careful," she cautioned.

"I always try to, Mom."

That seemed to satisfy her. I thought about how sad it was to have to lie to Mom about things she'd not understand and get upset with. I didn't feel good about the lie and was fearful that she'd find out about what really happened. Then I'd get another belting and more bruises.

Fortunately, for me, she never found out. And I thought now that I was initiated as a carrier I could talk more like a man. As Dad had told me, there just was a way men talked. I was learning.

CHAPTER 8
Route 7

"It's a good route and I like to deliver it because it's easy to throw, easy to ride my bike with little trouble, and most of the customers are nice and pay on time," I responded to Dad's question about my route.

"How's it different from the two you subbed?" he wanted to know as he sat in the green swing on our big front porch, smoking his Camel cigarette.

"It's hard to tell; throwing is throwing." I was sitting on the step of the porch, watching Mr. Capshaw, our postman, deliver the mail to Mrs. Gooding's house across the street as I talked with Dad. I liked Mr. Capshaw. Often I got him a glass of cold water on hot days when he put our mail in the mailbox. He delivered both in the morning and again in the afternoon, so he was very busy. I'd also gotten to know Mrs. Capshaw, who lived on Chuckwa Drive, as I'd collected on the far north sub job.

"My route is the largest I've delivered. And it seems as if I have two different kinds of customers. Those who live in houses that face Main have very nice ones. And the houses between their property and the Frisco tracks are OK but not nearly as nice as the others. But most pay me, and I am beginning to get to know my customers. And most treat me well," I told Dad, trying to answer his question.

"How long do you want to keep your route?" he asked, seeming to make conversation more than really wanting to know.

"Most carriers, or those who really like to carry, seem to stay through the seventh or eighth grade. So I guess if all goes well, three or four years."

"I've been thinking about what the men at Tyson's filling station are talking about. They say that if we should go to war against Hitler, the rubber to make tires and innertubes won't be available. I think you'd best go to Babcock's and buy four new tires and tubes," he said.

"How much would that total?" I asked.

"About $8.50. But I think you should do it. You've already got a new mower. And you'll need your bike."

When I bought all of the tires and the tubes, the salesman commented that I probably was smart to buy them. His comment, as well as Dad's, plus the news I read every day in the *Democrat* about war in Europe, kept me on edge.

Dad had designed a large storage attic and a swinging stairway, which could be pulled down out of the ceiling in our long hallway so we could easily climb the stairs. Many people had come by to see how Dad had fixed this. It was the talk over many cups of coffee when Dad was in his favorite café. I felt good because he had the idea, and the swinging staircase was the only one in town. After I had wrapped my tires carefully, I kept the tubes in their boxes, and I then used the stairs to climb into the attic to store them. Mom said I was hoarding them, and I had to look that word up in the dictionary.

Later that day, as I was looking through my route book, I discovered that I had some interesting names which amused me. I always had fun with names, so I had fun putting the customers' names together for a few laughs. It was also a way I could learn and remember them. I had Lively Bass, a Long Whale, some White Rice, a Carpenter, a Plummer, who liked to Work, a Hurt and a Payne, a Cason, who just kept Roland on, keeping away from a Battle, a Green Street, a Strong Pope, and a person who had been to hell and back (Helbach). He needed to meet Mrs. Sweet.

I walked into the room where Mom was ironing to share my amusement with her about my newly discovered combination of names. She, too, had a pleasant laugh after I read them, adding that if I had an Akin to go with my Hurt and Payne, I'd have to call a doctor. Then she said she didn't want a strong Pope, referring to her anti-Catholic beliefs. I ignored that.

She continued, "Do you know where your name, Paul, came from?"

"The Bible, I guess," I replied, wondering where this was going.

"Yes, and do you know what Paul's name was before he became a follower of Christ?" she asked.

"No."

"He was Saul of Taursus, and he persecuted and killed Christians. His conversion was so powerful and good that he took the name Paul. He affected history forever. I want your life to be that powerful, Son," she said with meaning.

"I like my name, Paul, but I like my new name, P.J., even better. That's what nearly everyone is calling me now."

"That's all right for now. But remember that you've always said you wanted to grow up and become a minister, and that's what I want you to do."

"Mom, I just don't know about that anymore. I've been thinking that when I have to fill out my fifth-grade data form, I'll write 'Businessman' on the line where I'm asked to tell them what I want to be when I am an adult," I replied, expecting a negative response from Mom.

"Haven't you always put 'Preacher' for that question before?"

"Yes, but I don't think I want to become one anymore," I responded, knowing it wouldn't please her.

She tilted the iron on its end, walked around the ironing board, and, looking me sternly in the eyes, said, "Now don't you begin to tempt God's direction for your life. I've always promised Him that you'd be His messenger, and He will speak to you soon."

I was more scared than anything. Her voice was different than usual, but I tried to hold my ground. "Mom, don't do this to me. I don't want to be a preacher. I don't like our preacher, I don't like how he scares everyone, and I don't believe that everything he says is a sin is a sin," I said, surprising myself that I could blurt this out to Mom.

"I'll have no more of your blasphemy, Paul. It's obvious that your being saved didn't take. You'll need to be saved again. I'll pray for you." And then she went back around the ironing board, picked up the iron, and touched the hot part with her thumb. She stuck the burned thumb into her mouth to let it cool off. In a couple of seconds she took it out and said, "See, Son, what you've said displeased

God, so He punished me because I brought you into this world. I'm responsible for you." She then vigorously applied the iron to Dad's khaki pants on the ironing board.

"I thought what I did with my route customers' names was funny," I meekly added, going slowly into the other room. I wasn't sure what *blasphemy* meant, either, but it seemed like I could somehow add it to my humor with words.

I heard her begin to hum "Amazing Grace." I didn't like that song either. I didn't like to think about myself as a *wretch*. Also, I thought Mom was responsible for burning her finger—not God. And I knew I'd write "Businessman" for my fifth-grade data form.

Because I had lots of other stuff to do, I forgot as quickly as I could Mom's and my get-together. I needed to do some chores, mow Miss Bertha's lawn, which was just across the street, and get on with the collection since this was Friday.

Having mowed and collected the 50 cents, I washed up a bit and put on some clean blue jeans and shirt, told Mom goodbye, jumped over the rail of our side porch, just barely clearing the spirea shrubs, mounted my bike, and took off to collect.

Since I had to collect from a few customers who worked downtown, I went into places I ordinarily wouldn't go. The first stop was the second floor of the Bryan County Courthouse to collect from Mrs. Jarrell. She was usually in an office that had something to do with property titles, even though she worked for Stewart Title Company on Third Street. She'd already made a favorable impression on me because she was so pretty and had a big smile, a pleasant voice, and an air about her that always made me want to linger. And another reason that I liked her was that she had tipped me a dime each time for always putting her paper behind the screen door of her screened-in front porch on West Main. She lived with her two sons, Jack and Dick, and her mother, Mrs. Stewart. Maybe she understood more about boys than Mom did, I thought.

She paid me, and wished me well. As I descended the wide white marble steps of the courthouse, I decided to buy an RC Cola and peanuts with my tip money.

And that's how I met Mr. Snow. He had the Coke, candy, cigarette, and newsstand on the first floor. A sign told me his name and that he was blind. I bought the cola and peanuts with my dime.

"What's your name?" he inquired as I paid. "You're new around here."

"Paul, but I go by P.J."

"What's the J. for?"

"Johnson."

"Are you Earl's boy?"

"Yes, that's my dad."

"He's a good man. Don't see him around here much, but I knew him when we were growing up as kids, especially before the war," he added.

"Thanks. I like Dad a lot," I responded, taking a big swig of the RC Cola to wash down the half-chewed peanuts. "You worked in the courthouse a long time?" I asked.

"Been here since '34 after I mostly recovered from the wounds of the war. I had to get a lot of special training to manage my blindness and my business. Don't misunderstand me, though; I'm a lucky man. Some of my buddies didn't make it back from the war. They were killed defending Belgium, and they're buried in Flanders Field."

I didn't know what to say, so I just took another long swig so I'd finish the RC and could be on my way. "It was good to meet you. I'll see you every Friday because I come in to collect for the *Democrat*," I said, trying to leave.

"Oh, you're a carrier, huh?"

"Yes," I said, moving back toward him.

"Who is your customer who works in here?" he inquired.

"Mrs. Jarrell."

"Oh, you've got a good customer. She's a fine lady. She'll always treat you right. Now see to it you treat her mother and her right, too. Understand?"

"She seems to be, and I've not met her mother. I try to treat all my customers right," I added.

"That's a good plan. I treat mine well and get a lot of repeat business. Always remember that."

"I'll try. Gotta go now," I said as I walked away. I vowed that I'd buy something from him as often as I could. Selfishly, my thoughts drifted toward hoping Dad would never have to be drafted, as some men were nowadays.

My next stop was just across the street at the city hall building, which also housed the Durant Fire Department. I had two customers who were firemen, Mr. Moore, who was fire chief, and Mr. Helbach. Since Mr. Moore paid once a month, I only collected from Mr. Helbach each Friday.

Several firemen were sitting outside in chairs, leaning back against the white brick building.

"Is Mr. Helbach here today?" I asked.

"Yeah, he's upstairs," one replied.

I climbed the metal spiral staircase and called out for him in the bedroom area.

"Be right out," was the response.

In a few seconds he appeared, finishing putting his belt through his trousers' beltloop.

"I'm here to collect for the *Democrat*," I said.

"You mean the *Durant Daily Disappointment?*" he responded with a big laugh.

I'd heard that before, so I just nodded my head yes.

"It's a disappointment to get it, and it's a disappointment not to get it," he said with an even larger laugh than before.

"But the price isn't bad," I teased back.

"Boy, you're all right," he said as he gave me a dime. "Be sure to put the newspaper on my porch."

"I always do."

"Have you ever slid down a firepole?" he asked.

"No."

"Well, only firemen are supposed to, but all the men are outside, so be quiet." He put his finger to his lips to tell me to remain silent.

He told me to wrap my legs loosely around the glistening clean steel pole, hold lightly, and slide. Looked easy enough, so I did. I was on the concrete by the firetruck in a second. I looked up to see him wink and wave goodbye.

Two collections and two new pleasant experiences. I wondered if they'd continue.

My third stop was down the hallway on the first floor of the city hall in the office of the city judge, Mr. Woodward. He wasn't busy, so his secretary told me to go in. An older man, he sat in a desk chair which tilted back and rotated around. His office was smelly with cigar smoke.

"What are you here for?" Before I could answer, he continued, "Oh, you're that new *Democrat* carrier, aren't you?"

"Yes, Judge, I sure am."

"Well, I'll tell you something. I get tired of people coming in here always wanting something from me," he said sternly. "You collect every Friday, don't you?"

"Yes, sir, I do. But if I bother you by coming weekly, I could set you up on a monthly or yearly pay," I responded, trying to be helpful. Also, I was trying to avoid him as much as I could, because he looked so stern.

"I'll pay weekly. Monthly or annually is always too much money to give to a youngster like you."

I didn't understand his reasoning, but I said that would be fine, holding out my hand for his dime as he dug in his pocket.

"Before I pay you," he said, "I want you to understand some things I'll always expect of you."

He got up from his chair, leaving his cigar smoking in a large green glass ashtray on his desk, and walked around just in front of me. Then he said, with a lot of authority in his judge-like voice, "You know where I live on West Main, don't you?"

"Yes, Judge, I do. It's the two-story red brick house just east of Mrs. Stewart's house and west of Chief Moore's house," I added proudly, thinking he'd be impressed that I already knew my customers. "And it pleases me to knock each day and take an unfolded paper inside to your daughter."

"And be sure you do that. You've already learned that she can't get around, so if she asks you to do something for her, be sure you do. Do you understand what I'm saying?"

"Yes, sir, I'll always be willing to do her a favor. Only last Wednesday she asked me to get her a glass of cold water, and I did. She wanted me to stay and visit, so I stayed a couple of minutes with her."

"She's my only child. She's been a special person to me for many years, even though she's not able to get out of the house without someone to lift her. Now, boy, you be good to her, or I'll call Mr. Story. Do you understand me perfectly?" he asked with his finger wagging up and down at me.

"Yes, sir."

"Well, here's your dime. Now go," he said with the same finger now pointing toward the door.

I left as quickly as I could. I wondered if all judges were as stern and grumpy as he seemed to be. I liked his daughter from our first meeting and always looked forward to seeing her each day. She always asked me to do something, even if it were unfolding the newspaper to a certain page. We had a moment or two of pleasant talk, and I'd be on my way. She surely seemed different from her father.

So, I thought, *three collections and three completely different people*. I vowed that I'd learn all I could from all my customers. The next stop was to collect from Mr. Shannon, an insurance agent on Main at the alley way just east of Montgomery Ward. A pleasant older man, he paid me quickly, and as I was leaving, said, "Your father needs to buy his insurance with me. I have five growing sons who are in their late teens or in college, so I need Earl's business."

"I'll say something to him, Mr. Shannon, but he talks about Mr. Rector Swearengin having his car insurance. Maybe he does business with him."

"I'm kidding, but I'd like to have his business."

And with that I left to go collect from Dr. Williams, a dentist. I saw his sign, *W. S. Williams, Dentist,* just before entering to climb a very long staircase to the second floor. Even for a kid, I was out of breath when I ran up the steps two at a time. I thought that most of his patients must be young because older people wouldn't enjoy the long climb. But then I thought that maybe they wouldn't be in such a hurry as I always was.

A woman came out of Dr. Williams' office when she heard me close the door as I entered. "Do you need to make an appointment?" she asked, and before I could answer, she continued, "If you do, you're too young to make an appointment. Either your mother or daddy will have to do that."

"No, ma'am, I'm here to collect for the *Democrat*. Ten cents, please, from Dr. Williams."

"You're new, aren't you?"

"Yes, ma'am, but I've been here before to collect. Dr. Williams paid me. He was out here in the waiting room when I came by."

"Well, I knew I hadn't seen you before. I need to check. Where does Dr. Williams live?"

"At Eleventh and Main in the two-story red brick house," I quickly responded, not thinking that she was testing me to make certain I was the doctor's real news carrier.

"I'll get your money."

As she opened the door to his dental office, I saw him working on a patient. The smell of his office was the same smell I remembered from the only time I'd ever sat in a dentist's chair after I'd chipped a tooth while playing football.

Dr. Williams paused, stuck his hand in his pocket for a dime, and gave it to the woman, who came back and paid me.

As I was leaving, she asked me my name. "I'm P.J.," I said as I turned back toward her.

"No, your whole name," she said.

"Paul Johnson."

"OK, Paul Johnson, are you going to always collect about this time each Friday?"

"Yes, ma'am. I'll try to."

"Well, look here," she said as she opened a drawer in a desk in the waiting room. "The dime will always be right here," as she pointed. "If I have to leave a quarter or half dollar, just put the change back here. Understand?"

"Yes, ma'am."

"And don't be bothering the doctor any," she said sternly.

I was surprised then by Dr. Williams coming out of his office, leaving his patient alone for a minute.

"Now, Mrs. Heard," he said politely, "boys don't bother me. You know I have two boys, Earl and Edward, who are dentists, and they were carriers of the *Democrat* once themselves. Who knows, this boy may become a dentist, too, someday."

I vowed that if I ever needed to go to a dentist, it'd be Dr. Williams.

I thanked them and left. Bouncing down the stairs, I heard the coins jingling in my jeans pocket, and I thought about how I liked that sound. Then I had a strange thought. If I didn't have some coins in my pocket, it was like I couldn't make a fist. Don't know why I had the thought, but I knew I'd always want to be able to make a fist when I needed one.

Our downtown had wide sidewalks, so I could ride my bike, easily dodging people who were walking. I pedaled slowly toward Long's Drug Store, going by Harrison's Appliance Store, the Ritz Theater, Boyet Drug, where I saw George inside with his dad, and bumped off the curb at Second and Main. Then I jumped my front wheel onto the sidewalk and put the kickstand down. I had an uneasy feeling about entering to collect from Mr. Long. On an earlier collection day, he'd kept me waiting around before paying me the dime. But maybe this day would be different.

I saw him at the back near the pharmacy area, so I walked by the soda fountain, the customer tables, and the cosmetics area to where he was. Since he didn't appear busy, I told him I was here to collect for the *Democrat*.

"How much is it?" he asked.

"Ten cents, Mr. Long," I said with some urgency, trying to get my dime and leave.

"Same as last time, huh?" he said, not really seeming to pay much attention to me.

"Yes, sir."

"That's too much for that paper, and there are too many ads in it. The Storys are making too much money," he said, matter-of-fact-like.

Not knowing what to say, I remembered about men's talk and tried what I thought might be good to say. "Well, Mr. Long, you know how you put so much ice in your glasses of Coke so you won't have to use much Coke? I guess that's what the Storys do when they fill their paper with things you don't like." I felt good to have come up with that. It seemed to fit. Sort of like Dad's customers teasing him about muddy water and vanilla.

But it wasn't the right thing to have said.

"You finding fault with my business, young man?" he said with a mean look on his face.

"No, Mr. Long, I was just teasing, just trying to get along with you," I said.

"How old are you?"

"I'm ten, be eleven next April." I was hoping to impress him that I was getting old enough to use men's teasing.

"Well, don't be impertinent with me."

I didn't know what *impertinent* meant, but it didn't sound good. "I'll not do it again, Mr. Long. I'm just here to collect," I replied, trying to get my dime and get out.

He turned away and walked behind the pharmacy window, not saying anything. He seemed to be stalling again as he had at other times. *What should I do?* I wondered. So I just stood and waited. I remembered that last week I'd bought a root beer while I waited to be paid and wondered if I should go do that again. It was a good root beer, maybe the best I'd had. It was served in a silver mug with chipped ice in it, which made the drink mighty tasty.

But I just didn't want to spend a nickel at his business when he was treating me this way. So I continued to stand near the pharmacy area.

Soon he came back.

"You still here?" he asked.

That seemed strange. He had been looking at me off and on the whole time I had been standing there.

"Yes, and if you'll pay me, I'll be on my way. Fridays keep me busy with collecting plus delivering." So he paid me, and I left. I wondered if collecting from him would always be this way.

Riding eastwardly on down Main, I stopped at the Bass Finance Agency and went in. There were three people, all named Bass, to collect from in this business. One Mr. Bass, who lived at Sixteenth and Main, also owned and managed the Durant Natatorium on North Sixth during swimming season. During the time he was at the pool, he always left the dime with another Bass. I didn't know how they were related, but they were always prompt to pay.

As I left, I thought about how Mom didn't want me to go swimming at the Nat because Nazarenes were not to have any part of mixed swimming, which meant boys and girls together. But Dad had told her to let me go there. He had said that no harm would take place.

Then I had another idea. The entrance price to the Nat was 15 cents, so I thought that the next time I was at the Nat I'd ask Mr. Bass if he'd let me swim once a week for a free paper six days a week. If he'd agree, I'd have me a bargain of 5 cents. I'd have to argue heavy that he'd get something six days a week while I got something only once a week. I liked my argument and my chances.

By this time I was in the alleyway behind Main at the Ideal Laundry. Mrs. Beal, who lived in the last house on my route, worked there. The lady at the front desk recognized me, and not saying anything because of the heat and the noise, motioned that I could go on to the back where Mrs. Beal worked. As I walked by the giant washing machines, the large ironers, and the sweaty women who were operating them, I felt a moment of sorrow for them. Mrs. Beal saw me coming, smiled at me, and had the dime ready.

"You are really doing a good job as a new carrier," she said.

"Thank you. And you seem to know what you're doing with that ironing machine," I said, as she went back to ironing another man's white dress shirt.

I had finally collected from all my customers who worked downtown. Riding rapidly to the *Democrat* building, I went in, checked the carriers' message board, found nothing clipped to route 7, loaded my unfolded papers into my two bags, and left for the rest of my collection and delivery.

Much of the rest of the route was normal that day. But one unusual event was that at Mrs. Madrea's house on South Eighth, a note was pinned to the screen door which read, "Paper boy, your dime is on the cabinet counter in the kitchen. Come in and get it. And while you are there, turn on the fire under the pan on the gas stove. A match is lying there to light the burner. But if you are here before 3:15, don't light the fire. Thanks. Mrs. Madrea." It was strange to walk into her house, but I did as she had asked since it was 3:45 P.M. A simple favor for a good and trusting customer.

Across the street Mr. Roberts was waiting for me. "So Mrs. Madrea is already asking you to help her, huh?"

"Yes, sir, but that's OK with me."

He told me about how good all the families were who lived in the four houses on South Eighth. I liked Mr. Roberts.

And when I got to Mr. Woodward's house, his daughter was in an especially good mood. She asked me to sit and visit, which I did for a couple of minutes, and then I excused myself, telling her that people would be waiting for their papers.

Collection day was different on all the routes I'd delivered, but route 7 seemed good, because all except four customers had paid. Three weren't home, and one asked me to collect Monday. I'd agreed to do so.

My pocket was full of coins, along with two dollar bills in my billfold. I got home, counted out what I had to pay Skip the next day, and found that I had $4.90 left over. And I'd been given 30 cents in tips, too, and had sold four *Democrats* for 20 cents. Four dollars and seventy-five cents went into my lock box, to add to my profits from lawns. I needed $2 to make a $20 bank deposit, so I felt good.

That evening I told Dad about Mr. Long's keeping me waiting. I didn't tell him what'd I'd said that caused Mr. Long to use the word *impertinent* when he talked back to me.

"Why would he keep me waiting?" I asked, expecting an answer which would help me understand more about men, and Mr. Long in specific.

Dad thought a bit and then said, "Son, I've always found that when you want something that someone else has, you ask in a polite way for what you want, and then you wait. The other person then has the power to make the next move. Do you understand?"

I nodded that I did, but I wasn't sure. I guess he said I needed more patience, but I wasn't sure. I was still learning, and sometimes it was hard to do. I asked Earleen to look up the word *impertinent*. She told me to look it up for myself. She spelled it for me, and I found that it meant being too bold or too forward. I didn't think I had been that way with Mr. Long.

CHAPTER 9
The Family Picture

On Sunday, the day before school began in September 1941, we got our neighbor Mrs. Gooding to come over and use our Kodak camera to take our family picture. It was a sunny Sunday morning, and we were dressed for Sunday school and church. Dad put on a suit for the picture, even though he wasn't going to church.

A few days later, on Wednesday of the first week of school, Dad brought the developed pictures back from Truby's Studio. We all looked, oohed and ahhed, laughed, and enjoyed the pictures. I noticed in one picture that Dad had one arm around Mom's waist and in the hand of the other arm was his ever-present Camel. I vowed I'd never ever smoke a cigarette, laughing inside as I remembered the peach tree tea I received at the age of seven when a neighbor, Mrs. Pierce, tattled on me to Mom when she saw me smoking corn silk rolled in a piece of newspaper behind the garage. The taste was horrible.

Mom's picture was pretty, just as she was in real life. She was five feet, two inches tall and had red hair that was braided and pinned tightly on top of her head. She was plump and had on a pretty Sunday dress along with her moderately high heels. She even had her purse in one hand. She had no rings, jewelry, or makeup because the Nazarene church had taught her to believe that women should not be adorned. She owned a diamond wedding ring but didn't wear it.

Modest and pretty, and she's my mom, I thought as I kept looking at the new picture.

And in front of Mom was little sis, Linda, only four. Her long curls hung below her shoulders, she had a cute smile, and she had a pretty bow on her blouse. I'd always tried to play with her and be nice to her, but my busy life kept me away from her most of the time. I thought that I'd try to help her learn to read soon, like Earleen had done for me when I was late four and early five.

By Dad's side in the picture stood my big sis, Earleen, who had just announced that her new name would be Tommie Earleen. She'd always wanted two names, but she'd just been named Earleen. Since Dad was Thomas Earl, she said it would be perfect to be Tommie Earleen. And so now Mom and Dad, along with her friends, had begun calling her Tommie. I still called her Earleen, partly because I wanted to pester her, but mainly because I envied her for almost getting a first-born's father's name—and she was a girl. Earleen was pretty and very smart. Sometimes I had to be smart-alecky around her to bring her around to being human.

During her eighth grade, she had taken elocution lessons from Miss Downs for six months. Dad even paid for them. I tried to mock her sweet-talking ways, but Mom always made me quit. She was still taking piano lessons from Mrs. Hunsaker, for which Dad also paid. And I had to buy my BB gun and bike. Not fair. But Earleen was nice to me most of the time, except when she wanted to boss me. Then I might tear into her, and she'd scream to Mom, "Make Paul leave me alone!" And Mom would always tell me to behave. It really was Earleen who should have been told to behave. But I tried to respect her because she sometimes helped me with my studies.

She'd just begun her junior year in high school and wouldn't turn fifteen until December. And she made all A's. High school boys were beginning to hang around, especially Raymond Taylor from the Taylor dairy family. The Taylors went to the Nazarene church, too. One night Earleen and Raymond had come in from their date and were sitting in the front porch swing. I hung around, trying to find out what people did on dates.

Out of the blue, Raymond said, "P.J., you look like you can run fast."

"Well, pretty fast. I'm not the fastest in my class, but I get by," I bragged.

"Can you run around two square blocks in four minutes?"

"Sure can. That'd be easy."

"Here's a dime for you. Go try."

"Really? You're going to give me a dime to run only that far?"

"Yes, I just don't think you can do it that fast," he said with a grin on his face.

"I think I can do it."

And so I was off into the darkening night. I don't know how long it took me, but with the dime already in my pocket, it didn't make me much difference.

When I returned, the swing was empty, and Raymond's car wasn't at the curb. It then dawned on me that he just wanted me gone so they could kiss. I was still learning, but anyway, I'd still made a dime.

Going inside, I knocked on Earleen's bedroom door.

"Come in," she said.

I entered and immediately said in a low voice, "He kissed you while I was gone, didn't he?"

"None of your business what we did," she said, trying to keep her face from blushing. "Now, go away and leave me alone. I need to get ready for bed. And Paul, please don't tell Dad about this evening. Promise me."

"I promise," I replied, thinking that it was a good thing for my sister to grow up and to have boys like her. Someday I wanted to kiss some girls.

Dad didn't like Raymond. As a matter of fact, he wasn't very nice to any of the boys who came around. I'd even had to defend Earleen's friend one time when Dad was going on about him after her date had left. I wondered if, when I started dating, the girl's father would disapprove of me. Something else about men I needed to understand, I thought.

And Dad. I looked at the photo again. It was unusual to see him in a suit. He said he'd bought it so he could be a pallbearer at funerals. He teased Mom by often saying he'd keep the suit so long that he'd be buried in it. And Mom would respond that he needed to wear it more often and go to church with us. He looked handsome in the family picture, except for his big ears that I'd inherited.

Once, I recalled, when I was a small kid living in Mead, a man had opened the blade of his pocketknife and told me that he was going to whittle on my ears until they were of normal size. I screamed and cried and ran home. Dad was there, and when I told him what had happened, he took me with him, asked me to point out the man who had said it among those sitting in a group playing dominoes. When I did, I saw Dad go into a rage. While he didn't hit him with his fists, he hit him with his voice. I felt good about what Dad did, but I never again liked my big ears. Looking at Dad's ears in the picture made me wonder if anyone had ever treated him badly because of the size of his ears.

And there next to Mom was my parent's only son. Ten, going on eleven, a fifth-grader in love with his redheaded homeroom teacher, redheaded and freckled-face himself, like his mostly Irish mother, big-eared like his dad, the owner of a bike, a Daisy Red Ryder BB gun, a lawn mower, a mostly unused treehouse, a lock box, a bank account, a nickname of P.J., good friends, and not yet a bank walker at Round Hole, still shy and one who didn't know much about life, a churchgoer who bet while sitting in church, and one who knew more about vanilla than any other ten-year-old in the world. I liked this guy, P.J., who looked back at me from the picture. I blushed when I thought about liking him. As Mrs. Wheat told me during fourth grade, my artwork needed improvement, so I knew he wasn't perfect yet. His pictures could improve. But maybe there were all kinds of ways to draw pictures. Maybe I'd get an S rather than an I in art some other way. And then I laughed at myself as I thought, *That's blasphemy*, still not knowing for sure what the word meant.

As I was finishing looking at the new pictures, I again saw the name *Truby's Studio* printed at the bottom. I made myself a note to ask Mr. Truby if I could mow his lawn and maybe try to sell Mrs. Truby some vanilla.

After supper, I was drying dishes while Mom washed. Earleen had cleaned the table and swept the floor and gone to her room. She asked, "Did you like our new family pictures?"

"Sure did, Mom. We have a good family. All beautiful and handsome except for the big-eared kid."

"Now quit that, Son. God gave you your ears for a purpose. Someday you'll find out His purpose."

I didn't think God was like that, so I just hushed.

Mom seemed sentimental about the family picture as she continued. "I am made to think of pictures of my Tate family. We have such a good family. There is Maude, who married Mr. Carter, and they have seven girls and one boy. Then there is Cecil, who married Dr. Hardy, and they have three boys and three girls. Cliff, my oldest brother, married Susy, and they have three sons and two daughters. Next was Watt, who married Julie, and they have five boys and four girls. And then my favorite brother, Don, who first married Mary, and after she died, married Delia. All told, Don has five girls and three boys. And then my closest sister, Lilly, who married Roy Hurt. That's where the Roy in your name, Roy Paul, comes from. And Lilly and Roy have four children—two boys and two girls. And then you saw our Johnson family's picture today. The Tates' last born, my youngest brother, Tillman, died when he was young."

I listened quietly because I knew this was important to her. Maybe I'd learn something more about the Tate family. I'd been around them frequently.

Included in my life had been the annual graveyard cleaning at the cemetery where the Tates, as well as many others, were buried. On the first Saturday after Memorial Day, many relatives of those buried in the cemetery at Enterprise, Oklahoma, northwest of Coleman and northeast of Fillmore, gathered for an all-day cleaning of the graves. More food was brought by the women than could possibly be eaten. All the men bragged about the pie or cake or meat dish, and the women thrived on the compliments. Enterprise was a typical small burial place. Nearby was a two-story school building with the second-story auditorium serving as a place for Sunday church and revivals for the area, teacherage, a big water well covered by a roof, and the fenced-in cemetery to the north. So I'd seen many, many of my aunts, uncles, and cousins at this graveyard cleaning day.

Mom said, "Son, you've got more Tate cousins than you can shake a stick at."

I agreed.

But my only close cousins were Aunt Lilly and Uncle Roy's children—Hamble, Erten, Fern, and Claudia. And of these, Erten was the closest cousin I had. The Hurts were sharecroppers, dirt poor, and hard-working. I had spent two weeks living with them when Linda was born, and I learned what living on a dirt floor was like, sleeping in the loft on a corn shuck mattress on cold nights, using kerosene lanterns, drawing drinking water from the well, going out back to the two-stooler, finding out what the real purpose of the Montgomery Ward catalog was for, exploring all the canned foods in the cellar, and seeing the salted meat in the smokehouse.

Erten taught me so much about farm animals, plowing, using an axe, milking a cow, and training farm dogs. Even though they were poor, in some ways they seemed to have all they needed. Well, except bologna. That was such a treat that Dad would frequently buy a whole round of bologna at a grocery store to take to them when we visited. And Aunt Lilly would usually send us home with one or two live pullets for us to have fried chicken. It was quite sad to see Mom wring the chicken's neck until its head came off its body. And then it'd flop around for a while before it died. But I surely did enjoy the fried chicken, biscuits, mashed potatoes, fresh black-eyed peas, and fried okra that Mom would prepare after a visit to Aunt Lilly and Uncle Roy's house.

We were finishing the chores in the kitchen when I decided to ask her about the Johnson family. The time seemed right.

"Son, there's your one cousin, Barney, Jr., but Dad doesn't know where he is. One of your dad's sisters-in-law remarried after her husband died, and she lives in Bristow, Oklahoma. You've met your dad's second cousin on the Wolfe side, Dr. and Mrs. Reed Wolfe, who live in Hugo. There are some other of Dad's relatives scattered here and there, but he's not close to any other than Dr. Wolfe. And somehow, he's related to Lizzie and Tom Johnson and their son, Crip Johnson, who is chief of police here in Durant. But Crip is not a relative on the Johnson side. Lizzie was a Wolfe before she married Mr. Johnson."

"So I'll go through life without too clear of a picture of the Johnson side, huh?"

"You've seen the family pictures of your Johnson grandparents and their four sons. You can see if your father will tell you more about the Johnsons whenever you can find him in the mood to talk about things like that. He doesn't seem to want to do that very often."

That Wednesday had been a good day for me. Not only had

things gone well in school and on my route, but also I'd had some good times with our family pictures and the stories and thoughts about our family.

When I came home from the Wednesday night prayer meeting service, I asked Dad if he'd talk to me about the Johnson side of the family.

"Someday, Son, but now you'd best get on to bed. Sunrise will be here before you know it. I'm going on the Ardmore, Davis, and Wynnewood run tomorrow, so I'll be gone when you get up."

That wasn't anything new. He was always gone when I got up, except on Sunday morning when I had to leave the house by 5:00 A.M.

I tried to tune in to KMOX to pick up the Cardinals game, but the clear channel wasn't too clear that night, so I turned the radio off and lay there awhile wondering what my future picture would be. But not for long, because I needed sleep. My prayer that night included thanks to God for a good family.

CHAPTER 10
Fall of '41

The fifth grade was going great. I had put *"Businessman"* on my personal data card. I didn't mention it to Mom, nor had she asked me about it. We'd finally progressed to the west wing of Washington Irving Elementary School and were far removed from those young kids on the north wing. Now we only had to protect ourselves from the snobby sixth-graders.

A great new guy had moved to Durant from Ardmore. His name was Bobby Nichols, known to us all as Nick. The girls seemed to like him. Nick was a good athlete, and he added to our fun at recess. He seemed to be friends with everyone.

I was pleased to again be in Miss Vaughan's homeroom. She had never disappointed me; she was always friendly and helpful. I kept wondering why all the teachers weren't like Miss Vaughan, but, I thought, not all my customers were alike either.

Mrs. Landers taught us arithmetic, almost literally to the "tune of a hickory stick," except her paddle was made from another wood. But it was fierce, and she used it often. We all said that she had eyes in the back of her head. Also, she'd explained to us that she had some hearing loss, so when we spoke, she said to speak clearly and loudly, but not too loudly.

Just yesterday, Earl and Wayne were whispering to each other while she was writing on the blackboard, and she heard what they'd said. And then she gave them three licks each, right in from of the class. I flinched with each lick, knowing how they hurt. But neither Earl nor Wayne flinched, and both smiled at the class as they walked to their desks. I vowed at that moment to never get paddled by a teacher or principal in my life. I knew it might be a difficult vow, but I vowed it nevertheless.

Our reading teacher was Miss Taylor. Both Mrs. Landers and she had taught for a long time. Miss Taylor was pleasant but like Mrs. Landers, a no-nonsense teacher. Since I read well, both silently and orally, I had no problems with her. She often called on me to read parts of the story in front of the class, an assignment I enjoyed. We all knew we'd better learn what she expected because she didn't mind, or almost seemed to enjoy, giving low grades.

And finally, as Mr. Garrison had promised me, I had a man teacher, Mr. Sharp, who taught us things about geography and events of our country's development. He was very patriotic, which seemed good at the time, especially with Hitler's war in Europe. He never really seemed to have his heart in what he taught, mostly just assigning us seat work. Occasionally he'd spend a whole class just reading to us from Halliburton's *Book of Marvels*. He said that we should imagine we were on a magic carpet and could fly away to visit the places he read about to us—just like Richard Halliburton did when he was young.

I usually could do just that. I could see in my mind a carpet, and I'd travel to the pyramids, or to the Golden Gate, or to China, or wherever the story he read took us. But after awhile, my carpet would run out of magic due to Mr. Sharp's boring voice. Several times I saw my friends, especially Billy Jack, with his head on his desk asleep. But from what I knew about Billy Jack's family, he needed to sleep. I often brought a peanut butter and jelly sandwich to school, pretending it was for me, but then I'd convince Billy Jack to take it for his lunch. It didn't take much convincing. Mr. Sharp never seemed to mind if kids went to sleep while he read. Billie Jean and I would look at each other and try to say, "What's Mr. Sharp doing?" Billie Jean was about as smart as anyone in our class. Her father, Mr. Parrish, an Indian, worked in the local office that helped Indians. I liked Billie Jean very much. She was kind, smart, and talented as a piano player. She also seemed shy, like I was.

For play time during recess, Mr. Sharp would tell some of us boys to get the play equipment, and he'd just let us go play. We liked that freedom, but often I wondered where he went during recess. Sometimes he'd be with us and try to teach, but we thought we knew as much as he did.

The girls played hopscotch or just sat around. Some would wander over and watch us play ball.

Occasionally, Mr. Garrison would join us for recess, and he'd always be playful and fun. But not Mr. Sharp. Behind his back, some of the kids called him Mr. Dull. I wondered if that were blasphemy.

My grades remained good. Learning was fun and exciting, and I couldn't let Earleen think she was smarter than I, even though Mom and Dad were already talking about her being the top student in her class and probably graduating from her senior class as valedictorian. (I had learned that word.) I vowed that if Earleen was, then I'd be, too. And that was a scary vow.

I was having fun with my paper route. Once already I had backed out of participating in an initiation of a new carrier, and I liked myself for that because it seemed so cruel to hit guys. And I seemed to be doing well as a carrier, or so Skip said. I was earning $5 to $6 a week, had five or six new customers, and could race around the route in almost record time when there weren't many delays to take a paper to a person sitting on a front porch. My bank account continued to grow. The teller at the Durant National Bank knew me by name and always chatted with me when I made a deposit, and that really me feel good. I now had $140 deposited, and I was very satisfied that I wasn't taking any money, directly at least, from Dad. I still felt OK about getting a room, food, and my clothes washed for my labor in the house, yard, and vanilla business.

The *Democrat* had just begun a new daily comic strip, "Boots and Her Buddies," in which there was a woman always wearing a Red Cross cap. And the *Democrat* had front-page articles every day about something going on concerning the war. I always read from one unfolded paper as I folded the others, and I never liked much of the news about the war. Several of us carriers talked about the war as we sat around waiting for our papers. But I enjoyed reading the "Chatterbox," a daily column about persons or events in Durant. It was a pleasant change from war news.

I was getting along better with Judge Woodward. I guess his daughter had told him how helpful and pleasant I had been when I brought the paper to her. He even smiled one day when I collected.

Maybe I was making progress. I thought, too, that his job as a city judge must be interesting, but it must have a lot of unpleasant things that went along with it.

Mr. Long continued to try my patience. I just couldn't figure him out. But he always paid, finally. Mrs. Mattox, who lived on South Ninth, had told me to begin collecting from her at the Plaza Theater, where she sold tickets in the little booth at the front. I liked the idea of collecting there because maybe people would see me talking with her and think I was buying a ticket to see the movie. Once she'd offered to buy me a ticket to see the show Saturday afternoon, but I thanked her and told her that I wasn't allowed to go to movies because my church was against it. She was surprised, but she didn't say anything.

On a Saturday morning in early October, Dad asked Mom and us kids if we'd like to go on a picnic. Mom responded, "Earl, are you sick, or something?" shocked that he had asked. "We haven't been on a picnic in so long that I can't remember when it was."

Immediately Earleen said, "I can't go. School activities."

"Maybe we four can go then," Dad continued.

"Where'll we go?" Mom wanted to know.

"I thought we'd drive to Colbert and go west to where the dam is being built."

"Is that the one damming the Red River?" I asked, almost feeling guilty for saying *damming* in front of Mom.

"Yes, and the dam is very high and long. We can look at the construction for a while and find a wooded area someplace nearby and eat and play awhile," Dad said.

"I'm ready," I said.

Linda said she wanted to go, too.

Mom added, "Now wait a minute, Earl. Do you just want to watch the men work on the dam, or are we really going on a picnic?"

"Some of both, I guess," Dad replied, in a somewhat discouraged voice.

"Let's go, then," said Mom. "I'll prepare us a picnic basket."

Linda and I both jumped around together in excitement about all of us being together on such an outing. I was sort of glad Earleen wasn't going because Dad and she would talk about the debate team and the debate contests she and her partner, Jack Hewett, were preparing to enter in high school competition. Dad liked debate.

We left just before noon and soon arrived at the area where the Red River dam was being built. Although we couldn't drive too close to the construction area, we could see what a giant project it was. Dad said that it was to be one of the great earthen dams in the country. He also said that the lake would have more than 1,200 miles of shoreline and would have water backed up nearly all the way to Tishomingo.

That made the lake more real to me because I'd ridden to Tish from Durant many times, and it was thirty-two miles one way. Dad said that the lake would not necessarily be thirty-two miles long, but that it would cover lots of valuable farm land, oil wells, and even small towns.

"Son, you've been on my vanilla run when we've sold in Aylesworth, east of Madill," he said with a desire for me to understand.

"Yes, I know the store where you sell."

"That whole town will be underwater, so all the people will have to move."

"Where will they move to?" Mom asked.

"Not exactly sure," Dad replied. "You remember that Governor Phillips and the State of Oklahoma filed a lawsuit trying to stop the construction because of the loss of productive land, oil, and school taxes, plus the simple fact that so much of the land to be covered was Oklahoma while Texas seemed to benefit from the lake as much as Oklahoma."

"What happened?" I asked, not sure I understood all of what he was talking about.

"The courts, Supreme Court of the U.S., I think, finally said it could be built," he said knowingly. "The bill authorizing the dam was passed in Washington in 1938, the best I remember."

I was very impressed with Dad's information. It seemed that Mom was listening and appreciating it, too.

"You know who was mainly pushing the bill through Congress, don't you?" he inquired, knowing that I wouldn't know. I hoped Mom would know. We shook our heads "no" and laughed when Linda did, too.

"I'll tell you who. It was the Highway 82 man, that's who. Son, do you remember who that is?" He looked at me as if I should know, which I did.

"Yes, sir, Mr. Sam Rayburn from Bonham," I smartly replied.

"And where did you learn about him, Son?"

"When I went on your Hugo, Paris, Bonham, Sherman run, Dad. I remember when we went west on Highway 82 out of Bonham, and you told me that your relatives had lived all up and down that highway."

"And what did I do when I got in front of Mr. Sam's house?"

"You stopped and told me what a great man he is. How he took care of the average person and how he knew everyone by name. I thought for a minute, Dad, that you were going to make me get out of the car and kneel down to honor him," I said somewhat jokingly.

"Well, that'd been OK, too," he laughingly responded.

Mom laughed, too. We were all having such a good time. It was quite different for us to laugh and play. So much of the time everything seemed to be focused on church, business, school, or study. Mom and Dad didn't seem to go out visiting much. They enjoyed taking us visiting to the Hubbards or to the Trammels, but most of the time Dad had his friends and Mom had her friends.

After seeing about all we could see of the dam's construction, we drove to a pretty wooded area, probably where an old farm house had once stood. The grass was still green, leaves on the tree were beginning to turn autumn colors, and, after Mom spread an old quilt to make a pallet, we were comfortable and pleasant. Mom had brought delicious crispy fried chicken, potato salad, homemade bread, and some red beans, along with a big jug of lemonade. And, of course, she'd baked some oatmeal cookies. We stuffed ourselves, laughed, and enjoyed being together.

After we'd cleaned up, I played chase with my little sis for a while, and once, when I glanced back to see what Mom and Dad were doing, I saw them kissing. Mom saw me looking and motioned for me to go on and play. She looked embarrassed.

Since I couldn't ever remember seeing them kiss before, I was embarrassed, too. But as I thought about it while playing with Linda, I liked seeing them kissing, and I hoped they did it a lot. But I certainly didn't know.

We drove on home before long, enjoying the ride in the Mercury. We had all four windows down, and Mom started singing, "Row, row, row your boat," and we all joined in. I discovered that Dad and I both must have deserved an I in music.

About the last four miles I asked Dad to turn on the radio so I could hear the last of the SMU football game. SMU won. I liked SMU because of the word "Methodist" in it.

The next morning during church service, I told Dan that I didn't want to count cars. So I sat and thought. I kept wondering if Dad had gone on the picnic knowing that he might have to leave for the army someday. He said that he wouldn't, but it still worried me. I hoped for more picnics.

About that time I heard the preacher say that the youth revival would begin next Sunday and run through the week. He said that we'd be blessed by having a male quartet from Bethany-Peniel College there to sing from Friday night through Sunday morning service. He told us who the preacher would be, too, but I didn't listen very well to that. Now Mom would make me go to every night's preaching. I didn't need reviving; I needed rest from all my activities. But the quartet and the college sounded interesting—that's where Earleen was going to attend and the one Mom said I'd go to someday.

After the service, Earleen eagerly talked about the quartet. But she had excuses for Monday, Tuesday, Wednesday, and Thursday nights with debate practice. Mom let her off. So I was trapped. It was strange to me that Earleen didn't have debate practice when the quartet would be at church. I was beginning to figure her out.

I told Mom that the Durant High football team had a home game Friday night, and Dad and I wanted to go. She said that she'd consider it.

I sat by myself for all the nights of the revival because Dan didn't have to come. I was so tired of the stories about sinful youth and all the long altar calls that by Thursday night I occasionally wished I were dead. But I laughed to myself because I knew I didn't mean it.

Dad and I saw the DHS Lions lose to McAlester 17-0 that Friday night, but it was a pleasant change not to have to listen to the preacher. Earleen was aglow with happiness about the college guys when I saw her after the game.

"Oh, they were so good," she told me. "You really missed a treat, Paul, by not being there to hear them," she said, almost blushing.

"Yeah, I bet they were good. Probably good looking, too. Did you get sweet on one of them yet?" I teased.

"This is serious. They are good Christians whom God has given wonderful voices to sing His praises. Now, you be respectful to me," she said with a raised voice.

I laughed. "Would they have had such wonderful voices if they'd been ugly?" I asked.

"Paul, that's blasphemy. Now, leave me alone!"

I decided, once again, that I'd have to learn what that word meant. But I laughed as I was getting into bed because I thought I'd won that debate, or whatever a debate was.

Much to my surprise, Mom had invited the evangelist and the quartet for dinner Saturday at 12:30. Dad went fishing at 7:30 A.M. but didn't invite me. Mom made me bathe and put on clean clothes. She didn't have to tell Earleen anything because she was dressed in her best.

When they all arrived, Mom had the fine china and stuff like that on our dining table. She'd had me put the two leaves in so it'd be long enough to seat everyone. Nine seemed to be a lot to feed, and Mom was surprised when the local preacher showed up, too. The evangelist said he insisted that Brother White come also. So we set another place. I thought I'd be OK until he showed up. Then I knew I'd do something that would get me in trouble with Mom again.

After a long blessing, we dug in. The college guys were fun. And could they eat! I wondered if they ever got fed at their college, the way they ate our food. I thought about how much it cost, but Mom seemed happy when they all bragged on her food. The preacher put away about three times as much as any one of the guys in the quartet did. I told him to save me something for leftover meals, and Mom looked at me sternly. After the main meal, Mom fed them five butterscotch pies. I thought I'd die watching them cram down my favorite pie. But I, too, got two pieces of the delicious pie, so it made me forget about how much they ate.

Then the guys, Earleen, and I went to the front porch while Mom, Linda, the evangelist, and Brother White sat in the living room and visited.

Three of the guys seemed to stay around Earleen. They called her Tommie. They were telling her stories about the college, which they called B-PC.

The fourth guy, Joe Norquist, from a town in Kansas, and I walked around to the back of our house. He seemed different from the other three.

"Do you enjoy college?" I asked.

"Yeah, it's OK. I enjoy dating a lot. College girls are OK. Do you have a girlfriend, Paul?"

"I'm only in the fifth grade," I said.

"I had a girlfriend when I was a fifth-grader. She liked me, too."

"Well, I don't." Trying to change the subject, I first asked, "How'd you become a Nazarene?"

"Dad and Mom were Lutherans, but Mom began to take me to the Nazarene church when I was about ten."

"Why did she change?" I wanted to know.

"She said that she just liked the preacher there more."

"That's what my mom told me when we left the Methodist church. She said the preacher at the Nazarene church seemed better."

And that ended the discussion of my first question. (Thinking of this switch in churches, as a future businessman I had a thought that it was the salesman, not the product, that convinced people to buy.)

Then I asked Joe, "Do you sing at many revivals?"

"One in the fall and one in the spring," he said rather matter of factly.

"Is it a fun thing to do?" I asked.

"The most fun is standing on the platform and singing during the altar call. That's when I look for white-knuckle sins. You know what a white-knuckle sin is?" he asked, smiling.

"No, tell me."

"I don't know whether I should or not, but I will. During altar calls, people who've committed the big sin hold on to the pew in front of where they're standing so hard that their knuckles turn white. And then I know what they are praying about if they come to the altar to be forgiven and saved," he explained.

"What's the big sin?" I asked.

"Oh, I forgot how young you are. The big sin has to do with what big boys and girls do to make babies. Does that help you understand?"

I blushed and wanted to leave, but I needed to stay and act big. "Do you see many white knuckles in our church?"

"No. There really aren't many young people who attend here. And those who are in church seem to be saved."

I thought I'd try something risky. "Earleen, I mean Tommie, was there last night. Did you see her?"

"Oh, yes, she was the prettiest girl there. She really stood out."

"Did the evangelist have an altar call last night?"

"Now, whoa, right there, Paul. I'm not going to answer any more of your questions," he said with a grin. "But Tommie never did even have her hands on the pew in front of her during the entire altar call. I watched carefully. Let's walk back to the porch."

And we did. I found a new way to entertain myself during altar calls. I planned to share this with Dan later, so we could watch and see if we agreed or not. When I did, Dan said, "You know that's not right. He was just pulling your leg."

"I thought so, but since he's a college guy I had to listen."

And during the altar call on Sunday morning, the evangelist said, "With all heads bowed and every eye closed and letting the spirit of God work among us, listen to the words of these wonderful Christian young men as they sing, 'Nearer My God to Thee.' And I want all sinners walking rapidly to this altar to confess your sins. Now sing, boys."

Dan and I never closed our eyes. We looked around and discovered others' eyes were open, too. I grinned at Dan as he looked for white knuckles. He grinned back.

And then I looked right at Joe while he seemed to be enjoying the song the quartet was singing. I watched as his eyes roamed around the congregation. Finally his eyes caught mine, and he grinned and winked. *Maybe,* I thought, *parts of college would be all right.*

The revival ended that night. I'd given my $3 pledge to "help pay the salary of this wonderful evangelist sent to us from God." It was worth $3 to get another revival behind me, and besides, I'd learned a little bit more, this time from a college man. And I always tried to remember to keep my hands in my pockets while I stood during the altar calls.

During the second week of November, Earleen and her debate partner, Jack Hewett, were to enter the area debate contest held at our Southeastern State College. Dad had told me the competition would be tough. High school teams from Ardmore, Ada, McAlester, Hugo, Idabel, Atoka, Antlers, and Denison and Sherman, Texas, and maybe a team or two from as far away as Muskogee would be there.

So a week earlier Dad was spending time during our supper asking Earleen to outline and review her positions, both affirmative and negative. It was interesting for me to hear, but I just ate rapidly and hoped to be excused from the table as early as possible.

Dad surprised me. "Tommie, tell Paul what you are debating this season."

As she turned to me, she said, "Resolved: That the expansion of the role of the federal government in President Franklin Roosevelt's time in office is good for the people of the United States. Then she asked snottily, "Do you know what that means?"

"Sorta," I responded.

Then Dad said, "Well, Paul, I want you to debate Tommie. I'll let you go first. You argue for the affirmative."

"What's affirmative?" I asked. Earleen laughed.

"You take the side that what President Roosevelt is doing is good for the country," Dad said.

I was silent for a few seconds, feeling trapped. But I thought about our *Weekly Reader* story about the REA, and our class discussion about what the Rural Electrification Act was doing to bring electricity to people who lived in the country. Since that was the only thing I could think of, I asked Dad when I could begin my debate.

"Now, Son. Make your points carefully."

And so I began. I used Aunt Lilly and Uncle Roy's house without electricity as my example. I explained about every way I could how electricity would be helpful, and, finally, I said that President Roosevelt had done well in leading us to a better country, and the REA was a good example of that. While I talked, I remembered that Mr. Rayburn had supported the REA. So, I thought, if Dad, the judge of our debate knew this, he'd favor me. And crossing my mind was that Dad was trained as an electrician. I didn't think of these things until I was well into my argument, but, again, I thought that Dad would be impressed. So I added these points, causing Dad to smile.

Then Earleen took the negative and disagreed with my points. She rattled on for a while. When she finished, she said she wanted to quit, adding that she thought it was a waste of time to debate me.

"Well, OK," Dad said. "But I have to declare a winner from what you've done already. And I declare Paul the winner. I think he was better prepared and had more facts to support his position than you did."

With that, I laughed out loud. And while my mouth was open with the laugh, I caught a large spoonful of mashed potatoes in my mouth and all over my face. Then the potatoes started falling on my clothes.

Surprised, I looked at Earleen reaching for another spoonful, but Dad stopped her. She got up and ran from the room, crying. Dad followed, and evidently consoled her in some way. I cleared the potatoes away, still enjoying my victory. I thought, with a grin on my face, it would be best to debate elsewhere other than at the supper table.

The next week Tommie Earleen Johnson and Jack Hewett brought the first-place trophy back to DHS from the annual Southeastern High School Invitational Debate Tourney. Dad was very pleased and even invited Mr. "Slew" Hewett, Jack's dad, to have coffee with him at his early morning coffee shop. As Dad later told us, "That was an event unto itself, since Slew is one of only two Republicans registered in Bryan County. And his brother Harry Hewett is the other. Slew thought that the team did the best with the negative. I said that their affirmative was the strongest, using the REA as an example."

I always read my *Weekly Reader* more carefully from then on. Miss Taylor, our reading teacher, was impressed with how well I could remember what I'd read and could discuss it in class.

And was I ever reading the daily news printed in the *Democrat* about the war in Europe! It was so frightening to me. And when I collected, several customers mentioned something about Hitler or the war. Several said it looked as if we'd be in it soon. I added to my nightly improper prayer for God to take care of Hitler, reasoning that God would know what I meant since He knew everything.

And then it happened. We had come out of church on South Ninth, had gotten into our Mercury, and were driving over the bumpy Frisco tracks, listening to Dad complain once again about how he hated to wait for us when the preacher kept us so long, when I heard over KRLD-Dallas a news bulletin. "Shhh!" I said. "Listen."

And the announcer told us about Pearl Harbor.

Dinner was quiet that day, and the food had no taste. Dad and Mom listened to the Atwater-Kent all afternoon. Occasionally, I'd walk in to find out the news. We didn't go to church that night, but our family prayer was eventful because Dad joined us.

I couldn't get rid of a picture in my mind of Mr. Snow, my blind friend at the Bryan County Courthouse, as I went to sleep that frightful December 7 night.

CHAPTER 11
The Months After

Monday was one I'll never forget. A fifth-grader, scared, not sure what I understood, but we, and that included me, P.J., were at war. President Roosevelt and Congress had said so. Mr. Snow had once told me that his injuries had been worth it if all wars would end based on his fighting in World War I. But his war didn't end wars. I wished he'd been right.

Miss Vaughan brought a radio, and we listened nearly all of the school day. Even when she said we could go outside for recess, no one really wanted to go. Some girls cried. I had heard the word *emotion* and had learned what it meant, but I had never understood it until that day, December 8, 1941.

My thoughts were mostly about Dad, as well as other men from Durant who might, or would, go to war. Some of us guys talked about wanting to go fight Tojo, Hirohito, Mussolini, and Hitler, but we knew we couldn't.

The teachers let us talk about anything on our minds that day. So unusual, so unreal. Mr. Sharp asked all students how old their fathers were. I thought that he was trying to find out whose father would go.

"My dad," I said, "is forty-two."

It seemed as if most fathers were between thirty and forty-four. I thought that Mr. Sharp shouldn't have, but he said that he believed the fathers between thirty and thirty-eight would be conscripted, explaining what that word meant. I knew that I shouldn't have, but

I thought that if anyone was conscripted it should be Mr. Sharp. And I immediately wished I wouldn't think that way.

I survived the day at school and pedaled my bike to the *Democrat* building. I was surprised to find men all around the building, filling Evergreen Street and North Third. They were also sitting on the city hall lawn and on the steps of the post office building.

And then, upon asking Skip, I learned that the Selective Service Office was on the second floor of the *Democrat* building, and all the men were there to enlist. Skip said that a photographer from the *Democrat* had been taking their pictures most of the day.

Skip called all the carriers in and talked to us. "This is a very special day in our nation's history," he said as he held up a copy of the *Democrat*. "Look at this. It says, 'Congress Declares War,' and the sub headline reads, 'Session Acts 33 Minutes after President Demands Vengeance Against Japan.'"

It was the largest headline I'd ever seen on the front page. The situation was really beginning to sink in on this fifth-grader.

Skip continued, "Mr. Story has decided we'll need extra copies of the paper today. So we're going to let you buy extra ones for two cents each. I'll sit at that table over there and take your order. Then, if you buy fifty extra, I'll bill you an extra dollar next Saturday. Do you understand? Any questions?"

And he went to the table. I thought I'd be able to sell as many as 100 at Ninth and Main after I delivered my route. Skip was surprised and tired to convince me against ordering so many. But I insisted that he give me 100, and he charged me $2.

I probably set a time record for delivering my route that day. By 4:30 P.M., I was at the corner trying to sell the special paper. Within minutes, nearly every other car was stopping to buy.

"How much, Son?"

"Only a nickel," I replied.

"This paper is worth more than that," several had said, with comments about Pearl Harbor, paying me anywhere from a dime to a dollar.

I sold every paper, all 100, by dark. When I got home, I told Mom and Dad why I was so late, and then I counted my money. I had $17.35. I felt good about the money I made, $15.35 profit, but I soon began to feel bad because I'd made money as a result of news about the war.

When I mentioned this to Dad, he reassured me that radio, newspapers, and magazines provided us with the only up-to-date account of the war and that it was OK to sell news as long as it was accurate.

We were mostly quiet at the supper table. Dad did discuss seeing all the men lined upon around the draft board office.

I asked him, "Were you there to enlist, too?"

"No, Son, I still don't believe they'll take forty-two-year-olds. It's better I'm home."

It was a relief to hear him reassure me, but then Linda began to cry, I guess because she had been scared that Dad might leave home for the army. Mother got her and went into the living room. They never did come back and finish supper. Earleen and I had to clean the kitchen. We listened that night, once again, to the Atwater-Kent. Finally I fell asleep on the carpet. Mom shook me awake and told me to go to bed. As I pulled up the covers, I wondered what would happen to our country, as well as to us in Durant.

Just before our Christmas break from school, Mr. Garrison spoke to everyone in the fourth, fifth, and sixth grades during an assembly program. He talked about the war and how we'd have to begin safety drills.

"They will be much like a fire drill to which you are accustomed, but this time you will hear the school bell sound the alarm three times, instead of the two for the fire alarm. Your teachers will ask that you get under the front part of your desk, be still, and remain quiet. Your teachers will assign two students in each room to pull the black shades on the windows so that light cannot come in and your room lights can't be seen from the outside. Then, in a few minutes, the all-clear bell will ring, and you will go back to your regular class activities."

Then a sixth-grader came on stage carrying his desk, and Mr. Garrison and he showed how to huddle under the desk. After a few more remarks about how our country would win the war, we all stood and sang "The Star Spangled Banner." It had a very special meaning to me that day. Then we went to our rooms and practiced the drill. About 2:00 that afternoon, the drill bells rang; we stopped our lessons and practiced again. Mr. Sharp was our teacher during that period, and he told us what a good job we'd done.

Then he showed us some maps of Europe and of Pearl Harbor.

I really became upset about the Japanese killing American men, sinking our ships, especially the USS *Oklahoma*, and destroying our airplanes. I vowed then to do everything a ten-year-old guy could do to help defeat Hitler, Mussolini, Tojo, and Hirohito.

Dad and Mom always tried to listen to the radio to hear President Roosevelt when he addressed the nation. I'd lie on the carpet near the heat coming out of the big coal stove and pay close attention to my president. His voice was so reassuring when he began, "My fellow Americans..." Then I was already better. I liked my president and just knew that he'd lead us to victory.

I noticed that men in our neighborhood were already joining the military. So had my cousin, Erten Hurt, who joined the navy, and my cousin Ralph Tate, who was a track star at Oklahoma A&M, who was mobilized when the Oklahoma National Guard was called to duty. The guard was the Oklahoma 45th Division. The McPhersons, just down the block from our house, had two sons and the father to enlist. And the man who rented our north rent house, an optometrist named Dr. Morrison, was soon drafted. The Housers, the Spragues, Mack's uncle, and many men on my paper route either enlisted or were soon drafted.

My friends, George Boyet, John Shaw, and Mack McElreath, and I were all playing together after school was out for Christmas on December 19. Tiring, we sat awhile, and the talk began about the war. All of us agreed that our dads wouldn't have to be in the army because of their age. I was relieved to hear them say that because maybe Dad hadn't been deceiving me about having to go.

That night I told him about our talk. He again reassured me that things looked like he couldn't go unless the war got real bad. If that happened, he said that all men might have to go.

Continuing, I asked, "Dad, will bombs fall in the U.S.?"

"Probably not. I imagine that if they did, they'd fall mostly on the West and East coasts, like in California or New York. We're probably in one of the safest parts of the U.S. right here in Durant. Why, who'd want to waste a bomb on Durant?" he asked teasingly.

He made a good point. Who would want to bomb Durant? But I didn't want any enemy invading or harming my country.

All of a sudden Dad asked, "What do you want for Christmas? I need to buy you something special this year."

I recalled what Mom had said when Dad asked us to go on a picnic last October. "Earl, are you sick or something?" I wanted to say, "Dad, are you sick or something? Since when have you planned for a Christmas gift for me?" But then I remembered that he'd given me a new kickstand and two fender reflectors the Christmas after I'd bought my bike.

"Dad, I'd like anything you'd get me."

"But I think you need something really special this year. What'll it be?" he asked enthusiastically.

"If you really want to know, I'd love to get a basketball," I said quickly, not wanting him to forget what we were talking about.

"Do you know where one is that I could buy that you'd like to have?"

"Yes, sir. I was looking at the Voit outdoor rubber basketball just the other day out at Thompson's Book Store near the college. One of those would be perfect. But it'd cost a lot of money."

"How much?" he asked.

"Best I remember, one cost $7.50, but you get a needle and a small air pump with that price," trying to show him what a bargain one would be.

"We'll drive there tomorrow and look," he said, finalizing our conversation.

I could hardly sleep that night. And when I did, it didn't seem any time before I heard him shaving and smelled the cigarette smoke. I thought about getting out of bed and reminding him of our trip to Thompson's, but then I decided he'd just have to remember it for himself. I'd test him to see if he had been serious last night.

Soon I heard the engine of the Mercury start, and he was gone for coffee. Would he remember?

About 8:30, as I was finishing breakfast, I grinned as I saw him turning into our driveway. I guessed he remembered. And he had.

"You ready to go to Thompson's?" he said with a smile.

"Yes, sir, in a couple of minutes." I rushed to finish, brushed my teeth, combed my hair, and then hurried back. We drove out North Fifth to College Street, parked, and went in. I brought $2 along just in case the cost had increased, and Dad wouldn't be willing to pay more than $7.50.

I led him to where they were on display and was pleased to see there were several all boxed up. A sign read: "A Christmas Special,

$6.95 Only." Mr. Wilder Thompson came to help us. I knew him because the Thompsons had once rented our north house.

"Good morning, Earl. How can I help you?"

"Paul needs a basketball for Christmas, and he thinks he wants one of these. These any good?" he asked, seeming to need assurance that what he was spending his money for was a good product.

"The best money can buy. This ball is used by nearly every school around here. Well, that is, the schools that have outdoor courts, and that's nearly all of the elementary schools," he responded.

"Let's put some air in one and see if Paul wants it," Dad said.

"Dad, I know I want it. I've dreamed of owning one. Please buy it," I said, almost pleading.

"OK, I'll buy it. Oh, it does come with the air needle and pump for that $6.95, doesn't it?"

"Oh, sure, come on over here to the register," Mr. Thompson said as he picked up a new boxed ball with pump and needle.

I was so thrilled, I could have exploded! It was too good to be true. Me—me—me with my own basketball. Now I'd be in charge of the game. When I would arrive with the ball, the game could begin. And when I had to leave, the game would be over. And right then I vowed that I'd never get mad and threaten to take my ball and go home. No-siree, I'd stay until it was time to go. No silly mad games.

Dad said, "Wilder, wrap the box for Christmas, will you, please?"

"Be glad to, Earl," he quickly responded.

My heart sank a little. It was only December 20, so I'd be without my ball for three and a half days.

"Dad, can't I just have it now? It's vacation time from school, and I could surely use it."

"No, Christmas morning it'll be."

I had no argument. After all, he'd just spent $6.95 on me for something I'd wanted for a long time. We picked up the brightly wrapped box and left. Dad carried it into our house and put it under the decorated Christmas tree, next to Earleen's piano. I thanked Dad.

Monday afternoon after I finished delivering my route, I was riding toward home when I heard boys' voices in the distance. And then I heard a basketball bouncing against the hard playground at Woodrow Wilson Junior High. I was still two and a half bocks away from the school and couldn't see the playground.

At that moment, it dawned on me why I had such large ears. I could hear better! I could always hear a ball bounce or a football being kicked or a ball batted. I grinned. Knowing that it wasn't true about hearing better, I remembered the line from "The Big Bad Wolf"—"the better to see you with." So I always had a response to anyone who teased me about my big ears: "The better to hear you with." And then I wondered if boys really didn't have gifted hearing for balls bouncing, balls being kicked, and balls being hit by bats.

I stopped and joined the game. I wanted so badly to brag that I was getting a basketball Christmas morning. I wanted to say, "Be here Christmas morning and we'll play with a new ball." But I didn't. I still thought something might happen, that the gift under the tree might disappear.

Christmas Eve was nice. Mom had made fudge, divinity, and date loaf candies as well as ambrosia. A big hen would be baked for Christmas dinner. I went to bed early that night, almost like I did when I believed in Santa Claus. My last look at the tree confirmed that my present was still there.

About 5:30 A.M., I was awakened by Earleen playing carols on the piano. Soon we were all gathered around, ready for presents. Our tradition was that I delivered all the packages and placed them in front of the gift receiver. Then we'd say a brief prayer of thanks and begin opening. We opened our gifts in order from youngest to oldest. So Linda began, opening slowly and admiring each gift. I guess she had eight or ten presents, and I thought she'd never finish.

Then it was my turn. I had four presents, but the one that was to bounce was the first I opened. The other three had a shirt in one and some socks in the other, and a game of Pick-Up Sticks in the last. I thanked everyone and watched as Earleen began with her presents. After a long, long, long time, all presents had been opened. The basketball was in my hands. I even took it to the breakfast table with me, but Mom made me put it in my room.

After Christmas dinner, I hurried to the playground at Washington Irving and started bouncing my brand new basketball. Within ten minutes five other guys showed up. I knew then that boys could hear well what they needed to hear. We played until nearly supper time on that cool Christmas afternoon. Dad didn't know what he'd done, but he provided me with the happiest Christmas day of my life.

Christmas vacation was always over too soon, but to return to school was all right, too. The new year, 1942, brought wishes from all of us kids in the fifth grade that the war would be over as soon as possible.

The *Democrat* was crammed full of war articles or of articles pertaining to what we'd have to do because of the war. The January 25 *Democrat* had an article that said sugar would be rationed to one pound per week per person. When I read that article to Mom, she said, "Oh, my, we don't use five pounds a week, so that won't bother us."

Then I asked Dad if he would have enough sugar to make his vanilla.

"I have to go before the rationing board and make my case for an adequate supply. I imagine I'll get plenty since my business depends on having enough."

"Will your business be hurt because women won't bake as much anymore?" I asked, wondering about the supply of money for our family.

"We'll have to wait and see. If it is affected, it'll probably be because there won't be as many men around to bake for. But I imagine the wives, mothers, and sweethearts of our servicemen will still bake a lot of cookies and cakes to mail to their men," he replied thoughtfully.

"I've learned that a lot of sugar comes from Cuba, so why is it rationed?" I wanted to know.

"Ships and boats have gone to war. And U.S. land vehicles, like trucks and trains, are involved in the war effort. We'll see hard times over and over again before we win this war," he said knowingly.

On January 26, 1942, I had a real tragedy to deal with. My customer and friend, Mr. Helbach, the fireman, had been killed when the firetruck and a car ran together at Fifth and Evergreen. I was saddened to think about him dying, and I remembered how he smiled and winked as he had let me slide down the pole in the fire station. He'd always been friendly when I collected and had paid me quickly. He was such a good man.

So the day after his funeral, I wrote a poem about him and how he and I got along so well, and I inserted it in the Helbachs' *Democrat*. When I collected from Mrs. Helbach on Friday, she asked me in to have a piece of chocolate cake, and she talked to me and cried. As a kid, I didn't know much to do but listen. I hoped then that no other customers would die because it was tough to listen to people talk about death, especially when trying to enjoy cake. I thought about Mr. Helbach and her almost the rest of that day.

For the next few days, everything had gone pretty well. Articles appeared in the *Democrat* about the OPM, the Office of Price Management, suggesting that some products would have fixed prices for the duration. A daily column began to appear entitled "War Bulletins" with events of the war within the last day. And I found it both sad and interesting when I saw an ad from our drug store, Swinney's, that said, "Due to rubber shortage, we will deliver purchases of a minimum of 35 cents, which does not include ice cream, candy, or tobacco."

It was interesting, because I had an idea that I could ask Mr. Swinney if I could ride and deliver purchases for less than 35 cents if the customer would pay me 10 cents for delivering. I knew that my schedule prevented me from actually doing that, but I liked my idea.

On February 3 the *Democrat* was filled with information about Ira Eaker, a local man who graduated from Southeastern, being promoted to brigadier general. It told about how he had been a hero in World War I. Durant's first airport had been named for him. And I'd never heard of him before. I was still learning.

Dad told me quite a bit about General Eaker that night. When he was through talking, I asked if he'd let me ask him some questions that I needed answers for.

"Sure, go ahead," he said, as he turned the Atwater-Kent sound to very low.

"The war concerns me to the point I don't know what to do sometimes. I love my country, and it seems sometimes I can't keep my mind on my studies and on my paper route and other stuff. I even have dreams about war. Is this normal for a boy like me?" I asked.

"I think so, Son. But you have to find a balance. Let me give you an example, even though I don't know how good an example it is. When you ride with me in the Mercury, do you constantly think about having a car wreck?"

I grinned. "What if I said yes?"

Dad kicked his foot at me teasingly.

"No, I don't think about wrecks, Dad."

"Is it possible we might have one, and we'd both get hurt or killed?"

"Yes, I guess so."

"But you don't go down the road thinking about it every minute. Maybe that's what you can do with the war. We need a good driver, and he needs to be cautious, but the passenger doesn't have to worry all the time, except in moments of danger. Does that make sense?" he asked. And after a thought, he added, "And besides, you are delivering all the war news to your customers, and that's helpful."

"So maybe I'm a passenger in this war, and I can help if needed, but since I'm not in charge, I don't have to be too worried. Is that what you're saying? And I'm helping by throwing the *Democrat*, which has the war news."

"I've raised a genius for a son. He not only beats his sister in debate, but he also understands his dad's poor example," he said laughingly.

"Dad, I think you're smarter than a lot of high school graduates I know," I said, proud of him.

"Well, in some ways I may be, but I'm still always about broke because I don't make much money."

And with that he turned the radio volume back up.

He always comes back to money, I thought. But anyway, he'd given me a reason not to worry so much. Maybe I could watch the road and help the driver fix any flats, but I didn't have to be the driver. And off to bed I went, carrying with me a blanket I'd warmed around the hot coal stove. Sleep went better that night.

Friday I was collecting again. It seemed as if every other day was Friday. Collection was OK, but it just took so long. I'd had a few minutes to visit with Mr. Snow and heard his version of the war. It wasn't much different from everyone else's, but, coming from him, I respected what he thought and said. Mrs. Jarrell had given me a tip again, which I spent at his shop. Tips from customers were nice. They made me want to try harder to please them. Since the collection just before Christmas when I'd been given $8.75 in Christmas tips plus four presents—a baseball, a hair brush, a book by Twain, *Tom Sawyer*, which I'd already read four times, and a bag of apples and oranges—I had found myself being friendlier to all my customers, except Mr. Long. Dad had told me that Mr. Long "gets your goat," an expression that I knew meant he really bothered me. And I guess he did "get my goat."

Later that day on South Seventh, just behind the Magnolia station, I went into what I called my beer joint to collect. It was always crowded on Friday afternoons, but today it seemed jam-packed with men drinking beer, smoking, and using language which wouldn't have been approved of by Mom. Some of the words were even new to me. As I waited for the owner to pay me, a man sitting on the bar stool near to where I was standing asked in slurred speech, "Well, boy, what do you think of this war?" and before I could respond, his words made my ears burn. I'd heard some profanity in my life, but not like this. He called Hitler every word that my dictionary wouldn't print. While I wanted to leave, I was interested in his language. I really didn't listen to what he was saying other than the curse words. I got my dime, plus a quarter for a paper I sold to the man I listened to, and then I left.

When I cleared the smoke from my eyes and nose, I rode on to the next business, a dry cleaners, to collect. But I kept thinking of all the curse words I could remember him saying. And I said them over and over to myself, but never out loud.

I got my dime at the cleaners and began pedaling up the alleyway to Mrs. Madrea's house, where I expected to have to light the stove under her pot. But I kept asking myself if it was a sin to say these curse words, even though they weren't said out loud. And I knew that some of them took the Lord's name in vain. I knew that if Mom ever heard me say any of them, she'd declare that I'd sinned, applying appropriate punishment and prayer. But what if I just said them in my silent talk? This thought bothered me for most of my collection day. I was about to Mrs. Harris' house, the wife of the preacher at the First Christian Church. They lived in the middle of the block between Eleventh and Twelfth on Main. I almost wanted to ask her about this problem that was bothering me. "Mrs. Harris, you're a preacher's wife. Is this a sin?" But I was too scared to ask.

I knocked and Mrs. Harris soon greeted me pleasantly. "Cold February Friday, isn't it?"

"Yes, ma'am. Sure is. I'd like to collect, please."

She left for a couple of minutes, and upon returning, she

opened the screen door and said, "Hold out your hand, P.J., because there are a lot of pennies."

I did, and the coins were soon in my hands. I thanked her and left. Before I got to my bike, I counted them. There were nine pennies and a dime. Immediately, I ran back to her porch and knocked. She opened the door quickly, almost like she was waiting for me.

"Mrs. Harris, you've paid me too much. You gave me nine pennies and a dime. Must not have seen the dime, or thought it was a penny," I said.

"Thank you so much, P.J. I knew I paid you too much money. I was just curious as to whether you'd be honest and return it. Here's the tenth penny. And I'll take my dime back. Thanks. Now I know you're a Christian young man. I'll tell Reverend Harris what you did."

I left, more puzzled than ever. In a few more minutes I'd finished collecting and delivering the *Democrat*. Riding home, I tried to sort out my thoughts about what Mrs. Harris had done. I just couldn't put it all together. So, as I'd done in the last two or three years, I just put this day into my "Will Figure Out Later" box of thoughts.

That night a "blue norther" blew through Durant. Saturday morning Dad had a warm fire going, and I was helping Mom clean house. Then she said for me to run to Montgomery's store to get a loaf of bread.

When I returned she said George had called and wanted me to phone him. *Good*, I thought, *maybe something is happening*.

I picked up the phone, and the operator said, "Number, please."

"Is that you, Miss Bertha?" I asked.

"Yes, Paul."

"Well, ring 960 for me, please."

And she responded, "Good thing. George just called you a few minutes ago."

Miss Bertha was my neighbor, whose lawn I mowed and garden I dug and weeded. She was a very nice lady, but I guess that what Mom said was correct: telephone operators know more about what goes on in Durant than anyone else.

George's mother answered the phone and called for him.

"P.J.," he said, "I've got five new comic books. Come on over and we'll read them."

"Sounds great." I asked Mom if I could go. "Be over in a few minutes."

Putting on my mackinaw, which I'd mostly outgrown, I pedaled over. George and I read, talked, and laughed. Mrs. Boyet brought us each a cup of hot chocolate with two marshmallows. It was so good on a cold morning.

After we finished, he loaned me a couple of comic books to take home, but for some reason, I said I wasn't interested. Then I told him about the two events while collecting Friday and asked him his opinion about cussing silently and cussing aloud.

"Oh, P.J., you make too much about some stuff. My dad cusses, not very often, just when he needs to. Don't you think he's a good man?"

"I guess so," I responded, not knowing whether I really knew or not.

In a few minutes I put on my mackinaw, thanked George and Mrs. Boyet, went outside, and started to get on my bike, still as confused about cussing as I was yesterday. Maybe someday I'd sort it all out.

CHAPTER 12
Dog Days

Before I could get on my bike, Mrs. Mason's mother, who lived with her daughter and son-in-law, Albert, next door north of George, called out, "Son, would you please help me?"

"Certainly, be right there," I responded, moving toward her rapidly.

"*The Daily Oklahoman* has been thrown in the shrubbery, and since I'm an old woman, would you please help me by getting it for me?"

"Be glad to," I answered, wondering why in the world any carrier would throw a paper that didn't hit the porch. I noticed that the Masons' bulldog, whom I'd seen many times while visiting George, walked up and stood by her.

Down on my hands and knees, I was reaching in and had the paper in my hand when it happened. *Pain! Pain! Pain!* The dog had his teeth in my right ankle, or at least in the tender part between the ankle bone and heel. And it wouldn't let go. The lady was screaming at her dog. "Boots! Boots! Quit that! Bad dog! Bad dog!"

I was almost paralyzed with pain and fear. But I did have the good sense to use the rolled newspaper to hit him hard two times, and he let go of me.

What a relief! But then I saw blood running everywhere. Thinking more about my shoe and sock than about myself, I took them off so blood wouldn't ruin them.

She said that I should go home and let my mother take care of the wound. So I rode home with my shoe and sock off, leaving drops of blood along the way. I didn't feel very good, and I was also very weak.

Dad had just come home from town when I got there. "What happened?" he asked in a very concerned voice.

I told him. He wrapped a towel around my foot, put me in the Mercury, and soon we were in the emergency room at the Evergreen Sanitarium, just west of the *Democrat* building.

A nurse cleaned the wound; it burned badly, whatever it was she used. Then a doctor looked at it, talked with Dad for a short time away from me so that I couldn't hear, then came back and bandaged my foot. The nurse brought in some crutches just right for someone my size.

Dad then asked, "Are you through now, Doc?"

"Yes, he'll need to stay on those crutches a few days. And I've given you new bandages. Change them daily until the wound heals. And I'll need to give him a series of rabies shots."

I froze when I heard "series of shots." Why me, Lord, why me?

"How much will your bill today plus the shots be?" Dad asked.

The doctor figured in his mind for a minute. "Today's bill is $15. Crutches rental is $3. The shots, all combined, will be about $35. That adds up to $53."

Dad asked me, "Son, isn't the dog a pet?"

"Yes, it's the Masons' pet bulldog."

Then he said to the doctor, while reaching for his billfold, "I'll pay you the $18 now, and we'll see about the shots."

And we left. My foot throbbed. The crutches were a new experience, but I was soon home with my foot propped up, which helped a bit. I decided I didn't like bulldogs—or at least the one that bit me. I called for Dad.

"What am I going to do about my paper route?" I asked.

Dad answered as I hoped he would. "I'll drive and deliver as you roll and show me your route."

"Thanks, Dad. I imagine I'll need your help for several days."

He agreed he'd help for as long as I needed. In a few minutes I heard him on the phone to the Masons' house.

"Well, where is Albert? Country Club. He's not playing golf on a cold day like today, is he? Oh, at a club board meeting. Thanks, I need to talk to him about his dog and my son. Goodbye."

He drove off to find Mr. Mason. In about an hour, he returned, and I could tell that he wasn't in a good mood.

"Dad, what happened between Mr. Mason and you?"

"We talked," he said abruptly.

"Will you tell me what he said?"

"I'd rather not. I'm still mad." He left my room.

I called him back and asked him to get my lock box and key. After he brought them to me, I got $18 and gave it to him for the doctor's fees and crutches. He took it, turning his head away from me. I felt my body tense up and was aware of being disappointed and hurt that he took my money because he'd always paid Earleen's and Linda's doctor bills. But I was more interested in whether or not I was going to die from rabies, so I asked. "Will I have to get the shots, Dad?"

"I think we'll risk it without them. The dog is mostly a house dog and won't be rabid."

I was relieved, but still frightened. "What if the dog is rabid, Dad? Will I die?"

"We'll not discuss that. The dog is OK, and you'll be OK," he responded as he left the room again.

After he left, I counted the money in my billfold and found $3.75 left. I was going to make another $20 deposit, but that would have to wait a while. Anyway, I now had $220 in my bank, and I grinned satisfyingly, knowing the money was in Uncle Barney's bank rather than in Mr. Mason's bank.

Mom came in to see me, and I asked her why boys seemed to get hurt more than girls. She grinned and said, "Son, it's harder to get hurt playing the piano than playing football or messing with dogs." We talked a few minutes, and then I slept soundly.

Dad woke me at 4:45 Sunday morning. As I put my foot down and reached for the crutches, the pain in my foot was really bad. But I let it hang down for a few minutes and then hobbled around and got ready. When we went to the garage, we saw that a light snow had fallen during the night. Dad guessed the temperature to be around 25 degrees, but there was no wind. Just a cold, snowy morning to introduce Dad to the world of throwing the *Democrat*. I kidded him about being my sub. He laughed and said I'd have to pay him.

Since I rolled the papers in the car, we didn't have to stay at the *Democrat* except long enough to insert the funny papers into the main section. The streets weren't slick, just snow-covered, so Dad could drive easily. I wished that our Mercury had a heater in it like some other cars had, but it didn't. I was cold, but, I realized, warmer than if I were riding my bike.

It was funny to watch Dad stop, put the long S-curved gear stick into neutral, get out, throw the paper to two or three houses, walk back to the car, and drive to the next place where he repeated his actions.

He missed several porches, and I laughed at him. Maybe I had a more accurate throw than he. Or more experience, or something. I told him to go get the paper and put it on the porch. It wasn't long before he'd walk up much closer to a porch before throwing.

We finished and got home. Mom said that I didn't have to go to church. *Well,* I thought, *maybe the dog bite had some blessing after all.*

By Wednesday, I was able to ride my bike and deliver again. Dad had been patient and very helpful, and I planned to buy him a new smoking pipe at Boyet's Drug Store to thank him. I picked up the crutches from my house on my way from school to the *Democrat*. The doctor saw me, asked how I was doing, and checked my ankle.

"Looks like it's doing just what it's supposed to do," he said, with a smile on his face. So my episode with the dog was over, except that I was still embarrassed and upset at Mom because when I stayed home from church, she'd told me that she'd stood up in church and made a prayer request to everyone to pray for me to recover rapidly. And she told me that the preacher had prayed a nice prayer for divine healing.

Since my foot was healing, and I wasn't getting rabies, how could I tell whether or not God healed me? More confusion. I had so much to learn, but no one to teach me.

School continued well. Mr. Garrison had sent me a get-well note while I was on crutches, and Miss Vaughan had asked the school nurse to look at my bandages on two occasions. Seemed like when I was on crutches, people wanted to take care of me more than I wanted, but I liked the attention.

On a Saturday morning, March 7, I was at George's house playing Monopoly. As usual, he had hotels on Park Place and Boardwalk, and I tried my best to get to "Go" without landing on his expensive property. I had hotels on Baltic and Mediterranean Avenue, but he never would land on my cheap property.

I spun my spinner and counted my eight spaces forward. I was aware that I'd lost again, that I couldn't afford, with the amount of money I had, to land on Boardwalk. But I did. George laughed, so I threw all my Monopoly money at him. And then his mother walked in. George told her that he'd won again. I groaned, then laughed, aware that he usually won.

Mrs. Boyet said she was glad we had so much fun together. Then she asked me if my foot had healed totally. "Yes, ma'am, it's all well. I have a scar on either side where the teeth went in, but there's no pain."

"I'm so glad Mr. Mason paid for all your doctor bills. He just stepped right up and paid your dad. That was the proper thing for him to do, don't you think, Paul?"

Stunned by what she told me, I didn't know how to answer. Curious, though, I managed to respond, "Yes, Dad was pleased that he was responsible. Did Mrs. Mason tell you how much Mr. Mason paid?"

"I'm not sure I remember correctly, but I seems she said around $65," Mrs. Boyet said.

"Well, that took care of the costs, I think," I responded, not really sure of what I said.

As I rode home later, I thought about why Dad took his money, but I just couldn't figure it out. On the one hand he'd take me fishing, take me on a picnic and on his vanilla runs, deliver my route for me, and advise me about things. But then, he'd take my money to pay the doctor and then get Mr. Mason to pay him. And more than it cost. *Money must really be a big thing to Dad*, I thought. *Could it be that Dad thought he was collecting for the pain I'd had? Or was it because he didn't like Mr. Mason because he was a bank officer and had more money than Dad? Or, again, since Mr. Mason's daughter, Dorothy Ann, was competing against Earleen for tops in their class, could it be some kind of "I'll show you who has control" thing?* Regardless, I knew I was upset, hurt, and confused by it all. But I decided it would only muddy the water to talk with Dad about it. And I vowed that I'd never tell Mom or Dad what Mrs. Boyet had told me.

On Tuesday evening, March 12, I walked into the living room

because I heard strange sounds from Earleen. She stopped talking, put her books down, and asked what I wanted.

"You were reading from your Latin book, weren't you?"

"Yes, why?"

"No reason, it just sounded funny. What were you reading?" I asked.

"Julius Caesar. Although tomorrow is just the 13th of March, we'll celebrate the Ides of March, which is on Sunday, March 15, and our Latin teacher has asked me to read several paragraphs to the class."

"What's the Ides of March?" I asked.

"You're too young to understand," she replied.

"Try me," I dared.

"OK, but when I tell you, go away. Promise me."

"I'll leave. I promise. Tell me about the Ides."

"Well, Julius Caesar was a very powerful ruler, even before Christ was born. You know what B.C. means, don't you?" she asked, trying to test me.

"Sure, B.C. means Before Christ was born," I added smartly and smart-alecky.

"If you're going to be that way, I'll quit," she said, knowing she had the upper hand. "So Caesar, this powerful ruler, had become unpopular with his senators, and they plotted to kill him, and when Caesar met the senators that day, even his friend Brutus wanted to kill him, too. Brutus stabbed Caesar, and Caesar, bleeding and dying, said, *Et tu, Brute?* and then Caesar died. It was on March 15, and it's known as the Ides of March. Now go on because I've told you all I have time for."

"Tell me what *Et tu, Brute* means and then I'll go."

"Thou too, Brutus? Caesar was surprised that his friend had turned against him."

"Thanks. Now I can use *Et tu, Brute* to show off," I said with humor.

"Well, you are a show off! Try *veni, vidi, vici*, too, and people will really know that you're crazy. Now go."

Knowing I shouldn't push myself with her anymore, I left. Several times before I went to sleep, I said *Et tu, Brute* and *veni, vidi, vici*," not knowing what the last three words meant. But they sounded good. *Veni, vidi, vici; veni, vidi, vici . . . Et tu, Brute?*"

While throwing papers on Monday, March 16, everything went normally until I got to Mrs. Work and Miss Work's house. As I approached, I thought that the next time I would collect from Miss Work, I'd say my new Latin to her since she was the teacher of Latin at Southeastern and would enjoy my new words.

But on this day, one day after the Ides of March, their bulldog Pugsy decided I was Caesar. He'd run at me and barked a lot of times before, and I'd always been able to kick at him and he'd leave. Not today. He lunged at my right ankle and grabbed hold. I gave my leg a strong kick, and it knocked him loose, and he ran away still barking.

Getting off my bike, I examined my right foot, the same one that had just healed from the bite of the Masons' bulldog. My sock was torn, and two or three small scratches were there. Trickles of blood were there, too.

I decided I'd show Mrs. Work or Miss Work my wound.

After I knocked, Mrs. Work came to the door. I showed her the wound and the torn sock, and explained that her dog had done it.

"Not my precious Pugsy," she responded, almost angry that I'd accused her dog of anything.

"Yes, ma'am, he did." And I tried to explain how he did it.

"My dog has never attacked anyone. He's gentle and a sweet pet," she responded, beginning to close the door. Upset and confused about how she was treating me, I decided at least I'd ask for her help.

"Mrs. Work, would you at least get me some medicine to put on my ankle?"

"Oh, I guess so. Wait right here." As I waited, I wondered how in the world she could deny what her dog had done. In a couple of minutes, she came back with a wet white cloth and iodine. I wiped the blood off and then put the iodine on. It burned like fire. She took the cloth and iodine and left, almost as if it was a relief to get rid of me.

Still confused about her unwillingness to believe that her dog had attacked me, I continued on my route, making plans for any time he ran at me again.

Soon I was laughing when I'd say, *"Et tu, Pugsy?"* My day after the Ides of March had been with the bulldog of the college teacher of Latin. I didn't tell my parents about this event with the bulldog.

The next day I put a good-sized rock in my paper bag, just in case, and Pugsy charged me again. When he was about ten yards away, I hurled the rock, and it hit him right in the middle of the head. Instantly he flipped on his back, with all four legs in the air, wailing as if he were dying.

I was scared to death. Should I go to the dog? Should I go tell Mrs. Work? Should I watch the dog for a few minutes to see if he survived?

Panicked as I was, I couldn't think very clearly, so I rode away, thinking that I'd be arrested or something bad. And I knew that I'd have a great difficulty stopping to collect any time soon. But, as I got to thinking about how to defend myself, I decided that the way Mrs. Work had treated me, the dog had it coming. Still, I never could come up with a very good answer.

That evening at supper, Earleen asked me if I was the slightest bit curious about what *veni, vidi, vici* meant.

"Sure, tell me," I said, knowing that I really did want to know. I liked words, even Latin ones.

"They mean 'I came, I saw, I conquered,'" she said. "That's what Julius Caesar did a lot."

"Thanks. Now I can show off even more."

That night I thought about how I'd hit the dog. Even though I didn't like what I had done, it was worse not knowing how Pugsy was. After a while, I grinned, saying to myself, "*Veni, vidi, vici*," as I fell asleep.

I didn't collect from the Works for four weeks. And I hadn't seen Pugsy at all. When I finally did knock to collect, Miss Work answered the door, and beside her was a healthy Pugsy.

"Here to collect, Miss Work," thanking my lucky stars that Pugsy was alive and well.

"Haven't seen you in several weeks. How much do I owe you?"

"Forty cents, Miss Work."

"I'll get it. Be right back."

Pugsy stayed inside the screen door growling at me.

She returned with the 40 cents and paid me.

"Thanks. Pugsy looks good," I said with some risk.

"Yes, he's a healthy and happy bulldog," she answered with a smile on her face.

"Did your classes at Southeastern read about Julius Caesar and the Ides of March?" I asked, knowing she'd be surprised.

"Oh, yes. The Ides of March is a big day in the lives of students of Latin."

As I was turning to leave the creaky, wooden porch, I said, "*Veni, vidi, vici*" to her.

"That's great, Paul."

I thought as I rode away that maybe I had some new experiences which caused me to learn a good deal about how people handled life differently. But I wasn't sure I'd conquered very much, though. Maybe I wouldn't be so fearful in the future to admit that I'd done wrong, like hitting Pugsy. I wasn't sure yet, but I was feeling better all the time because I had defended myself against Pugsy. I wished I'd had enough courage to have stood my ground and made Mrs. Work admit that her dog had bitten me. *Maybe the courage will develop*, I thought.

CHAPTER 13
Which Way Is Up?

Mother was still laughing with me about the April Fool's Day prank I played on Dad. A Durant merchant had called early Saturday morning and said he needed a dozen four-ounce bottles of vanilla. While Dad had been changing into better clothes to deliver the order, I replaced the twelve full bottles with a dozen empty ones, put a piece of paper on top on which I'd written "April Fool's," closed the lid, and put the box back into the Mercury.

Dad left and soon returned. He enjoyed my joke, or at least he said so. I got the filled bottles for him, and he left again.

Mom said she was happy that Dad and I got along so well. I agreed that we did but that sometimes I got confused about how he treated me.

"Mostly about money?" she inquired.

"Yes, ma'am, mainly that."

"Your dad's a proud man. It hurts him not to make much money, and sometimes he takes it out on all of us. You'll understand him better when you get older."

"But I want to understand him now," I said, showing my lack of patience. "I have $240 in the bank. Do you think he needs some of that?" She shook her head no and turned slightly away.

"The Bible says that we only see through a glass darkly now, but someday we'll see better. It means that we just can't understand everything in this life."

I changed the subject. "Just wait until next April Fool's Day to see what I'm going to do to you."

We both laughed, and I went outside before it got too dark to shoot baskets through a rim that I'd nailed to my treehouse tree. I didn't climb up to my old treehouse much anymore.

While bouncing the ball, I had an idea that I'd try to talk to Mr. Garrison about the things that confused me so much. Liking my new plan, I made a long, long shot that went through the rim. Then I went in, washed a bit, and was off to bed.

"Miss Vaughan," I asked just after arriving the next morning for homeroom period, "may I get an appointment to talk to Mr. Garrison?"

"Is it something I can help you with?" she asked.

"I'd really like to see him."

"It's OK to go now," she said, as she gave me a hall pass.

A bit scared and unsure of what I'd do or say when I got to talk to him, I told the secretary I'd been given permission to talk with Mr. Garrison.

She knocked, went in his office, and in a few seconds, Mr. Garrison, with his usual big smile, invited me in. He closed his door, which I liked. I needed time alone with someone I trusted.

"What's on your mind, Paul? Or is it P.J.?"

"I like P.J., Mr. Garrison." Getting up my nerve I said, "I'm not very clear about some things going on, and I thought that maybe you could help me—or do something."

"I'll try," he said reassuringly.

And in a way that surprised me, I said, "Mr. Sharp has the world globe on the table next to his desk, and we study where lots of countries and cities are located. I like that a lot because I like to learn, but the other day while he was teaching us about Australia, I began to wonder some silly things."

"Like what, P.J.?" he asked.

"You said you grew up as a Nazarene and went to Bethany-Peniel College, didn't you?"

"Yes."

"And you were taught that heaven was up, weren't you?" I asked as I pointed my finger toward the ceiling.

"Yes, as a child that's what I was taught."

"And that hell was down?"

"Yes," he said with a puzzled look.

"Well, Mr. Garrison, looking at that globe made me think that if I pointed 'up' in Durant, and a person in Australia pointed 'up' from where he was standing, that 'up' would be different. And if heaven is 'up,' then where is heaven? And if I pointed 'down,' I'd be pointing into our earth, and the Australian pointing 'down' would also be pointing into our earth. And if hell is down, is hell inside our earth?" Whew, I didn't know what I was going to say to him, but I was relieved to get it all said that way.

"P.J., I'm glad you've told me this. Let's talk about these thoughts because I, too, got confused about heaven and hell when I was young. Remember that I'm a principal, not a minister, so I'm not an expert about heaven or hell, but I do like what I believe about them."

"Will you tell me what you believe?"

"Hmm, let me think a minute before I answer you."

And he thought. Then he smiled and began. "Did you ever believe in Santa Claus, P.J.?"

"Oh, yes, and that was fun. It was sad to learn there wasn't one."

"It was sad for me, too, when I learned that years ago. What was it like for you to wait for Santa Claus to bring you presents?"

"I tried to be good, always wrote him a letter that I gave to Mom, and ran to the tree on Christmas morning although sometimes I didn't get what I'd ask him for."

"And after you learned there wasn't a Santa Claus?"

"I'd ask Dad or Mom or my sisters for gifts."

"And when you knew there was no Santa, and when you didn't get the gifts from your family that you'd asked for, what'd you do?"

"I was usually sad."

"And suppose you'd have asked for a bike and didn't get one, and you knew they'd never give you one. Then what?"

"What I *did* do. I found one at Babcock's that I liked, earned and saved money, and bought it myself."

"Were you pleased with yourself for doing all that?"

"Yes, sir. It took me awhile, but I liked what I did."

"See, P.J., what I think you've learned is very important. It took me a long time to learn what you seem to be learning. Maybe sometimes Santa is 'up' at the North Pole, maybe God is 'up' in heaven, and maybe sometimes we believe that Santa drops 'down' bicycles, or God brings 'down' His will, but I've learned to be more comfortable with the words 'in' and 'inside' than I am with 'up' and 'down,' at least in the way you've used them. Let me explain as well as I can."

"I'm a bit mixed up, Mr. Garrison," I said, knowing that I wanted to understand.

"I think that as you grow, you learn that God is inside of you. And He gives you the opportunity to make enough money to buy your own bikes and other things in life. Sometimes other events get in the way, like the Great Depression, which people seemed not to be able to control for a while, or like the war now, but for the most part they like to manage their own lives. And I think they are best able to do that when God is inside, not outside, or up, or down."

He paused, saw that I was trying to understand, and then asked, "What about that?"

"So you think God is inside me?"

"Well, not like your stomach is inside you. But I think of God as love, and I'm capable of loving, yet love is something you can't put on a scale and weigh. If I can love and God is love, then God must be a part of people. And further, P.J., your namesake, Paul, wrote, 'I can do all things through Christ which strengtheneth me.' So I think you get your strength from God to learn your lessons, earn money, love your parents, and find ways for you to be responsible."

He paused, leaned back in his chair, and chuckled, "P.J., I'm sounding like a minister rather than your principal—you'd best ask your minister about this. Remember, I told you I'm no expert. Maybe I shouldn't be telling you these things."

"But, Mr. Garrison, what if someone lies to me, or hides facts from me, or treats me mean? I'm confused as to what to do then."

"I am, too. Confusion seems to be tough to know how to manage sometimes. But I know that it's my responsibility for whatever I do back to them. I can wish they'd not done it, but whatever was done is done. Then it's up to me to make a decision as to how I'll respond—or if I'll respond at all. And my right to respond, my ability to respond, is what I call independence. And I think that God gives us the opportunity, as we grow, to be independent and responsible people who don't do unusually cruel things on purpose to hurt others. And that seems to be because God is love, and He wants us to love others. But you have to love and take care of yourself first."

"Do you think that when I love myself I'll love even those who do mean things to me?"

"I find that I'm angry and upset not so much about what they've done, but that the person hasn't yet learned to love himself. And God teaches us to love our enemy, and that's difficult to do. But maybe I can love the person, Hitler, but strongly dislike what he does."

"Maybe that's helpful. I'm not sure that it makes sense yet, but I'll think about it. Oh, before I go back to class, I want to ask you that when I pray, would I pray for God's love to give me energy to do things for myself, as well as use this energy to help others?"

"Perhaps so, P.J. Just remember that bikes don't fall from 'up' to 'down.' They come because you use your 'in'side energy to ask for one, and if that doesn't get you one, then you use your own energy to earn the money in a proper way so that you buy it for yourself."

"And if someone does something to me that I think is cruel, I can still like—or love—the person who did it, just not like what he did. Is that right?"

"P.J., you're a quick learner, and that's what all your teachers tell me, too. I know that your sister, Tommie Earleen, is the smartest in Durant High, and it looks like you are just like she is.

I was embarrassed. "Thank you, but she draws a lot better than I, has a lot better penmanship, and plays the piano," I said, trying not to blush anymore.

"Well, I know that you are an excellent student. Miss Vaughan says that you really like to learn new words. Is that right?"

"Yes, sir. After my dog bite at the Masons' house, Earleen taught me one that I really do like."

"What's that?"

"I'm still not certain that I can pronounce it, but I'll try. It's *onomatopoeia*," I said, trying to say it syllable by syllable.

"I'm not sure that I know what it is," Mr. Garrison said with a laugh. "Please tell me what it means."

"Earleen said that it's the word used to define what a dog's bark sounds like. *Bow-wow*. Or a cat's sound, *meow*. That's onomatopoeia, I think."

"You'll probably know all the words in the world soon," he joked. "How'd you get so interested in words?"

"Don't know for sure. Earleen taught me to read when I was four when we played school. Then I'd always read signs along the road when I went with Dad on his vanilla run. And maybe it has to do with Dad teasing me when I was real young. He'd say, 'Son, I heard that you slumbered in bed last night.' Or he'd say, 'Son, now don't you hesitate on the doorstep.' And if anyone else was around, they'd all laugh, so I just had to find out what *slumber* and *hesitate* meant. And then I just wanted to know what every word I saw or heard meant. I just like words, especially those that you can have fun saying, like *onomatopoeia*, and another that's easier, which I like, is *celebrate*. It just sounds fun to say."

"I'll try to find new words for you to learn. I'll write them on my notepad and occasionally send them to Miss Vaughan to give to you."

"I'll like that."

"And I'm glad to see that you still have excellent grades and perfect attendance. Keep up the good work."

And with that I went back to my homeroom. I thought a lot that day about what Mr. Garrison had said. And when Mr. Sharp used the world *globe*, I drew a circle on my tablet paper and thought of it as the world, my world, and how I can love it, maybe a tiny bit as much as God loved it.

That night, when Mom, Earleen, Linda, and I read the Bible and prayed silently, I prayed a little differently. "Thy kingdom come" became "heaven is in me already and I know that I'm to love and not be cruel, and that I have energy from God to earn my daily bread and all other things. And I can love people who trespass or hurt me, and I can try to keep from hurting others, maybe even Pugsy, if he won't try to bite me anymore. And I don't want to create evil like Hitler is. And, God, I still don't like what he's doing." *There*, I thought, *I said "what he's doing." Maybe if I'd known him as a kid like I am now, we'd have done things as friends that might have helped him grow up differently.*

I liked my thoughtful and different prayer. After we finished, I said, "Mom, I think I'm saved and always will be."

"That's good to know. You're such a good son. God has a purpose for you in your life."

"Maybe to say over and over again *onomatopoeia, onomatopoeia, onomatopoeia*. That's my purpose," I laughed, so as not to be cruel to Mom.

The next day I unlocked my lock box, took out my four-leaf clovers and my rabbit's foot, and threw them away. I vowed I'd never believe in luck anymore, but I would believe in my ability to do whatever I could, even moving mountains, maybe. I'd be stubbornly independent. Earleen had always said that I was the most stubborn person she'd ever known, so I'd add that word before *independent*. That's what I'd be—*stubbornly independent*.

CHAPTER 14
Energized

Now that I knew I was saved, I didn't have to worry about that anymore. And I decided I wouldn't worry Mom about church. I'd rather please her than to tell her that I was going to be a Methodist someday, so I just let her continue to think that God's voice would direct me into the ministry. I just wasn't going to make an issue of church anymore. That was her problem, not mine. And her butterscotch pie was too good to risk her wrath. She might not bake anymore, and that'd be a catastrophe. That was another word I liked to say. It has a nice sound—*ca-tas-tro-phe*. If I couldn't say *onomatopoeia*, that'd be a *catastrophe*. I enjoyed laughing inside as I used big words.

Mr. Garrison, as he had promised, sent to me five new words a week. I'd learned *catastrophe, metaphor, simile, prompt, celebrate,* and several more. And I had begun reading the new vocabulary in the *Reader's Digest* when we went to the school library.

Mom was treating me cruelly, I thought, because she made me do so much more around the house than she did Earleen. And if she were cruel to me, wouldn't that mean she wasn't saved? I made a plan to try to seek some fairness in the amount of housework between Earleen and me. I made a list of things I was told to do and a list that Earleen was told to do.

For P.J.
   1. In winter, bring in coal and kindling daily.

2. In winter, clean ashes and clinkers from coal stove and carry outside twice a week.
3. Remove food and dishes from table 3 times a day.
4. Sweep kitchen and breakfast nook area 3 times a day.
5. Take out garbage 3 times a day.
6. Dust furniture 1 time a week.
7. Sweep front, side, and back porch when dirty.
8. Get up by 6 A.M. on Mondays to fill washing machine and 2 rinse tubs with water, run pots of clothes through machine cycle, and 2 rinse cycles, and carry clothes to clothesline.
9. Mop kitchen and breakfast nook every week. Wax both once a month.
10. Put folded clothes away on washdays.
11. Make my bed and Linda's bed and keep my room clean.
12. Mow the lawn in spring, summer, and early fall.
13. Rake leaves when necessary.
14. Dig ground for victory garden and plant onions, lettuce seed, radish seed, and tomato plants. Pull weeds when necessary.
15. Water garden, flowers, and shrubs when needed.
16. Clean gutters on house as needed.
17. Wash Mercury when needed and wax twice yearly.
18. Attend Bible reading and prayer at our house.
19. Attend church 3 times a week and sometimes more.
20. Take care of Linda when necessary.
21. Help Dad with his vanilla bottling at least 3 or 4 hours a month.
22. Trim peach tree where I've gotten limbs for switches for peach tree tea many more times than necessary!

For Earleen
1. Dry dishes when made to, probably twice a day.
2. Make her bed.
3. Clean her room.
4. Dust her piano because I won't do it.
5. Dust front porch swing when date is coming.
6. Run dust mop over floor where there isn't carpet.
7. Pester me.

 I gave the lists to Mom when I thought she was in a good mood and asked her to read both lists before she said anything.

She did. Then she looked at me, "Son, you probably do more than these on your list. And you may not remember because you were so young at the time, but Earleen did the housework and much of the cooking when I was sick when we lived on North Sixteenth. Earleen's list is about correct now. I guess the reason is that Earleen, as a junior in high school, is so very busy." And then she added, "We'll probably not have many more peaches if you don't stop getting into trouble so that I have to switch you."

"Mom, you mean that as a fifth-grader, I'm not busy? I didn't even put on my list that I deliver papers six days a week, go back and collect from some people who didn't pay on Fridays, mow lawns, sell vanilla, work on my bike that frequently needs repairs, and have to find time to study and play. You're not fair to me, just like you weren't fair for not letting me go to a movie when you let Earleen go, or punishing me for lying when I went to the carnival when you let her go to the Texas Centennial," I said with as much courage as I could muster. Fairness seemed important if I were to be responsible.

"You've made a strong argument, Son. I guess why you'll continue all those chores is because I need you. You work about four times as fast as Earleen, even though I think she may dust better. I've told her a hundred times to hurry up, but that's not her nature. But she can do some things fast because she's the fastest typist in high school. Why, in a ten-minute timed test she typed 78 words a minute without one error," Mom bragged.

"If I worked slower, Mom, would you make her do more then?" I asked, already knowing the answer.

"I don't think you'll ever slow down, Son. You were just born to do things quickly," she said with a big grin on her face. "So you just put aside any idea of less work around the house."

"Mom, you're cruel, which means you aren't really saved," I almost shouted in my disgust.

"I am saved, and I'm not cruel. You're my son, and I'll always depend on you."

That word *depend* got me. So I knew that Mom's definition of *cruel* and my definition didn't match. I'd been through so many initiations that this just seemed like another one. *Maybe boys get initiated forever,* I thought again. I wondered what kinds of initiations Earleen had to go through.

Just to satisfy myself, I found an empty Prince Albert tobacco can, filled it with dirt, and when no one was around, sprinkled a little bit around the corners of Earleen's room. I wasn't being cruel. I just wanted to make her clean her room more often.

After the third time I put dirt in her room, Earleen told Mom about it.

And so, when asked, I had to tell Mom that I'd done it. I tried to argue with her about why I did it. Later, I had to trim the peach tree again.

Birthday time came on Sunday for both Miss Vaughan and me. Mom told me that there'd be no party this year because there wasn't any money to spend on those kinds of things. That was fine with me, because if I had a party Patsy Hall would probably try to kiss me again. On Monday, I took Miss Vaughan a bud vase and put a homegrown rose in it. She gave me a big hug.

When I came in from delivering papers, Mom said she had several things to show me. Going into the living room, I saw a tall bookcase filled with all sorts of books and next to it was a wooden table with a built-in checkerboard.

"These are ours now. But the table is for you. Mrs. Laird gave them to us and specifically said that the table was a gift to you for your birthday, even though it's a day late."

I rubbed my hand over the highly finished table. *Perfect*, I thought, *for all kinds of games.* "May I move the table into my room and then to the screened-in porch when I live out there?"

"Yes, that'd be a good idea," Mom responded, smiling because I seemed so happy.

"And that's a special bookcase, isn't it, Mom?" I asked as I began to pull the handle to one of the glass doors on a shelf. Pulling the handle out, lifting it up, and pushing the door backwards until it was out of sight gave me access to any number of big books. I closed the door and looked at the books on all six shelves. The first fifty or so that I saw all had *Harvard Classics* on the rib of each. The titles didn't mean too much to me, but I thought that as I grew maybe they would. Then I saw a set of five large books with *Children's Classic Stories and Riddles* printed on each of the books' ribs and three volumes about Theodore Roosevelt. I knew that he'd been a president of the U.S., and I remembered looking at a picture that we had of President Roosevelt as he was waving to a crowd of people in Durant as he was riding away on a train on April 5, 1905. So I had some interest in these books. And Mom had already filled the rest of the shelves with books from around the house.

The bookcase looked great. It added something to our living room that I liked.

"Mom, why did Mrs. Laird give these to us?"

"You may remember that her husband, Paul Laird, died in January 1939. He had seen you around the neighborhood and had told Mrs. Laird that he liked you and someday wanted you to have the table and books."

"I don't remember him at all, Mom."

"He taught at Southeastern, was the football coach there for a few years, and had a great following among students. As a matter of fact, he was there when I was getting my teacher's training in 1922. Now, as you know, they've named the football field the Paul E. Laird Field. Mrs. Laird wanted to carry out his wishes, and we decided that your birthday would be a good time to do it. Also, Mrs. Laird said that she knew Earleen would enjoy the *Harvard Classics*."

It was truly a great birthday present, and I was very happy. I pulled a book of riddles off the shelf and read the first one I saw. I laughed and then read it to Mom, knowing it would be her kind of riddle.

"Mom, do you know why Eve couldn't have measles?" I asked with a grin on my face.

"No, why?"

"Because she had Adam."

"What was that again?" she asked.

"Mom, listen. Because she had Adam."

Then I explained further. She said she got it and laughed. No need to read her any more children's riddles, I thought.

"Read another," she laughingly said.

"OK, but listen carefully to this one."

"As I was walking down the lane, I met a British scholar. He tipped his hat and drew his cane. Now tell me the name of the scholar, and I've told you his name in the riddle."

"I know that one," Mom grinned. "'Andrew Cane' is his name."

"Sure," I said, not knowing the answer myself, so I bluffed that I had figured it out when I read it.

"I've got work to do. Stay here and read or move your table to your room. And come help me in a few minutes."

I put the book away, closed the bookcase, and thought I'd enjoy reading about Theodore Roosevelt or some more riddles. Then I moved my new table to my room, got out the checkers, and placed them on the board so they'd be ready to play. I vowed that George would never win a game when he played on my new table. I wasn't sure whether John could beat me or not.

Forgetting that Mom had told me to come help her, I pushed my mower the block to Mrs. Laird's house and mowed her weedy lawn. Just as I was finishing with the last bit of daylight, she came out with a glass of water and a smile on her face.

"How much do I owe the birthday boy?" She was holding her big black purse.

"Not one cent. And I want to thank you for the gifts. Mr. Laird and you will always be high in my thoughts. And when I'm in Durant High on the football team, I'll always play my very best on his field."

"Oh, that's right. The Durant Lions do play on the college field, don't they?"

"Yes, ma'am. And I'll read some of the books and really enjoy the table."

"Mr. Laird made the table in his woodworking shop, so it's sturdy and will last forever," she added, with a look of sadness on her face as she talked about him.

"I'll enjoy all of the gifts, and thank you." I pushed my mower home, cleaned up, ate, and got a book about Roosevelt from the shelf to begin my reading about a man I was soon to discover was a real adventurer. Mom called and told me to set the table and straighten up the sitting room.

At the supper table I had three gifts that they had decided to give me a day late, to go along with Mrs. Laird's gifts. I got a pair of blue socks from Mom, a Captain Marvel comic book from Earleen, and a Red Ryder comic book from Linda. Dad gave me a pat on the shoulder and a promise of another fishing trip to Blue River. Then they sang "Happy Birthday."

I grinned when I saw the socks. Mom said that she couldn't find one pair of mine, and she thought I'd need this new pair. What she didn't know was that I'd thrown away the pair that Mrs. Work's bulldog, Pugsy, had torn. At least, he'd torn up the one on my right foot, and I couldn't leave just one sock around.

And so I was finally eleven. Earleen said that she knew why I was so stubborn.

"Why?" I asked, putting the last bite of the third piece of chocolate birthday cake into my mouth.

"Because you were born under the sign of Taurus, the Bull, and bulls are stubborn just like you are."

"I thought Taurus was where Saul of the Bible was saved and changed his name to Paul," I kidded.

"You're so silly sometimes. You know that was Tarsus," she said disgustedly, like my big sister would.

"Well, now I know why I'm stubborn."

And Mom added, "Tommie, you know that I don't want your reading anything about those signs."

We cleaned the kitchen, I did my homework, read some riddles, and was preparing for bed when I looked at my new checker table. Linda was already asleep, so I moved the table a bit closer to the closet light so I could see, and I played a game of checkers against myself. No surprise, I beat myself. *Let George or John just think they can beat me!* I thought.

Lawn mowing had begun, so I hurried as much as I could around my route, and I would usually mow two, sometimes three small 50-cent lawns before and after supper. I had made another $20 deposit and now had $260 in the bank. But it seemed as if the money was not coming in fast enough. Vanilla sales to my customers had slowed, as well as Dad's sales to the grocery stores. That meant more troubles at home.

On the next Tuesday, May 5, Skip called all of us carriers together. We knew something must be up because he rarely did this.

When he got us quiet, he said, "Boys, the owners, the Storys, have decided to increase the weekly delivery price from 10 cents to 15 cents. The announcement is in today's paper. So when you collect this Friday, tell everyone to pay you 15 cents since they always pay a week in advance. The monthly price will be 75 cents. You'll like it, too, because that will mean you'll make more money. You now pay 5 cents per week for each paper, and beginning Sunday, you'll be charged 8 cents per week for each paper, but you will be getting 7 cents profit for each customer who pays. Also, there will be no more rubber bands for Sunday papers. Rubber is needed for war. But we'll give you, free of charge, string to tie the Sunday paper. It'll take a bit more time to tie."

I quickly used my new multiplication skills. Now I would get ninety papers x 8 cents, meaning I'd pay 8 x 0 = 0, 8 x 9 = 72, add the 0 and put in the period—$7.20 to the *Democrat*. Then 90 x 7— 7 x 0 = 0, 7 x 9 = 63, add the 0 and put in the period—that's $6.30, a week's profit. I liked that, even though after I thought about it for a while, I wanted to ask Skip why it wasn't 7½ cents to each of us. But I didn't.

The thought of more profit for the same work gave me more energy. And when I'd folded the papers I rode my usual way down the alley behind Montgomery Ward on my way to my route.

"Son," a man in the back door said.

"Yes, sir."

"What's your name?"

"P.J."

"I mean all of your name."

Wondering if I'd done something wrong, I was hesitant to say, but I did. "Paul Johnson."

"I've noticed you frequently as you come by our store, and you seem to go by about the same time. That means to me you're reliable, and I need a boy who is reliable to throw our Montgomery Ward circulars once a month beginning in June. You interested?"

Not knowing anything about the job, I just said yes.

He continued, "I'm Mr. Warner, and I'm the assistant store manager. We'll need the circulars thrown to 1,000 houses. Still interested?"

"Yes, I am, Mr. Warner. How many pages will there be?"

"Usually six pages. You can fold them like you do your *Democrat* papers. And you can throw the circulars in the yard rather than on the porch. And we'll pay you $12 each time you throw a thousand, and if you're still interested when school begins in the fall, you can throw them on Saturdays."

Twelve dollars sounded good. "I'll need to get my parents' permission before I can tell you, though."

"That's fine. Let me have an answer in a day or so. By the way, if your dad has a car and would be willing to do it, the best way to throw this many is by standing on the running board and throwing as someone hands the circulars out the window to you. You think he might do that?"

"I'll see." And with that I pedaled to my route, thinking that would be an easy $12.

Dad and I arrived at home about the same time. Before he went into the house, I asked him to stay outside a minute. He walked around to the side porch, where I was putting my bike up for the night.

"What's up, Son?"

I told him about the Montgomery Ward job.

"I think I'd need your help, Dad, and the Mercury, too. And Linda, too, if she's willing to hand the papers out the window for me to throw."

We discussed the pay, the amount of time involved, and the rationed gasoline issue.

"It'd probably take two or three gallons because of slow driving. I could probably swing that on my A stamps. I just don't want to use my B stamps because I use that gasoline for my vanilla runs."

He had both an A sticker and a B sticker on his windshield. He had to get approval for all stamps from the local rationing board, just as we did for sugar and for meat. But we seemed to manage all right as far as I knew.

"So I can tell Mr. Warner 'yes,' Dad? If you'll let me, I'll buy your gasoline and pay Linda 50 cents for helping."

"She'd like that. She's five now, and it's time she earned a bit of money."

"Should I ask Mom for permission, too?"

"No, I'll tell her about it, and that'll be that."

So, with all my newfound inner energy, the next day I told Mr. Warner I'd be glad to throw the circulars in June. He said he'd call me when they arrived, said I'd have about four days to fold the 1,000 before the deadline to throw, and he told me to be careful standing on the running board while I threw. He said when I'd finished to come by the business office, which he showed to me, and he introduced me to a woman who gave me a Montgomery Ward business card to identify myself so I could get paid.

I left Mr. Warner with a feeling that I was soon going to be rich. Well, not rich, but adding to my bank account more than I expected. It was a good feeling.

Collection day Friday wasn't what I expected. Mr. Long delayed me more than usual, complaining that the paper wasn't worth 15 cents, but he finally paid me. In my first seven houses, three customers stopped their subscriptions, complaining about the price increase. I really got scared about what would happen on the rest of the route. But only four more told me to stop their paper due to the price increase. The only tip I got that day was from my first collection, Mrs. Jarrell.

When I paid Skip on Saturday morning, I told him about my stops.

"Should I decrease my paper purchase by seven?" I asked.

"No, P.J., most, if not all, will begin again. They'll miss the paper too much, especially all the war news."

He was right. I got six new starts the next week, three on Monday, two on Tuesday, and one on Wednesday from my old customers. And two new customers started. So I had gained a customer. I'd learned from all this not to make too quick a decision about things when change occurs.

School was rapidly coming to an end, much to my pleasure and that of all of my classmates. Summer in Durant was great. Hot, but that's the way God wanted it to be, I said to myself. Shoes didn't exist except on Sundays. The feel of the green, wet grass, early in the mornings as it wriggled through my toes, seemed to be like new freedom.

Mr. Garrison organized an end-of-school play day. We had a three-legged race, a tow sack race, a bike race in which the slowest rider won (but if you put your foot to the ground during the contest, you were out of the race), tug-of-war, softball pitch, basketball free throw shooting, a boy-girl relay, and a jump rope contest for both girls and boys. This was topped off with a free lunch and soda pop.

I was on the winning tug-of-war team and was third in the slow bike ride. Nick won, with Mack coming in second. Miss Vaughan also brought ribbons for everyone in her homeroom to wear. They had *Vaughan's Champions* printed on them. It was a good day. And as the school day was finishing, we made a big circle around Mr. Garrison, and much to his surprise, gave him lots of applause and cheering. I thought he almost blushed.

In two more days my fifth grade was all over. I had made all S's, had perfect attendance, and teachers' comments written on the report card helped me feel good. I told Miss Vaughan that I looked forward to being in her homeroom again in the sixth grade. She smiled, gave me a hug, and said she'd look forward to having me again.

Freedom—energy—jobs to do—money to make—swimming—checker games—papers to deliver—circulars for the first time—fishing with Dad—and, as the war news was suggesting, scrap metal and scrap rubber to collect for the war effort.

One bad thing, though, was that there was no more chewing gum. Tin foil was gone, too. Lucky Strike green had gone to war, but that didn't bother me. And Uncle Sam's picture in front of the U.S. Post Office showed his finger pointing and his eyes looking right back into my eyes regardless of where I stood to observe him. The writing below his picture said, "I WANT YOU." I thought that Miss Wheat would have given whoever drew Uncle Sam's picture an S+ grade. I vowed I'd help my uncle in any way that an eleven-year-old could.

CHAPTER 15
Worms, Donuts, and Nose Pickers

Mr. Warner called on Monday, June 1, and said I could get the circulars. They had to be delivered Friday, June 5. Dad drove me, and we loaded ten bundles with one hundred circulars in each bundle into the Mercury. I mowed a couple of lawns and then spent some time folding before going to the *Democrat* at 3:00 P.M.

That evening I finished folding the first 500. Dad sat watching me and suggested that we go fishing the next morning.

"I'd like that, Dad, but I sure do need to get these all folded, just in case. If we go, promise me we'll be back by noon."

"That's fine, Son. We'll have caught them all by then," he laughed.

So we were at our favorite crappie hole on Blue River by 6:45 A.M., after we stopped to buy two dozen minnows. I paid 35 cents for my dozen, and Dad did likewise.

They weren't biting. Not even a nibble. We moved our lines here and there and still hadn't caught a fish.

And at about 9:30, Dad said, "We're just not having any luck at all today, are we, Son?"

I shook my head no, but then, after thinking about it, said, "Dad, I don't believe in luck."

"What do you mean you don't believe in luck? There's two kinds, good luck and bad luck, and today we're having bad luck."

"I'll try to tell you what I mean, Dad. I believe that we are either not putting our line where the fish are, or that we're fishing too shallow or too deep, or that we bought the wrong kind of bait, or that the fish aren't hungry, or something. But I've decided that luck doesn't have anything to do with it," I said, proud of the way I'd put my words together to explain it.

"Are you learning that stuff in school?" Dad wanted to know.

"Not exactly. Well, maybe Mr. Garrison helped me think about some things. But I guess I just figured it out."

"Well, you just believe the way you want to, but I will always believe in luck. I've had my share of bad luck all my life."

We didn't talk anymore. Soon Dad had caught a small black bass, and since it wasn't a keeper, he threw it back. Then he landed a large crappie.

"See, Son, my luck is changing."

"I hope so, Dad. I really hope so."

We left at about 11:00, had a Coke and a Moon Pie in Armstrong, and were home at 11:30. I started folding circulars.

While folding, I thought about the worm trough that the bait man kept his fishing worms in and how he sold them for 20 cents for two dozen. *If he can sell worms, I can, too,* I thought. I used my arithmetic again. If I sold two dozen worms for 15 cents, I might get a lot of business, and if I could sell twenty dozen a day, that'd be $1.50 profit each day. *But then,* I wondered, *how'd I keep my worms alive and all that stuff?* I decided I'd try a new business. I finished folding all but 100 of the circulars, and this was only Tuesday. I always had liked to get everything ready before time.

Wednesday morning I mowed four lawns and made $2.25, and then I rode my bike to Cash Noel's second-hand store on North First and bought two slightly rusting washtubs for 35 cents each. They rattled around noisily as I rode my bike home, carrying them as best I could in the front basket, one tub inserted inside the other. I filled the tubs with dirt from near the garden, and, grabbing a bucket and shovel, I headed to the grain storage silos just east of the MKT tracks. I turned over gobs of worms with each dig. My bucket squirmed with big earthworms. Soon I had hundreds, so I pedaled home.

I put them in my tubs, covered then lightly with dirt, and poured a little water over them. I was about ready, I thought, to go into a new business.

After delivering, I stopped at Piggly Wiggly grocery store, and they gave me two wooden apple boxes. At home, I took the nails out of the boxes and had perfect-sized boards for my new signs.

With a black Crayola I wrote in letters as large as I could make on two boards:

Fishing Worms For Sale
2 dozen 15 Cents
Open only 6 A.M.—9 A.M.
Closed Sundays
Knock on Back Door

Nailing a stake to each board, I hammered one into the ground on the Fourth Street parkway and the other on the Liveoak parkway. Then I went through several garbage cans in the neighborhood and found about 25 cans that I could put the worms into as I sold them. I'd ask Mom to save her cans for me, too.

Mom hadn't noticed what I'd done, and when Dad came in from his long Hugo–Paris–Sherman run, he saw the signs and called me.

"What in the world are you doing, Paul?"

It was unusual for him to use my name because he usually called me "Son," so I thought I was in some kind of trouble.

"You mean with my new business?" I said with as much of a businesslike voice as I could use.

"Yes, those worms. You know you can't sell worms in our neighborhood," he said in a really loud voice.

"Why not?" I asked.

"The neighbors won't like it, that's why."

"May I ask them if they don't like it?" trying to get him to change his mind.

"No, don't ask. Just take the signs down." And then he called Mom. "Allie, come look at what your son has done."

No longer was I just Dad's son. I was now Mom's, too. Mom came, saw the signs, and frowned, as she said, "Son, there's probably a law against selling worms in our neighborhood. If there's not, there should be."

"So you're embarrassed, too, huh, Mom?"

"Quite frankly, yes," she replied.

I decided I'd better make my case. "Look, Mom and Dad, if I'm to go to college someday like you say I must, I've gotta make a lot of money. If my worm business is any good, I can make up to $9 a week—maybe more. That's more than I make on my route. And Mom, notice that I close on Sundays. I'll even have more money to tithe to the church."

I'd done my best, using college, the $9, closed on Sundays, and more tithe. I couldn't have done much better, I decided. Then I added, "Please let me try."

I won. They agreed that I'd have to get up early enough to sell to any customer. And that I had to stop selling if any neighbor complained. I agreed. So I was in the fishing worm business.

Then I reminded Dad and Linda about throwing the circulars the next day. I piled all 1,000 into the back seat of the Mercury and showed Dad my plan for throwing street by street.

Friday, about 9:30 A.M., we left. Linda seemed pleased to be helping. Fortunately, the weather was perfect. With windows in the car all rolled down, I held on to the car frame where the doors closed with my left arm. I stood on the running board and threw every one of the advertiser circulars. My arm was really tired, and when we got home, I paid Dad 75 cents for gasoline and gave Linda 75 cents, a quarter more than we'd agreed to, even though she wasn't as much help as I'd hoped, and then I rode my bike to Montgomery Ward and collected my $12.

On Saturday, only three days after I'd gone into the worm business, I had four customers who bought ten dozen worms. *Not bad*, I thought as I counted my 75 cents and put it in my lock box. It was only 9:00 A.M. with most of the day left. And the grass was too wet with dew to mow until about 9:30 anyway. I rode to the *Democrat* to pay my bill and told Skip about my new business.

"Let's see, P.J., you have your route, you mow lawns, you sell fishing worms. Anything else you do to make money?"

"Yes, sir. I also sell vanilla that Dad gives me for helping him bottle it. And I throw Montgomery Ward circulars once a month."

"You should be written up as the young businessman of the year. I'll tell one of our writers to do just that."

"You mean an article in the *Democrat* about me?" I asked.

"Sure, why not?"

I finished my account with him and left, feeling like it'd be good to see my name in the *Democrat*. I mowed four 50-cent lawns that day and later swam with the guys in Round Hole until suppertime.

I was ready to make another $20 deposit Monday. That made $280 and counting.

The worm business was good. The next week I sold eighty dozen for a profit of $6. And the fishermen who bought were fun because they teased me a lot about what I was going to do with all the money I was making. I liked their teasing.

And then, there it was, right on the front page of my favorite newspaper, and on Sunday, too. It was down on the bottom left of the page, and it wasn't a long write-up, but it told about my business adventures and successes. The other carriers really gave me a bad time on that early Sunday morning as we inserted and folded. They all said they wanted to borrow money, or was I going to spend it on girls?

The article helped my worm business. I really had to dig and find a lot more worms, but I kept a good supply. By Saturday, June 20, I put into my record books that I'd made $13.50 from my worms, $6.50 from my route, $7.50 from mowing, and $1.25 from vanilla, for a total of $28.75. Not bad, I thought, and on Monday I deposited another $20, which now gave me $300.

Later that day I told Mom about my new bank total. She was surprised, but she went back to her usual kind of talk. "Have you tithed regularly?"

"Yes, ma'am, always 10 percent."

"Good ... do it cheerfully because the Lord loveth a cheerful giver. And He'll continue to bless you and allow you to be successful."

Without thinking, I responded, "Don't know whether the Lord has much to do with it or not. I'm the one who gets the jobs, does the work, and gets the money."

"Watch your tongue, young man! Why, the Lord might rain fire on you right now."

I was silent for a few minutes. Then I decided to try another way, thinking that this, too, would probably get me into more trouble with her.

"Mom, didn't you get a teacher's certificate at the college in your younger days?"

"Not too long ago, yes, I did. I think it was in 1923, when I was nineteen."

"Did you study any science?" I was thinking about what I'd studied in the fifth grade about cause and effect.

"Yes, I remember some study of science. Why?"

"Did you study cause and effect? Like, if I do this then the effect is that?"

"Don't remember studying much about that. But, yes, I do know about cause and effect," she replied as if I were insulting her.

"I cause a lot of things to happen because I work so hard and one of the effects is that I make money."

"Well, yes, that's right. But God shows you the path to your success. And always thank Him for His willingness to lead you in the right way."

Unwilling to talk any longer about this subject, I said that I would, and I went on to other things.

Several guys came by the next morning in a pickup truck with Mr. McElreath driving. Mack, John, George, and Nick were in the bed of the pickup, and they hollered at me as I was watering Mom's flowers.

"We're going to collect scrap metal, and we need you. Come on."

"Let me go tell Mom," I said as I was turning off the handle of the faucet. I quickly returned and got into the pickup, having picked up a pair of work gloves. Mack's dad knew where there was a bunch of old scrap iron near the end of East Main, so we worked among the weeds and gathered rusty metal until we'd filled the pickup. We drove to the collection depot, and the total weight of the metal was 1,142 pounds. We were thinking about the money we'd get at 7 cents a pound when we heard Mr. McElreath say, "No, no money necessary. But you send the proceeds to the Red Cross because the boys want to give this to a good cause. We'll be back again soon with another load." And later we kept that promise.

They took me home, just about time for my noon meal. I told Mom that we'd collected over a ton of scrap metal and that the Red Cross would benefit. She was pleased and complimented me.

"You need to do more of that, Son. Also, collect any old rubber you find. You'd best close your worm business and collect stuff to help us win the war."

"I can do both," I replied.

My worm business remained OK, even though I had a tough time getting out of bed about 5:50 A.M. six days a week and 5:00 A.M. on Sundays for my paper route. But Dan's and my Ford-Chevy game helped keep me awake in church. And I fell asleep nearly every night listening to my Cardinals on KMOX. It looked like the Dodgers and Red Birds would fight it out for the pennant, or at least it seemed that way by the standings in late June.

On the next Saturday, Dad cooked some new vanilla, even though he'd complained about how sales were down. He said that a company in Austin, Texas, the Adams Company, had begun to hurt his sales. But the vanilla cooking in the big vat smelled so good that afternoon, and since I'd mowed a lawn out near the college that morning, I couldn't tell which smelled sweeter, the vanilla or the thousands of magnolia blooms on the campus of Southeastern. Both smells would tie for the win, I decided.

That night I helped Dad bottle the vanilla. He seemed moody and wasn't easy to talk to in our usual way. So I just stayed quiet. Finally he said that he thought he might have to go to work as an electrician because there just wasn't enough money from vanilla sales.

"Does that mean we'll have to move?"

"No, I like our house, and you and Tommie need to stay in school here. And Linda will begin school soon. Durant is my home. I'll probably ask Oscar Laymance, who has the electrical shop on Third Street, if I can help him out some. It'll be hourly wages, but if I can get a good reputation with him, more than likely he'll use me when he needs another electrician," he said as he filled eight-ounce bottles and I capped them.

"Did you learn electrical work in Oklahoma City?"

"Yes, and I got pretty good at it, even though there are quite a number of new techniques now."

"Can you do jobs for yourself when you're not working for Mr. Laymance?"

"Yes, I've been thinking about that, too. Many, many houses out in the country have gotten the REA lines there a couple of years ago but haven't run a line from the main line to their houses. Maybe some people can now afford to get their houses wired. So I'm going to check into the possibility of wiring some of those houses."

"I'll help you if I can. I'll learn."

"I'll let you know. But now let's get these labels on the bottles because I want you to go with me someplace."

"Where?" I asked.

"My friend, Mr. Barker, is the telegraph operator down at the MKT station, and he said I should bring you some evening and let you watch him work."

So we hurriedly finished, cleaned up the bottling room, told Mom where we were going, and were soon climbing the outside steps to the second floor of the small brick building, where I could hear the keys of the telegraph machine even before we went in. Mr. Barker nodded to us, but he kept clicking the machine in a constant motion. It was fun to hear him talk about what he did and interesting to see how he put a message on paper out on a line for an incoming freight train. The train engineer used a hook-like device to secure the message as the long train kept rolling north toward Kansas City. I learned some new things from Mr. Barker.

When we left, Dad said we'd stop at Wilhite's bakery and buy some donuts for breakfast.

"Great idea," I said.

The smell of the frying donuts was, ummm, so good. Dad talked with the cook, wearing his long white apron for a few minutes, and then they turned to me.

"Your dad says you really like donuts. Is that right?"

"Yes, sir, I bet I could eat a dozen right now."

"That's what Earl said you'd say. So I've got a deal for you. If you eat a dozen, I'll give you a dozen free to take home with you."

"How much does a dozen sell for?" I inquired, just knowing I could eat a dozen.

"Thirty-five cents, and that's a bargain," he said as he grinned.

"OK, then I'm ready."

And he put twelve freshly cooked sugary donuts on a tray and told me to start eating. Dad brought me a big cup of water.

The first eight went down easily. The ninth I managed in time. After a big drink and a couple of minutes, I got number ten down. I was beginning to feel queasy, but I just couldn't lose. After a couple of minutes, with the cook and Dad both laughing at me, I started on number eleven. When it was half eaten, I knew what was about to happen. I guess by my expression, the cook knew and pointed to the bathroom.

The donuts and everything came up. I kept flushing the toilet to get them out of my sight. But then more would come up. After about three or four minutes of throwing up, I felt somewhat better, so I went back. They were about to die laughing. Another cook had joined them, and he, too, was laughing at me.

I told Dad I wanted to go home because I felt awful. The cook gave him a dozen donuts free for my good effort, but I told Dad to keep them out of my sight.

Needless to say, I wasn't ready for any donuts Sunday morning. I didn't feel good as I delivered my route, and I was ready to go to bed when I got home. Mom scolded Dad for what he let me do. Then she said I could stay home from church. *Well,* I thought, *one good thing came out of this.*

As I lay in bed, it came to me that one more time I'd had to be initiated by someone older than I. It was getting tiresome to me, so I thought I'd better wise up when people offered me a deal that sounded too good. As Mom had said over and over about food, "It looks like your eyes are bigger than your stomach."

On July 6, Mr. Warner called from Montgomery Ward and said the advertising circulars were ready to be picked up, so Dad and I got them. Mr. Warner reminded me that they had to be delivered on the 10th. Folding seemed especially boring, so I waited until nighttime and took my radio to the porch so I could listen to my Cardinals. Papers seemed to fold easier when the Cardinals were winning, but I noticed I folded faster when there was a need for the Cardinals to play better.

Dad, Linda, and I delivered on the 10th, I collected, paid Dad and Linda, and once again felt good about making my profit. And I made another $20 deposit on the next Monday. If I could save at that rate, college would be no problem, as far as money was concerned.

But I was slowed down. Dad called me to the front porch, where he was sitting in the swing.

"What's up, Dad?"

"I don't think the Mercury can stand the slow driving anymore like I have to do when you are delivering the Montgomery Ward circulars. Since no cars will be available until after the war, I'm really going to have to take good care of our '39 model. I've got close to 85,000 miles on it already, and it's already using oil. So unless you can figure a way to throw those circulars on your bike, you'd better tell the man you need to quit."

Since I just couldn't, or didn't want to, ride my bike and deliver 1,000 circulars, I stopped by and told Mr. Warner that I wouldn't be able to work for him anymore. He was understanding and thanked me for working. I didn't like to quit a job so soon, but it seemed as if I had to.

Then another job was taken away. Thursday, Mom told me that Miss McKinney, who taught at the college and lived across Liveoak Street to the south, had mentioned to her about the early morning traffic and the "worms for sale" sign not being very nice for our neighborhood.

"You remember," she said, "we told you if one neighbor complained, your worm business would have to stop. Now, go take the signs down and get rid of your worms."

"Aw, Mom, not really," I said in a disgusted way. "I thought the McKinneys were my friends."

"They are, and I want them to continue to be. Mrs. McKinney will probably be glad to see the signs go, too. You know, she's a sophisticated lady."

"What does *sophisticated* mean, Mom?" I always wanted to learn a new word.

"I guess it means she's worldly wise, or socially high-up, or something like that. Why do you ask?"

"Need to learn words." Then I asked, "Are you sure I have to take my signs down?" I asked, almost pleading with her.

"Yes, just go and get rid of them now."

And so the worm business was gone. I put about one-half of the worms out near the garden area, where the soil was fairly loose, and took the rest back to where I dug them.

"Money setback, big time," I said to myself. "I'll have to figure out some better ways so that I can depend on myself and not bother Dad or Mom." But I had difficulty coming up with new jobs. I did have more time to enjoy my summer vacation by playing, swimming, and enjoying friends. I'd even gotten Mr. Bass to agree to give me two swims a week at the Natatorium for one week of the *Democrat*, which was an even better deal than I'd first thought about.

On July 6, a Sunday, I was reading the paper as I usually did while I rolled. One front-page story told me that 4,000 U.S. war planes had been built in May 1942. Another war story was sad to me. It told about thousands of Polish people being killed by German soldiers. Then another article urged us to buy defense stamps and bonds, so we could help finance the war. And on the inside there was a full page of war-related pictures.

A couple of weeks later, on July 20, I read an article about twenty-one boys from Durant and forty-three from other county towns who were to be inducted. And many, many others had already enlisted or had been inducted. I could remember reading about several men from our town being killed, but I had known only one of them.

On the inside of the *Democrat* was a large article, almost like an ad, with this head line:

An Emergency Statement
to the People of the United States

There was a picture of a man named D. M. Nelson, the chairman of the United States War Production Board. He talked about the great need for us to collect scrap metal, which he said was just junk metal that was around everywhere.

I thought about our effort when we collected over a ton of junk metal. I knew I'd better find a lot more. Mr. Nelson's words in the paper said that twice as many battleships as there were in the whole world or enough 2,000-pound bombs to drop three per minute from big bombers incessantly for more than three years could be built from the steel and iron lying around on farms alone, if this junk were used with other materials. There was more information which helped me understand why we needed the metal. I needed to find out what the word *incessantly* meant. It was a word Mr. Nelson used.

And after I read Red Ryder, my eyes moved to a small-print ad, which said, "Is Your Child a Nose Picker?"

I laughed so loud that a couple of carriers asked me what was so funny. "Look on the bottom of page five for the ad," I said. And they did. It was in small print and began with a question, "Are there nose pickers in your family?" And then it went ahead to give information about what the medicine did to stop nose-picking. An address to order it from Chicago was listed, along with the price of

$1.98. Nick said that we ought to order some of the nose picking medicine for Tom, another carrier, who picked his nose so much that he'd been given the nickname "Booger Boy." But the nickname hadn't stopped him from picking. We'd all watch him fold, pick, fold, pick, over and over. Some of the carriers teased him about the ink from his hands feeling good in his nose. Tom never seemed to care. He just picked.

Nick decided to get twenty of us to give a dime each so we could order the nose-picking medicine from Chicago. I thought it seemed a bit cruel, but I contributed my dime. The words in the ad said that if it didn't stop your child from nose picking that you could send the unused medicine back and get all of the purchase price refunded. The ad finished with the words "Mail delivery guaranteed in one week after receipt of money."

Nick got the Durant phone directly and looked up Tom's address. He said he'd mail the money, and he filled out the purchase request, which the next day he said he had done. Then our daily chore was to watch the "Booger Boy" pick his nose. It was disgusting but still I watched, as least from time to time.

By August 6, we knew he should have received his package of medicine. We began laughing and betting dimes on whether he'd stop picking.

While we were discussing the bet, I said, "You know, if I got that medicine, I'd quit before I used any of it. I'd have gotten the message and known that others were watching me pick my nose."

Nick said, "Why would the medicine cause you to stop if the name 'Booger Boy' hadn't?"

"I don't know. But maybe the medicine arriving at my house would have a bigger message than my friends calling me names. Maybe a name was like a badge, sort of like my nickname, P.J. But I'm not sure."

And on the next Monday, "Booger Boy" folded all his papers without picking even once. We were very surprised. Mack won all the bets and got 90 cents from the betting money we'd put up. We talked about starting another bet on whether he'd start again, but I talked them out of it. "Let's just leave him alone and see what happens," I urged.

We agreed that if he stayed stopped, we'd call him Tom again. In a couple of weeks, we were all calling him Tom. We never knew whether the medicine worked, or whether just getting it through the mail caused him to quit.

We all laughed that we'd be scared if any package came in the mail to any of our houses. Then we joked about what each package would have inside if we got one. My package, Nick said, would have some medicine that'd cure me from being so shy and blushing so much. They all laughed. Later, as I delivered, I thought about my "medicine" and wished they'd send me that package. I knew it was up to me to get over being so shy, but it wouldn't be easy. I vowed I'd try.

It was a good feeling to have friends who wanted me to be better.

CHAPTER 16
As Time Goes By

Mid-August of '42 meant school wasn't too far away. I'd worked hard most of the summer and now had $380 in my Durant National Bank. Well, not my bank, but I thought I owned a large part of it. The paper route was just great. I had ninety-two customers, and I continued to sell, on the average, a dollar's worth of papers each week. It seemed as if my bike and I could deliver the route blindfolded since I'd thrown it so many times. And I made good acquaintances of so many of my customers.

One of these, Mrs. Lively, who lived in the third house from the end of the route, regularly sat on her large front porch awaiting her paper during warm weather. She was older, maybe in her seventies, and she always wanted to talk when I'd walk to the porch to hand her an unfolded paper.

"Mr. Johnson," she'd say—she always called me Mr., which I never could understand. "Have you worked hard today?"

"Yes, Mrs. Lively, I have."

"Well, good. Hard work is good for the soul, you know."

"Yes, ma'am, I've heard that. I guess I have a good soul then."

"Come inside, I want you to help me."

That wasn't just one day. I'd been inside her house on so many occasions that I sometimes thought I lived there. And so, one more time, I handed a cane to her, opened the screen door, and followed her into the kitchen.

"Get that chair right there and push it up to that high shelf," she said as she used her cane to point. "Now, do you see those quart jars of green beans?"

"Yes, ma'am."

"Well, get down two of them."

And I did. Setting them on the cabinet counter, she picked them up and wiped the jars carefully and then handed one to me.

"You take this one home for your supper. And open the other one for my supper."

And I did. Over and over, customers like Mrs. Lively had been good to me. Whether they were on Main Street or whether they lived nearer the Frisco tracks, most seemed to like me, trust me, and kid with me about lots of things that I somehow knew were meant to help me grow up.

But there were sad, sad things, too. All over town, the blue stars on some of the banners hanging in the front windows were replaced with gold stars, which meant a serviceman who lived in that house had been killed. Two gold stars were in houses on my route. And this was just August. I was scared to think how many gold stars would eventually appear. I hoped so much that the scrap metal we'd collected would hurry up and help end the war. And I just knew we'd win because Uncle Sam kept looking like he was a winner on the sign which always said, "I WANT YOU!"

I'd read that six German Gestapo agents had died in the electric chair. They had come to the U.S. by U-boats on orders to blow up and destroy our war factories. I just thought that if we could do this to more of the Nazis, the war would be over sooner. I daydreamed a lot about being a soldier and whipping the Nazis.

It was about time to begin work on Durant's new, improved airport, the Ira Eaker Field. I liked that. A military hero should have his name on something like a new airport. And there was some talk that a naval air station might be built at the airport. I'd even thought, from time to time, that Washington Irving school should be named Harrell Garrison Elementary. It seemed to me that he was a hero, too.

Just before school began for my sixth grade and final year at Mr. Garrison's school, George excitedly told me that his cousin, Miss Aggie Boyet, had been hired to teach English at Durant High

School. We laughed together as we thought about being taught someday by George's cousin.

Dad's name had finally come up to buy two new tires for the Mercury. It was interesting to read in the *Democrat* the occupations of people approved to buy new tires, new tubes, retread tires, or truck tires. Doctors' and farmers' names seemed to be listed the most. War wasn't pleasant, but Mom kept reminding me that God had spared our country from actual invasion of Hitler's troops. Sometimes when I thought about war, and I did a lot, I kept wondering what in the world would cause people to get so mad at others that they'd want to kill them. It just didn't make sense to me.

Two days before school started, I was mowing our front lawn when I noticed the Western Union delivery boy pedaling his bike toward our block. I stopped mowing, and my heart almost stopped beating. Seeing the Western Union boy in one's neighborhood was scary because many times the news wasn't good.

He stopped across the street at Mrs. Gooding's house, where one blue star was hanging on her front window banner. I almost panicked. And then I watched as Mrs. Gooding, after talking to the delivery boy, fell to her knees screaming. I ran for Mom, and Mom ran for Mrs. Gooding. I don't guess I'd ever seen two women hold each other so tightly and cry as much as they did. And I cried, too. Bruce Gooding was dead—killed in action. I saw the telegram. It said, "We regret to inform you that your son, Bruce Gooding, has been killed in action." Our neighborhood was stunned. Women and men kept coming to see Mrs. Gooding. Mr. Gooding didn't ever seem to be around home, and he didn't come home then either, or at least that I knew. Mrs. Gooding's children, and their husbands and children all came. All I knew was that I liked Mrs. Gooding, was very sad about Bruce, and wanted more and more to pray an improper prayer, as Mom called it, that God would cause Hitler, Tojo, Hirohito, and Mussolini to die.

Shortly after I entered the sixth grade, a gold star showed up on Mrs. Gooding's banner. I saw it every day. I got mad at our enemies every time I saw it. Why must war occur? Everyone I asked gave me the same reason, but I just didn't want war. I even told Dad that if I were ever in charge of the world that war wouldn't be allowed. He laughed a small laugh and told me to hurry up and get in charge of the world.

School activities and time passing seemed to help, even though I took Mrs. Gooding food for some time that Mom fixed for her. Mom visited her daily.

About three weeks into the sixth grade, Mr. Garrison called all the fifth-and sixth-grade boys into the school auditorium. All, I guess, except for Bobby Dale, who was a new student in our homeroom, but not new to our school. Bobby Dale was much taller than any of the other sixth-grade boys because he'd been kept back twice. He acted differently in the classroom, where he sat on the back row and sometimes just hollered over and would turn his desk over backwards while he was sitting in it. Then he'd just laugh and laugh. It was embarrassing to us all, even though we'd laugh, too. And so Bobby Dale had become "Goofy Dale" to us.

Mr. Garrison told us that he wanted to help us be better citizens. "Anyone here who doesn't want to be a better citizen, raise your hand," he said.

No hands were raised.

"Everyone here who likes Bobby Dale, raise your hand," Mr. Garrison said.

Every hand went up.

"Now, boys, everyone here who thinks Bobby Dale likes the name you call him, raise your hand."

No hands went up.

"Good. You've learned an important lesson today. While many of you have nicknames which you like to be called, your name for Bobby Dale isn't good. As a matter of fact, it's close to being cruel. And I don't want anyone in my school, or any place else as far as I'm concerned, to be cruel. Now, everyone who will call him Bobby Dale, raise your hand."

All of us raised a hand.

"I can count on you to do this, can't I?"

"Yes, sir," was said by us all at the same time.

"Any questions?" he asked.

No questions were asked.

"Good. You learned an important lesson today. Now go quietly back to your classes and learn what your teacher is teaching today."

And we did. I never heard anyone ever again call him anything but Bobby Dale. He became a special friend to many of us. Mr. Garrison seemed to help us understand things better.

Before delivering on September 17, I told Skip that I usually saw several servicemen in uniform at the Eat Well Café, next to the bus station on my route, waiting for the bus to go on to their military base. "Skip, I'd like to be able to give each one of those men a free *Democrat*. Maybe five to seven papers a day would be enough. Could I buy seven for ten cents extra each day for 60 more cents per week? I kinda think it'd be good for them to get our paper free."

"Sure, I can do that, but wait here a few minutes." He went into Mr. Story's office. When he returned, he told me, "P.J., Mr. Story said it'd be OK to give you seven more papers each day. And if you don't find soldiers to give them all away, just leave them in the café."

I did. I met servicemen from almost everywhere. I started writing their hometowns on a small notepad that I carried, and later I looked at a map to see where their hometowns were located. That really got me interested in maps. I learned to like even more what our servicemen were doing.

Patsy Hill, the girl who'd kissed me on the cheek at my tenth birthday party, invited a lot of us sixth-graders to a party on a Saturday night, September 26. It wasn't a birthday party. It was just a boy and girl party, which seemed to be a fun idea to me.

About twenty boys and girls came, and we were having fun just doing mostly nothing for a while. I was, how do I say, mostly awkwardly comfortable until Patsy brought an empty quart milk bottle, told us to sit in a circle, and prepared to spin the bottle. The person who spun and the person the bottle pointed to, if the opposite sex, would go into the darkened kitchen and kiss.

I hadn't ever kissed before. I couldn't even remember Mom ever having kissed me. And since I hadn't been to the movies to see kissing scenes, like my friends talked about, I knew I didn't know how to kiss. I panicked. I sort of wanted to try, but I could feel the sickness in my stomach as the bottle was spinning. I thought that if it ever pointed toward me, I'd kick it real quick away from me, even though I knew they wouldn't let that count.

Each time a boy and girl went into the kitchen, they'd stay a minute or so and come back. Then there were a few teases made about how good a kiss Nick gave, or if Donna Newberry was a better kisser than Julia Ann. Gwyn blushed when she returned with John. We all laughed, and they seemed to have more fun than I was having.

Then it happened. Patsy Ruth spun the bottle, and when it stopped, it pointed directly toward me. It seemed as if I became totally paralyzed. I couldn't think, either. I did hear Nick say that this was part of the medicine he'd ordered for me from Chicago. I did understand that and found enough courage, along with Patsy's hand pulling my arm toward the kitchen, to walk in almost a stumbling way with her.

She said, "Kiss me, P.J." And I somehow managed to press my lips against her cheek.

"No, on the lips. Right here on my lips," she said.

I tried. And Patsy seemed unhappy. "P.J., have you ever kissed before?"

"Well, I guess not," I admitted.

"Here, let me show you."

And she did. After three or four, I learned a little bit better. I didn't have anyone to compare her kisses with, but I thought she was a good teacher, and I knew I liked how she was teaching me. It made me feel good all over.

"Now, P.J., you do it by yourself. You hold me and kiss me like I've taught you to do."

"Shouldn't we go back? We've been in here for a long time."

"Yes, after you've kissed me."

And so we kissed. It seemed OK, even though I could feel my heart pound and other parts of me respond.

We returned. Did I ever get teased! I must have turned blood-red from blushing. Nick asked me if I took my medicine. I grinned and nodded yes. Margaret Rose asked Nick what he meant by medicine, and Nick was nice enough not to answer her.

It was a nice party. Patsy was a good helper and friend. We weren't sweet on each other; we had been good friends forever. I thought about a lot of things before I went to sleep that night.

On the following Monday in music class, I began to understand more about the party. After we'd sung all of the military songs from the Army, Navy, Army Air Corps, Marines, and Seabees, and "Remember Pearl Harbor," "Don't Sit Under the Apple Tree," "Coming in on a Wing and a Prayer," and "Any Bonds Today," Donna Newberry asked if we could sing "As Time Goes By."

I didn't know the song. As a matter of fact, I'd never heard of it. The teacher said that it would be OK to learn it and sing it. She said it was a song in *Casablanca*, a movie most of my classmates said they'd seen. Another moment when I felt cheated. The teacher, Miss Dyer, wrote the words on the board so we could learn them. "A kiss is still a kiss, a sigh is just a sigh..."

And then I understood about Patsy's party. When we sang the song, more girls seemed to enjoy it than boys. Some of the boys seemed to like the sigh more than the kiss. But I had a good feeling about the kiss, even though I sided with the boys, trying to act disgusted about the song. I guess girls just grew up faster than some of us boys did.

That night I got out my map of the world and found the city of Casablanca in the country of Morocco on the northwest part of the continent of Africa. I tried to imagine kissing Patsy Ruth or Donna or Jeanne or Gwyn in Casablanca, but I never could. I just thought about Patsy's kitchen.

My St. Louis Cardinals did it. They won the World Series over the Yankees four games to one! It was exciting for me. After listening to KMOX all those years, my team won it all. Stan "The Man" Musial was my favorite. I'd gotten a baseball glove that had his name on it, and I almost couldn't let it out of my sight during the series. And to think that they had won 106 games and lost only 48 was almost unbelievable.

I guess the Cards were my team because they were the only one I could ever listen to on the radio. Also, I liked St. Louis because it was on the Mississippi River. I liked Twain's book *Tom Sawyer*, so I'd read about the big river.

Rivers I liked. Maybe because I'd fished the Blue, Washita, and Red rivers. And Chuckwa was only a creek, but it had a good, steady stream. Dad taught me that. Rivers always seemed to be going someplace. Lakes, on the other hand, were pretty and tame, but they never went anywhere. So the Cards were near a river and were going places, especially in 1942.

Shortly after the series was over, I tried to tune in clear channel KMOX, but weather conditions prevented me from receiving the signal. Instead, I received station XEG, Del Rio, Texas. What they were attempting to get the listener to buy was a simulated diamond for only $5.95. And later they were advertising an autographed picture of Jesus Christ for $4.95. Even stranger, I thought.

The next morning at breakfast I asked Earleen what the word *simulated* meant.

"It's best you look it up in the dictionary, so you'll never forget what it means," she said, almost ignoring me.

"Oh, so you don't know what it means, either," I replied.

"Of course, I know what it means. I'm just not going to tell you." And she kept eating her oatmeal.

After finishing breakfast, I did look up the word *simulated* in my dictionary. No wonder. A fake diamond, probably a piece of glass, I concluded. I had added a new word to my vocabulary. Then, on my way out to go to school, I asked Mom how station XEG could have autographed pictures of Jesus Christ to sell.

"Think, Son, what the advertisement said. It said *autographed*. Did it say who autographed them?"

"No ... oh, I get it now. Anyone could autograph it, couldn't they? They said it was an autographed picture, but not autographed by Jesus Christ."

"Now you're learning. Go on to school," Mom said as I was on the porch getting my bike.

Dad surprised me that evening when he told me that he was giving two grocery store accounts to me to call on and sell vanilla.

"Which two, Dad?"

"B&H Grocery and White House."

"Why, Dad?"

"I'm not getting along very well with either of the store's owners, and they aren't pushing my brand, so I've just decided that you can do a better job than I. Do you want them?"

"Sure. Do I get an order book with the carbon sheet between the order pages?"

"Yes, I'll give you your own. And you can put the boxes of vanilla into your bike basket to deliver them."

"Are they low in stock now?" I was readying myself to go make sales.

"You'll need to check them. I haven't been in either store in quite some time. When you do call, introduce yourself to Mr. Bailey and Mr. Henderson and tell them that I've given you the account. Do the same with Mr. Kenner at the White House Grocery."

"Thanks. I'll call on them soon." And I did. Both stores' shelves were vacant where Tri-Pure Vanilla usually was displayed. I sold a dozen four-ounce and a dozen eight-ounce to both stores, rushed home to get all the vanilla, proudly shelved the vanilla, and wrote up my first sales slips. I felt important when they paid me. Dad let me keep all of the money, even though I offered to split it with him. About once a week I went by the stores and pulled the bottles to the front of the display shelf so maybe more customers would see them and buy. I'd seen Dad do that time after time.

I'd made two more $20 deposits and now had $420. Lawn mowing was over for the summer, worm business was history, and there were no more Montgomery Ward circulars to deliver. My money record-keeping book was slowing down on new earnings. Dad seemed to get more cross with Mom about money being spent. I'd grown a lot and had to buy some new school clothes. I gave Mom $15 to buy Linda some new clothes, and I made her promise she wouldn't tell Dad. Dad had worked some for Mr. Laymance's electric company, but he didn't seem to like coming home tired, sweaty, and dirty. He did, however, talk about putting in a fuse box and a single pull-chain light in farm houses that had never had electricity before. He seemed to enjoy seeing the happiness on the family's faces when the chain was pulled and the light came on. He said that he always liked for the woman of the house to be the first to pull the chain. And he'd laugh when he told that story. I never did quite understand why he laughed, but I thought it might refer to some man's joke, or something. I thought, once again, about how Speaker Rayburn helped get electricity to the farmers by getting the REA bill passed. And I liked President Roosevelt, too, for signing it into law. It made sense to me that all people should have the opportunity to have electric lights.

For a new source of money, I turned to collecting scrap rubber and selling it at the Atherton Magnolia Station at First and Evergreen. They paid me a penny a pound, so it didn't add up very fast. All of us sixth-grade boys, as well as many other boys, kept finding scrap metal and taking it to a huge stack that was on the junior high school playground. I could hardly imagine that there was that much scrap metal in the world.

The fall revival began November 15 and would run through November 22. I almost liked the evangelist because he told funny stories, but then he'd get to the reason he came—the altar call. The singer for the revival was his wife, and she'd sing as he opened the altar for sinners. I wondered if any money had ever been spent to teach her voice lessons, because she was a horrible singer. The heads of the worshippers were usually lowered when she sang her special during the service. Even Mom couldn't look at her directly, as she always tried to do. She liked to give people her support since she had become the leader of all women's groups in the church.

After church, I asked Mom if, while the woman was singing, she was praying for her.

"Why do you ask, Son?"

"Because your head was bowed in a prayer-like fashion," I teased.

"With a voice like she has, she needs a lot of prayer, and we need a lot of God's grace to listen to her," she responded, laughing as she said it.

I think Mom's slight illness that week may have been the first time I could remember that she'd not attended every service of a revival. I, too, got to miss four nights when she stayed home. After the revival was over, I worked up enough courage to ask her if she just got sick so she wouldn't have to hear the woman sing.

"Of course not," she answered, as her face turned as red as mine when I blushed.

I knew that I'd finally heard Mom tell a lie, even though I thought it was just a little fib. But I wasn't about to ask her any more about it.

It appeared that Mom and I were getting along much better. Only occasionally did we have the Bible readings and prayer. She told me to promise to say my prayers before going to sleep, which I did. I recited the Lord's Prayer in about fifteen seconds, and that was that. A promise kept and a prayer said. I knew God would hear my rapid prayer. Time was going by, and I needed my sleep.

As winter weather approached, Dad and I put up the big coal stove once again. He said that the heat from gas made his feet swell and the coal heat didn't. I'd asked a lot of people if gas heat caused their feet to swell, but none said it did. Some laughed and thought it was a silly idea. Nevertheless, Dad liked the heat from the coal stove. I wondered if burning coal was cheaper than heating by gas, but I kept that thought to myself.

And then Mom told me I had to begin taking a tub bath every other night unless I was dirty enough to take one every night.

"No more spit baths, Son. You're growing up now, and you know that 'cleanliness is next to Godliness.'" She'd told me that over and over. I really didn't think that God cared whether my body was clean or not, but Mom insisted on frequent tub baths.

What I occasionally did was turn the water on in the bathtub and then get my washcloth and scrub here and there. Then I'd turn the water off, dry off, and look clean and godly. Mom never questioned, so I got by. But I did take a tub bath before going to boy-girl parties.

A local dentist came to our homeroom and talked about brushing our teeth. He gave us all toothbrushes to take home. He brought small round disks hanging on a short string. One side of the cardboard disk was white, the other black. So Miss Vaughan put the name of each student just above the disk. And she began calling roll each morning by asking us to turn our disk to either white, if we'd brushed, or black for not brushed.

That surely did put a lot of pressure on me to remember. I didn't want a black disk, so if I forgot to brush, I kept a tiny elm tree stick in my desk with the end chewed enough to make it feel like a toothbrush. By covering my mouth with one hand, I could brush the elm stick around my teeth before she got to the Js on he roll. I'd proudly say "yes" and turn my disk to white. But I soon began to remember to brush at home. Things seemed to be changing in my life.

Mom called Earleen and me together in early December and told us she needed to talk about Dad, money, and the family. She left Linda out because she wasn't old enough to understand what she was going to tell us.

I was scared about what she was about to say, but I thought I already knew. Then she began.

"Dad and I have had a little talk, and I need to tell you what we've decided. Our income has never been much, but we've always had enough to get by. Don't you agree?"

We nodded yes.

And then she asked, "Tommie, don't you have enough money and clothes to make it all right in your senior year?"

"Yes, I'm OK, Mom," Tommie replied.

"And, Son, you have your own money that you earn and save. Do you need anything more?"

"Not really, Mom. I do wish I could find more ways to earn money, but it's difficult. I have $440 in my bank account. I hope that by the time we go to junior high, I have $670 total. And I think I can do that."

Mom said, "That's so good, Son. Dad said that you've refused to take a dime from him since as long as he can remember, and we both appreciate you for being that way."

"Oh, Dad's bought me Cokes and things, so I have cost him some money. But I try not to be expensive."

Then Mom dropped the "big one" on Earleen.

"Tommie, you'll be only sixteen when you graduate. And you want to go—and we want you to go—to Bethany-Peniel College. Dad and I think it would be best for us financially if you would work for a year here in Durant, live at home, and save all you make for college. What do you think?"

I was surprised. Earleen immediately agreed that she'd do it. I was proud of her and later told her so.

After that, I noticed Mom sewed more clothes for Linda and Earleen. She even got large flour sacks from one of the bakeries and, after bleaching them, sewed them together for bed sheets. She used some to make me some undershorts until I complained about how scratchy they were. Mom cooked a lot of red beans and cornbread. She told me once again to eat a lot because they'd "stick to my ribs." That was fine with me because red beans topped with Mom's chow-chow that she and Aunt Lilly always canned, along with cornbread, were really tasty. I had some picture in my mind of my ribs being covered with red beans.

Dad got moodier. Christmas of '42 wasn't pleasant, but we acted like it was. I bought Dad the nicest long-sleeve shirt I could find at Perkins Bros. Dry Goods. It even brought a smile when he tried it on. And we all survived with smiles, songs, and a baked chicken and cornbread dressing, along with Mom's delicious candy and ambrosia.

Sixth grade seemed to be passing too quickly. But one event brought it to a slow down. While I'd still been, on occasion, bringing my peanut butter and jelly sandwich and giving it to Billy Jack, he'd continued to lose weight. He didn't look much bigger around than a pencil. On the playground on a cold February day, Mr. Sharp's substitute had us boys running laps around the playground. Billy Jack had stopped running, was breathing hard, and leaned over and put his hands on his knees, trying to catch his breath. George was talking to him, when all of a sudden the sub came up, shouted at him, and told him to keep running. Then he used his knee to kick him in the bottom. Billy Jack struggled and kept running.

The next day Billy Jack was absent. And the next day. And the next. I could tell by the number of people visiting Mr. Garrison's office that all was not well.

On the fourth day, our class was told that Billy Jack had run away and had been killed by an MKT train between Durant and Armstrong. It was a sad time for us all. I cried and then cried some more. I felt guilty that I hadn't helped him more. Both Miss Vaughan and Mr. Garrison let us talk about how we liked Billy Jack. And I cried even more when Bobby Dale said, "Billy Jack was like me. He and I have difficulty sometimes."

I often wondered, if he had not gotten a knee to his bottom, would he have still run away? I never would know.

His funeral was in another town. So we all wrote a letter to his mother, telling her how much we liked her son. I guess I tried the hardest I'd ever tried in my life to use words that I thought she would like to hear about Billy Jack.

Time passed. I continued to have perfect attendance and all S's. I'd avoided Mrs. Landers' and Miss Taylor's paddle. Few could say that in our class. Billie Jean, Nettye Ann, Jeanne Paul, and I were still on the "no paddling" list.

In early April our class, as usual, had library time once a week in Miss Taylor's reading class. When it was over, as we walked back to our room, Miss Taylor heard pupils talking in the hallway. When she entered the room, she gave us a stern look and said, "Everyone who said a word between the library and the classroom stand up right now." And everyone stood up except me. I just knew her too well and knew what she'd do, so I'd walked by myself as rapidly as I could and was the first one to get back to the room.

It was a scary scene. Twenty-nine students standing, admitting that they'd talked in the hallway, and one sitting. It became scarier when she began asking each student if they'd heard me talk. By the time she'd asked all twenty-nine, I'd almost wished I would have stood earlier. I just knew that one of my friends would think I deserved a spanking and tell Miss Taylor I'd talked. But none did, and I watched as she gave three licks to twenty-nine of my friends as they bent across the table in the front of the room. It was unfair.

And especially when Billie Jean, a kind, intelligent, and caring friend, got her licks. Even though I made it without a spanking in school, I'd almost have rather had one than watch Billie Jean take hers. She sobbed for a good fifteen minutes.

I vowed that if I ever became a father or a teacher, I'd never spank anyone.

The sixth grade was full of events. And then it was over too soon. Miss Vaughan hugged me goodbye, and Mr. Garrison told me to keep learning vocabulary. I knew that I'd miss them both. I hoped they'd miss me, too.

I'd visited with my neighbor, Mrs. Gooding, once or twice a week. She was still sad about her son's death, but she was so strong that she hid her sadness a lot. Mom said that she'd make it. She also told me that Mrs. Gooding would be paid $10,000 in life insurance by the U.S. government to help make up for her son's death. While I thought that was a lot of money, I could tell that nothing could make up for her son.

Somehow I thought she began to treat me a little differently, too. Maybe I could help take the place of Bruce in some small way. I had vowed that I'd always be her friend.

CHAPTER 17
The Friday Double-Hitter

The summer began well for me, a twelve-year-old. Boy Scout Troop 117, sponsored by Skip's church, the First Christian, had invited me to become a scout. Since Skip was the scoutmaster, it was easy for me to make up my mind. Also, a lot of other carriers were in 117. So now I was a Tenderfoot Scout, and I bought my scout shirt, scout neck scarf, cap, shoes, and Boy Scout handbook from Pullen's Store, the official scout uniform store. It didn't take very long for me to learn the scout's motto and other things all Tenderfoot Scouts had to learn. And Skip was a patient and good teacher and leader. Learning to tie knots was easy because he'd show us while telling funny stories about how each knot could be used. And our campouts at Hickory Hollow were fun and challenging.

Mom had some reservation about me becoming a scout because I'd told her that occasionally the troop would go as a group to other churches, but I convinced her that, at least, I'd be in church.

Mowing kept me busier than I ever expected. I felt that I had so much business because I had such a good mower and did a good job. But Dad reminded me that another reason was that so many men were away in the military and weren't there to mow their own lawns.

Wiring houses with Dad also increased. I was learning about fuse boxes, romex wire, hot wires, neutral wires, using a sledgehammer to drive ground rods, hooking up pull-chain lights, and watching the family smile as an electric light came on for the first time in their farm house. Dad convinced several to let him put in one or two electrical outlet plugs for $2.50 each, and he would let them pay gradually when they saw him in town.

Dad seemed happier now that some extra money was coming in, but he still talked about the Mercury not doing well mechanically, something about rings, pistons, oil use, and needing an overhaul job.

Tommie, and I called her Tommie now since she'd graduated as the top student in her class, had immediately been employed at the Durant Peanut Company, just across the MKT tracks on East Cedar. She began for $25 a week as a secretary and figured that she could save at least $80 a month, work for eighteen months, and have between $1,400 and $1,500 saved for college. She liked the idea of being a year older when she went away to Bethany. I heard Dad say that the $1,400 would pay for two years of college. She also had been awarded a scholarship for her good grades.

Linda would be starting first grade at Washington Irving in the fall. Other than the news of the war, our family seemed better. Other than the Mercury, that is.

I'd learned to get along well with my two owners at the B&H and at the White House grocery stores, even selling them more vanilla than Dad said he had when he called on them, especially since vanilla sales continued to slow in almost all stores. The various Adams extracts were really our competition.

When I collected every Friday from Mrs. Jarrell at the courthouse, I'd become used to staying around Mr. Snow's business and talking to him, especially about the war. I thought that if anyone should know about war, he'd be the one. And I liked to hear his way of being patriotic.

"P.J.," he'd say, "why, when the GIs get rid of those Nazis and Japs, we'll have the biggest parade in Durant's history, and it won't be too long now. I'm going to lead the victory parade. You can count on that." Then he'd smile like he knew what he was talking about.

I always left feeling better and knowing we'd win. He told me a lot about Winston Churchill, things I'd never heard. Mr. Churchill, according to Mr. Snow, was a great leader. I'd tell him things I knew about Theodore Roosevelt that I'd learned from Mr. Laird's books, and Mr. Snow would laugh as he told me that he wished he would have been a "Rough Rider" along with Mr. Roosevelt.

I spent a good deal of time finding scrap rubber to sell at a penny a pound. I even kept a special box on the back of my bike so I could pick up bits here and there and save it until I could sell it all.

And one day in July, while I was putting Dad's freshly washed socks and underwear in his drawer, I saw a small box of rubbers down under his clothes. I was shocked because I was just learning things like that from the big boys, but it was difficult to believe that my mom and my dad really needed those things. After thinking about it, I knew that people who loved each other do need these things, so I finally gave in and assured myself that the supply in his drawer was OK. But for a few days I felt strange around Mom.

Now, as I was looking for scrap rubber, I laughed as I thought about asking Dad to save his used rubbers for my scrap collection. But then, I thought, they wouldn't weigh very much anyway.

Several of us had discovered the *Sunshine and Health* magazine, which was displayed on the bottom shelf at the back of the newsstand store on Main Street, near Wilhite's Bakery. Mack said it was published by a nudist association, but it didn't make me much difference who published it. What did make a difference was whether I could put the magazine down quickly enough, stand up and get a *Mechanics Illustrated,* and quit blushing when I heard the front screen door slam. I learned that routine well. We agreed that *Sunshine and Health* was better than the occasional pictures in *National Geographic* in our school library, and those pages seemed to disappear quickly. We all blamed Miss Taylor for tearing them out. I had some troubling thoughts looking at pictures and then listening to the preacher. But my friends convinced me that the preacher had looked, too, when he was our age.

The *Democrat* had added "Joe Palooka" as a comic strip that we carriers enjoyed. And an ad frequently appeared, which said,

> **Palooka says you kiddies who want to grow up big and strong
> like Uncle Sam's soldiers and sailors
> must drink plenty of good, wholesome body building MILK.
> Pasteurized Milk
> Hewett & Echols
> Phone 244**

I liked the ad, even though I wasn't a kiddie, because one of the Hewetts of the ad was Tommie's debate partner's dad, Mr. "Slew" Hewett, and the other Mr. Hewett, Harry, lived at Tenth and Liveoak. I occasionally played tennis with his son, Harry, Jr., who had a cute younger redheaded sister, Norma Ruth. I enjoyed talking to her when I went by to get Harry, Jr. to play tennis. She attended Russell Training School on the Southeastern campus. I thought of her as a precocious girl, another word that Mr. Garrison had given me to learn. And the Hewetts went to the Methodist church. I liked redheads and Methodists.

Taylor's dairy called me about the first of August and asked me to help deliver their milk early each morning. Tommie's old boyfriend, the one who'd paid me a dime to run around two blocks, told me that they needed someone to work for three weeks. So I had a new adventure, totally easy to do. And they paid me $30, which I thought was easy money.

I'd almost met my money goal before September. Instead of my planned $670, I had $660 and thought I was rich. I even began to think about quitting my route after the next summer, as I had noticed other carriers quitting about then. But I didn't mention that to anyone. I'd had to see Dr. Williams, the dentist, for a tooth problem, and he'd treated me at no cost because, as he said, I'd been such a good carrier. He told me that one son, Edward, was in England in the U.S. Army as a dentist. And another, Earl, was in Dallas practicing dentistry.

Mr. Long, the druggist, and I had some scary moments. I decided I'd throw his paper in the yard rather than on his porch because he always kept me waiting before he paid. The first collection after doing this, he was really upset.

"Young man," he said in an angry voice, "why have you stopped putting my paper on my porch?"

Almost trembling, I said, "Mr. Long, I'm just doing that because you keep me waiting too long to get paid." And then I quit being scared and almost laughed when I heard that I'd used the word *long* twice in my sentence.

"What difference does that make?" he asked, still angry.

"You slow me down too much. I have lots to do, and I don't understand why you can't just pay me my 15 cents quickly and let me go on."

"If I do pay you quickly, will you always put my paper on the porch?" he asked in a less angry tone.

"Yes, sir. I'll always do that. And if you want to, you can just leave the 15 cents at the fountain or tell the clerk to pay me 15 cents so I won't have to bother you." I was still thinking I needed a way to avoid seeing him each week.

"Well, then, that's what I'll do. I'll tell my soda jerk to pay you when you come in."

And I got my 15 cents and left, feeling I'd won. My cousin, Erten, who taught me so much when I had visited him on the farm, had a saying: "We taught that snake to quit sucking eggs." I took that to mean the problem didn't exist anymore. So as I rode on down Main Street to collect from the Basses, I had the thought that I'd taught Mr. Long to quit "sucking eggs." While my experiment had been scary, it had worked.

And school began. Woodrow Wilson Junior High School was right across Cedar Street from Durant High School, where we could watch the goings-on of sophomores and juniors and seniors. Well, from a safe distance, that is. No longer did we stay in one room, with the teachers coming to us, but now we had the responsibility to move from one room to another to learn that teacher's subject. My teachers were Mrs. McKinnis for reading, Mrs. Vaughan for math, Mr. Burton for health, Miss Swinney for music, Miss Morton for English, and Miss Ellison for geography. I liked the idea of having new students who'd come from Robert E. Lee and George Washington schools to join us from Washington Irving because we had a lot of new friends.

The first Friday night of our new school year, Tommy Alley had a boy-girl party. And was I ever ready to go. But when I got to his house, I heard the music playing and saw my friends dancing on Tommy's porch. My heart almost stopped. I didn't know how to dance and, like not being able to go to movies, I couldn't even learn to dance. So I stood around and watched. Our reading teacher, Mrs. McKinnis, who'd just moved from McAlester to Durant, had a daughter, Barbara Ann, a seventh-grader who, I thought, was really cute. She asked me to dance, and I said I couldn't for religious reasons. She was nice to me for a minute, but left to dance with Nick. I hurt. Patsy smiled at me while she was dancing with Tommy, but I knew I wouldn't be able to let her teach me how to dance like she'd taught me how to kiss. I hurt even more. All my friends seemed to be having so much fun, and I stood there watching. I went home early and prayed a strange and different prayer before going to sleep.

Then a big "hit" came the next Friday. The eighth-graders had warned us about our principal, Mr. Hall, who at the first of every school year gave his orientation speech to the seventh-graders. They told us it was funny, scary, and threatening, but to ignore it. I wasn't used to ignoring adults.

Our homeroom teacher, Mrs. Vaughan, whose husband was a brother to my favorite Miss Vaughan in Washington Irving, read a note that said all seventh-grade boys would meet in the auditorium last period to hear the principal speak.

We went. I sat on the second row on the middle aisle on an old green steel folding chair. I guessed that there were about sixty-five or sixty-seven boys there.

Mr. Hall came in and began, "Welcome to Woodrow Wilson. I'm most pleased to have you here. I'm Mr. Hall, your principal, and I want to give you an orientation to the way things happen here in our school.

"First, I want you to be proud or our building and take care of it. Anyone found to be disrespectful will have to talk to me. Do you understand?"

And we all said, "Yes, sir."

"Second, we have good teachers here, and they want to help you learn and become good citizens. So do what they tell you to do. Hand in all your assignments on time, don't take any answers from anyone on tests or give anyone your answers, and act like young men whose mothers would be proud of their sons' behaviors. Do you understand?"

And all together, we said, "Yes, sir."

"Next, I want you to know that I've heard that some students call me 'Pappy Hall' behind my back. Well, I don't want to ever hear you call me that, but I do want you to know I'm also like your pappy, who wants the best for you. But also I'm like your pappy because if you deserve licks, I've got one of the strongest arms and the best paddle that any principal in Oklahoma has. And I'm very willing to use it. I'm always eager to be a good principal and help you grow up in this difficult year for most of you. Do you understand me? And are you willing to let me help you?"

Again, a chorus of "Yes, sir."

"That's good. I expect your seventh-grade class to be outstanding. Now, before I dismiss you, there's one other topic I need to discuss."

I heard coughs and feet moving around on the floor. We'd been told what was coming.

"Now, boys, I want you to listen carefully. What I have to say is very important for you boys at your age. We have a good and clean boys' restroom, and I want it kept that way. The custodian always gives me a report about its cleanliness. And one way to help keep it clean is not to stay there very long. Some of you may think it's clever to do things in there that you're not supposed to do, but don't even think about it. Remember, most doctors tell us that if you do this too often, you probably can't have babies when you grow up and marry. And I know you'll want to be a father someday. So let's keep the boys' restroom very clean. Do you understand?"

And there were quite a few saying, "Yes, sir," but not as many as before. I said, "Yes, sir."

He then said, "I'm glad we've met today like this. I'll get to know you individually as the semester goes on. If you have questions, ask your teacher to let you come and talk to me. But remember, you don't want to be sent to see me. Now we're dismissed."

I had been oriented to a new life. As I was getting my papers that day so I could go collect, I heard James Attaway, Nick, Mack, and David Westbrook discussing Mr. Hall's talk.

I asked if Mr. Hall meant what I thought he meant about keeping a clean boys' room, and Attaway shook his head "yes" and everyone laughed. Attaway, who was a few months older than the rest of us seventh-graders, and one who seemed to always know more about worldly ways, said, "Hey, Mr. Hall must know what he's talking about because Mrs. Hall and he don't have any children."

Everyone laughed except me. I thought I knew better than the way Mr. Hall explained things, but I wasn't as sure as all my friends. And then they teased me and told me not to stay very long in the boys' room. I was puzzled. If he was correct, then I had big worries. And if my friends were correct, which I mostly believed, why would a principal lie to us that way? I thought about Mr. Garrison and knew he'd have spoken to us differently.

I started to bike toward my route, but I had an idea, so I rode back to the courthouse and went in to see Mr. Snow. It was good that there weren't any customers.

"Mr. Snow, it's P.J. again."

"Yes, I recognized your footsteps. Surprised to hear them, too, because you've already been in here today."

"I need your help, and I need you to keep it between you and me."

"Are you in trouble?" he asked.

"No ... well, I'm confused."

"Talk to me, Son, and it stops here."

"You've told me that you're married and have two children. Is that right?"

"That's right. Good kids, too."

Then I quietly began to tell him the part of Mr. Hall's speech about keeping the bathroom clean.

He stopped me right in the middle. "Oh, I've heard about that speech several times. It's all over town. Now, P.J., trust me, and I really mean trust me; he's deceiving you. He's just trying to scare you boys so his job will be easier. There's not one ounce of truth in a boy's not being able to make a baby. And I should know. The story usually goes that if you stay too long you'll go blind. Some of my very best men friends tease me that I didn't lose my eyesight in the war, but really because I stayed in the boys' room too long." I was surprised when he said, "That's a smile of relief, isn't it, P.J.?"

"Yeah, it really is, and thanks. Remember, this is between you and me."

"I gotcha, P.J. Now go do your route. I'll see you next Friday."

Collection was easy. Mrs. Taylor, whose husband owned the Taylor Barber Shop just north of Sandefur's jewelry store on North Third, asked me to bring her an eight-ounce vanilla the next day. Mrs. Woodward's daughter had me fix her a fresh lemonade, and I drank the leftover. Tasted good on a warm September day. Mrs. Pope was ill, and when I knocked she asked me to come in and get my 15 cents. She also asked me to get her a glass of fresh water so she could take her medicine.

And Mrs. Lively had a man working in her yard transplanting

irises. She gave me some iris bulbs to give to Mom. Only one problem with that: I'd have to plant them. So I went down a back alley and threw them away.

After I got home, I was in a good mood and ready for Patsy's party in a couple of hours. After we'd cleaned up the supper dishes, Mom said she wanted to talk with me. "I'll meet you in the living room in a couple of minutes," she said.

I didn't know what to think, and I wondered if someone had told her I'd dumped the iris bulbs. Did she know about Mr. Hall's talk to us that day? Had someone seen me looking at *Sunshine and Health* magazines and told Mom on me? I knew when Mom called for a talk, it wasn't about how nice the weather was.

I was sitting on our big blue divan when she came in, and I could tell that she'd been crying. She sat next to me and took my hand in hers. I was terrified, expecting her to tell me that someone was going to die, or something.

"Son, your father and I have talked about our money situation for several days now. You know that the Mercury needs repairs, and Dad depends on it for just about everything he does to make money. He's had it checked out at Cason's Ford House, and they've told him a total overhaul would cost in the neighborhood of $380-$420. And they told him that if the war doesn't last forever, that the Mercury would run OK for another five years or so when overhauled."

"Mom, why are you telling me this? I know the Mercury needs repairs."

She continued, "Dad could borrow the money from the bank, but he'd have to pay it back monthly with interest. And his income is never steady. So we've decided to ask you to lend him $400. He'll pay it back, but not on a regular basis, just when he can afford to."

Another big hit—two in the same day.

She began to cry again.

"Mom, I'll be glad to. Please stop crying. I guess that's what money is for. But, why didn't Dad ask me?"

"He's just too proud to ask, I guess, Son."

"Well, when does he want it? Dad can take me to the bank Monday during lunchtime, and I could draw out $400."

"He won't need it quite that soon. It'll take several days for them to work on the car, and he'll tell you when to get the money. Thanks, Son. He'll repay you."

I went to Patsy's party that night, but I didn't enjoy myself. All my friends were dancing and laughing. Several girls tried to get me to dance, but once again, I told them it was against my religion to dance. No one made fun of that, but I could tell that they thought it was strange, just as I did.

Sleep wasn't easy that night. I figured $400 from $660 leaves $260. I'd been working so long to earn the $660. I was subbing, doing my own route, vanilla, errand running, worms, advertising circular delivery, milk delivery, even winning a few dimes on Dan's and my Ford-Chevy bet—to almost be rich by my own standards. And I just knew I'd never get totally repaid. I was angry and confused at Dad, yet proud of the fact that I had enough money to lend. It was almost as if I could make two really big fists the way I felt, one to hit at him and one to protect myself. I'd really had a double hit today, I thought. I went back to when Dad and I would listen on the radio to the Joe Louis fight. It always seemed he had his opponent just knocked punch drunk before he'd knock him out. And I was just punch drunk that night. Mr. Hall's speech didn't seem important anymore.

Dad didn't go to town Saturday morning for coffee. He even had toast and coffee with me while I ate my Wheaties. He was mostly quiet, as was I. The sound of my crunching the bits of Wheaties sounded especially loud. Finally, he broke the silence. "Mom talked to you last night, didn't she?"

"Yes, sir. And I'm really pleased I can lend you the $400. Just glad it's there in the bank. That old Mercury needs a good fixin', too."

"You know I'll pay you back," he quietly said, with his head held low.

"Sure do, Dad. You can pay me anytime, any amount, and I'll deposit it again in my account. Bet that Mercury will run good as new again. Maybe it'll be in good shape when I get to be sixteen, and I'll learn to drive it." I tried as much as I could to stay away from talk about the money for fear I'd cry like Mom had.

"Tommie has said she wants to buy a heater to put under the dash on the passenger side while it's being worked on. That'll keep us warm in the winter."

"Sounds good, Dad. How much does the heater cost installed?"

"It's around $49-$53. But that's top of the line. That's what Tommie wanted to buy," he responded.

"When do you want the $400?"

"I'll let you know. It may take a week for the mechanics to overhaul it."

He left to go to town. A thought kept running through my head, one that I'd learned at church about honoring your father and mother so that you'd live a long time, or something like that. I hoped I was doing that, even though it left a funny feeling in my stomach.

On Monday, when I delivered the *Democrat* to my three customers who were mechanics at Ed Cason's Ford House, I saw the maroon Mercury with its hood raised. The mechanic working on it was my customer, Mr. Gibson.

"Hey, Mr. Gibson, I see you've got a great machine there. Now you take good care of it for Dad, you hear?" And he laughingly replied, "This old jalopy will hum like new when I'm finished."

One of the vocabulary words Mr. Garrison had given me was *perseverance,* which I remembered meant something like continuing a course of action, sometimes in spite of difficulties.

I vowed to persevere. And I hoped that no more Friday double-hitters would come along for quite some time.

CHAPTER 18

What's Money, Anyway?

The Mercury came home running smoothly. We even tried out the new heater, even though the weather was still warm. The hum of the heater fan and the warm air it produced gave me a good feeling for Dad as he'd be selling vanilla and doing electrical work during cold weather.

I'd already deposited another $20, but the bill for the Mercury was $418.57, so I loaned Dad $420, leaving a balance of $220. But somehow, money in my bank account didn't seem as important as it used to. I liked it, but I liked Dad more, even if I was still angry with him. And it seemed as if in the last couple of weeks I had felt I was reaching young manhood. It was a strange feeling, and maybe it was partly about my voice changing, or something, but I really did feel good about myself and had partly gotten over being angry.

And I'd put my arithmetic pencil to college costs and figured that I could manage that, too. If worse came to worst, I could work for a year after high school, like Tommie was doing. And maybe I could even quit my paper route after the seventh grade and do other things.

I washed and polished the Mercury on an October Saturday while listening to an SMU football game on the car radio. SMU won. I thought that someday I'd like to play football for SMU. The Mercury, even though the maroon paint was fading, looked real spiffy with my wax job as I thought how I owned a part of it now.

On Monday, in our music class, we were singing the patriotic songs when all of a sudden Miss Swinney stopped us with a wave of her arms, and then she started laughing. "Class, I've been teaching music for several years, but this is my first year to be a seventh-grade teacher. I'm learning a lot about boys and their changing voices. So as we start singing again, boys, please sing a little softer so I won't hear you squeak so much."

I was embarrassed, and I thought several others were, too. The girls seemed to enjoy what Miss Swinney said. As we began to sing "Any Bonds Today," I just opened my mouth and pretended I was singing. I liked how I didn't sound.

I thought that seventh-grade teachers must have a lot of perseverance. Especially music teachers. Then I changed my thought to include all seventh-grade teachers.

School was tough, probably tougher than I'd ever known. Miss Ellison, our geography teacher, had an assignment that I had to draw a map of South America, locate on it all its countries, major cities, and major rivers, as well as represent its exports. I got it in on time, but it took a lot of effort for me to draw in everything she wanted.

Our English teacher, Miss Morton, made us learn in alphabetical order all the prepositions which were listed in our *Walsh Plain English Handbook*. Then we learned prepositions, phrases, objects of prepositions, nouns, pronouns, adjectives, and adverbs. And she gave us ten new words a day to learn to spell and define, with a daily test. One wrong was a B, two wrong a C, three wrong a D, and more than three an F. Besides being tough, she was what most of us called "mean." I learned not to smile while I was in her room, fearful that she'd think I was misbehaving.

The written problems in math were a catastrophe. They would be like, "If two men were in a row boat on a river rowing against the current which was twelve miles an hour, and each man rowed his oar twelve times a minute, how many strokes would each man have to row in order to go upstream for one mile?" Or at least when I read the math problems, they seemed like that. I could get them, but it took a long time for each problem. And Mrs. Vaughan gave us five problems for homework every day. Several of my friends called me at home or came by my table during study hall for me to help them with their math problems.

Mr. Burton, my health teacher, didn't seem very interested in health. His fat stomach sticking out below his belt told me he wasn't very healthy himself. He was weird. He told us stories that he'd laugh at, but we didn't think were funny. I learned to laugh at them. Then he'd say, "Good, Paul, you liked my story." And we had to memorize how many calories a carrot stick, medium-sized, had in it, and stuff like that. A really boring class, not healthy at all.

But reading class was super. Mrs. McKinnis was fun, hard, and ready to let us laugh and enjoy what we read. She was always asking us not to lip read or subvocalize, like hearing yourself say the word to yourself as you read.

I'd already learned not to lip read, and long ago I had given up pointing my finger at each word as I read or using a marker to move from line to line as I read. But I still subvocalized. That was new to me, and I think new to all of us. Several in our class still pointed at each word while reading. But I tried to learn to see the word and gain meaning without hearing myself say it.

Reading was fun. And our library time was good. I read several books about the military academies. One of which I especially liked was *Navy Blue and Gold*. It was not only about life at the academy, but it was also about their football team. I chose that book as my first of three book reviews for semester one, and I received good comments from Mrs. McKinnis, along with an A+. My second book was *A Plebe at West Point*, which I also liked and got an A+ for my review. The last period I had study hall. About the eighth week, along around the first of November, I stopped by Mr. Hall's office early before school began to ask him if, on Fridays, I could skip study hall because it took me so long to collect my route. He asked me in.

"Good to see you. Tell me your name, please."

"I'm Paul Johnson, but I go by P.J., Mr. Hall."

"I'll call you Paul, if that's all right with you."

"Yes, sir, that's fine."

"How can I help you, Paul?"

I told him about my route and collection and asked to skip last period study hall.

"Are you making good grades?"

"Yes, sir. My first six weeks' grades were A's with an A- in math."

"Have you always been a good student, Paul?"

"I've tried to be, sir."

"Are you Earleen Johnson's brother?"

"Yes, sir."

"She was the best student I've ever had in this school. If you live up to her standards, you'll do well, too."

"Thank you. My sister is very smart."

"Last period off on Fridays. Is that what you want?"

"Yes, sir."

"I'm going to give you a permanent permission to be excused from the last period so you can do your route early every day. That is, it'll be permanent as long as you keep all A's. Is that understood?"

"Yes, sir. And thank you, sir."

And with that permission, I found a new way to earn some more money. Skip hired me to prepare the *Democrat* for mailing to those subscribers outside of Durant. And I earned $4 more a week for that job.

The only different thing that had happened on my route was that a woman came to the door to pay me, and she didn't have a dress or slip on. Women customers had answered my door knock in all sorts of dress, but this was the first one with as few clothes. She gave me a dollar bill, and I thought I'd never find 85 cents in change. I thought that part of it was out of embarrassment, but the other part of my thought was I was staying as long as I could. She didn't seem to care. Growing up was causing new thoughts and feelings.

The *Democrat* continued to print lots of war stories. General Eisenhower, who'd been born in Denison, Texas, just eighteen miles south of Durant, continued to be in the news. General Ike said this, and General Ike did that. It seemed as if the Allies would gain four miles and lose three. And General MacArthur, the *Democrat* reported, was having some success in the Pacific area fighting the Japanese. Since our troops had recaptured Guadalcanal in the Solomon Islands last February, a marine and army force had just invaded the Gilbert Islands. Hundreds and hundreds of our men were being killed, but the war news seemed to me, a seventh-grader, like we were winning.

Miss Ellison helped us in our geography class to find many of the islands and countries where we were fighting. And then she would discuss with us the latitude and longitude of the various islands. On Fridays, she would give us a test by listing twenty-five latitude-longitude degrees and having us write the name of the island, country, or city. I enjoyed that type of test and usually got them all correct. The fun part was she just gave us ten minutes to finish, and I always was through before time was up. I liked working rapidly.

The men from Durant kept getting killed or wounded in battle. Mack's uncle had been injured twice. Two more gold stars showed up on North Fifth and North Sixth, but I didn't know the families.

Dad sat by the Atwater-Kent night after night listening to the war news while I studied. Sometimes I just had to stop for a while and think about the number of people who were being killed.

The news announcers would talk about the large number of Jews whom Hitler had put to death. It didn't make sense. How could one person become so deliberately cruel? I put that question into my "Will Figure Out Later" box of thoughts.

Linda was adjusting well to first grade, although she didn't seem to make friends very easily. But I was extremely shy at that age, too, and thought she'd get over it sooner than I did. Or maybe I hadn't yet.

Mom worked more at the church now that all of us were away from home during the day. She helped pack bags of Red Cross supplies, was president of the Women's Missionary Society, and did part-time secretarial work. It seemed as if she were happier doing that than doing more sweeping and dusting in our house than I thought was necessary.

Dad had paid me $10 of the $420 loan, but he told me it might be until January or February before he could make the next payment. He talked about Christmas expenses. Mr. Laymance worked him more often doing electrical work, but Dad never seemed very happy. And he'd increased smoking to three packs of Camels a day.

Tommy Alley had our bunch of friends over for a Christmas party. We drew names to give gifts, each boy getting a girl's name and vice versa. I drew Iris Ann Maxey's name. We'd known each other all our school years. She was nice, short, and not the type for me to think of as a sweetheart, but I liked her and bought her a nice book, which she seemed to enjoy as she unwrapped it at the party.

Phyllis Woodruff had drawn my name, and she gave me a book also—*Black Beauty*, which I liked. When the dancing began, Phyllis got my hand and pulled me toward the action. I resisted with every

· 194 ·

ounce of energy I had. I thought of the several times in the fourth, fifth, and sixth grades when the whole class would go to the rhythm room and do various group dances, like "Put your right foot in and take your right foot out ...," and I'd remain alone back in the classroom because Mom told me that was dancing. I had hurt a lot during those hours.

And now Phyllis' tug and my pulling back were clashing. Finally, Phyllis let go and left me alone. But I didn't want her to. I wanted the courage to try, but I didn't yet have it.

We read Dickens' *Christmas Carol* in Mrs. McKinnis' class. There were parts of it that caused me to look at my family. Scrooge seemed so mean and unhappy since he was so selfish and controlled by work and money. It seemed as if the story helped me become less a Scrooge, or at least I wanted to enjoy spending a little more of my money to have more fun, but I knew I hadn't been like Scrooge in some way because my loan seemed to help Dad, whom I compared in some small ways to Bob Cratchit.

The story continued to be on my mind during the Christmas holidays of 1943, when I got only a few clothes. Since the basketball that Dad had given me a few Christmases ago was about worn out, I had wanted a new one. Coach Bloomer Sullivan at Southeastern, where I had watched a zillion games, bounced an old leather basketball toward me on Sunday when I'd sneaked into his gym to play. I was stunned to see him inside the gym on a Sunday, but he was smiling when he said, "You're Earl's boy, aren't you?"

"Yes, sir," I replied, just knowing that he'd call Dad and tell him I'd sneaked into his gym.

"You need a basketball, Johnson?" he asked, as I held the one he'd bounced to me in my hands.

"Yes, sir, I really do. This old rubber one of mine is worn out."

"Take that one home with you. Consider it my Christmas present to you," he said. And he didn't even know me, or at least I thought, and as I biked home I thought about how I'd received two great gifts from Southeastern Coach Laird and Southeastern Coach Sullivan. I vowed I'd consider being a college coach someday.

I wrapped the basketball in Christmas paper and put it under our tree. On Christmas morning, I unwrapped it and explained how I'd gotten it. Dad seemed pleased and embarrassed, but my pleasure in getting this ball seemed to outweigh his embarrassment. Tommie had spent quite a bit of money for presents, which everyone seemed to enjoy.

And the new year of 1944 began. I deposited another $20 to make my savings become $300. Dad had paid me $5 in early January, so he now owed me $405. The Mercury ran well, and the car heater kept us warm on the cold January days. Tommie's gift of the heater was just perfect for Dad.

My 7B classes began. Health class was over, and I had Mr. Burton's industrial arts class. And Miss Ellison's geography class changed to U.S. history. Other classes remained with the same subject. I was pleased that I continued with all A's and still hadn't missed a day of school since the second grade.

I don't know whether it was Mr. Burton or the subject of industrial arts, but I liked neither. A tool in my hands just didn't fit. I'd turn a nut on a bolt the wrong way, or I'd hit my finger with the hammer, or I'd saw off line. Then Mr. Burton would make fun of me in front of the whole class. After class, my friends would talk to me about how they didn't like how Mr. Burton treated me. By the second week, I vowed that I'd never get a full-time job that required me to saw, measure, glue, hammer, or use tools to build or repair. That just wasn't something I did well or that I liked to do.

Miss Ellison's U.S. history was fun. She made it so real and understandable. One class period Gwyn couldn't come up with the name of the U.S. president when Oklahoma became a state, so Miss Ellison took time out to teach us a way to remember all the presidents.

"OK, you all know the song 'Yankee Doodle Dandy.' We'll use the tune to sing about the presidents."

And she began, "George Washington, the choice of all, by Adams was succeeded. Then came Thomas Jefferson, who bought the land we needed..." Finally she came to Theodore Roosevelt, whom I knew so much about from reading the books Mr. Laird had given me, and she told Gwyn that President Roosevelt was in office from 1904-1908, when Oklahoma became the forty-sixth state in 1907.

School continued to be difficult. Life just seemed to be school, homework, paper business, war news, church, and some social life. And social life was becoming more important. Nick and Barbara Ann had broken up, and Barbara Ann started being nice to me. In her mother's reading class, she'd hand me nice notes. Mrs. McKinnis would see her pass the notes but wouldn't stop her. I was too scared to hand my note back to her during class, but I would give it to her in the hallway. Barbara Ann held my hand one day, and I liked it, but I pulled away.

Some things I'd never even seen or heard about began appearing on the playground. Attaway brought little sex books which used cartoon characters doing sexual things that he showed around. We'd hide behind the trees next to the playground to look, and I just had to look. I guess I was learning, but I was scared that God would punish me. Parties, dancing, hand holding, little cartoon books, perhaps not being able to have children, customers coming to the door without many clothes on, kissing—all seemed to be on my mind a lot more than earning money, delivering, church, or news about the war.

At the end of seventh grade, I spent the summer mowing lawns, delivering papers, and preparing the *Democrat* for mailing. In August 1944, I had $540 in my bank account. Dad had paid a total of $105 on his loan.

I wondered why I needed so much money. I thought that I was really ready to do other things. So I told Skip that I'd quit my route August 20. He was disappointed, but he understood. He got Bob to take my route. I'd already told my customers that I was quitting.

And on my last collection day, my customers did all kinds of nice things to me. I got $15 in tips, several "best wishes" cards, and hugs. Miss Woodward even cried. I hugged her. Mr. Long shocked me by giving me a $1 tip and buying me the best root beer in town.

As I rode my bike home that August afternoon, I thanked my $7 *Adventurer* for holding up for those hundreds—perhaps several thousand—miles it'd taken me. I'd been hit by only two cars with no serious injuries. Mom and Dad didn't know about the accidents. It had been an adventure, but now I was ready for a new one—or so I thought.

CHAPTER 19
The Route Continues

I began walking the four blocks to school the fall of '44. Eighth graders seemed to leave their bikes at home for some reason. I guess my thoughts were already about driving. Dad would even let me drive a bit when we were on a country road or somewhere else where there wasn't any traffic. But letting the clutch out smoothly and shifting the S-shaped gear stick weren't easy, especially when I got nervous trying to learn.

Tommie had left for Bethany-Peniel College, and two long distance phone calls made by Mom had convinced her that Tommie was OK. Dad cautioned about long distance phone calls, saying a three-cent stamp was cheaper.

My classes and teachers seemed great. Math with Miss Casada, English with Miss Harrison (who had lived on my route), Oklahoma history with Miss Willis, and choir with Miss Swinney, plus two library study halls—one of which was last period—made for an easier schedule than seventh grade. I hoped I'd never have as tough a year as I had in the seventh.

After school I began to hang around to watch the high school football team practice, thinking that it wouldn't be too long before I'd be playing on Friday nights at Paul Laird Field. The football equipment manager had even allowed me to help him some, so I was feeling important.

The second Thursday of school, Miss Casada told me that the

principal's office had a phone call for me. When I got to the office, the secretary handed me the phone.

"Hello, this is Paul," I said, not knowing who to expect to be on the other end.

"P.J., hi. This is Skip. I need you to do me a big favor. Bob, the boy who took over your route, has suddenly quit, and you're the only one who knows it. Will you come back for a few days or weeks until you can teach someone else?"

Not too pleased to do it, but pleased that I was needed, I agreed.

After lunch, I got my paper bag and rode my bike back to school and headed for the *Democrat* after the last bell rang.

Skip was waiting for me. "P.J., thanks for helping me. Now something else has come up. Mack just told me he wanted to quit his route. You know, it's the route that starts westward at Fifteenth and Main just where yours loops back eastward. Mack has only thirty-five customers. If you'll agree to deliver yours through at least August of '45, I'll give you his route, too. That'd give you about 125 total customers and close to $9 profit per week. And if you can get your last period off as you did last year, you can go back to your job at the mail prep room. What do you think?"

I thought it was a good offer, and I agreed. Mack waited for me at the first of his route and showed me the houses to throw. He explained that Mrs. Archibald didn't ever pay because her husband had been a part owner of the *Democrat* before he died. Mack said he would go with me Friday to collect.

So what I thought would be an opportunity to sleep later Sunday mornings stopped before it started. Mr. Hall excused me from last period study hall. Again, he said it would continue only if I made all A's. The route extension worked out well except that I had to ride to far West Main past Foote Nursery into an area called Toonerville. This was just a group of houses located on the western edge of town on Highway 70. It added about a mile to my bike ride. On the new route I had, among other customers, Mr. Shaw, who owned a shoe store downtown; Mr. Hewett, whose son Jack was Tommie's debate partner; Mrs. Archibald; Dr. Colwick, an M.D.; the Footes of the Foote Nursery; Mr. Ben Siegel, whose store I was told not to go into; Mr. Cason, who owned the Ford-Mercury Agency; Mr. Leonard, who owned Leonard's Floral; Mr. Miller, an electrician; my friend, Jerry Lou Winchester; and Mrs. Smith, who had a small family grocery on South Sixteenth. Her son, Billy Wayne, and I were the same age and good friends. Also I had Mr. Taylor, the county sheriff, so I got to collect in the sheriff's office in the courthouse on Fridays.

I thought about the opportunity I now had to go into Siegel's store every Friday to collect. I told Dad about it, but he made no comment.

I was embarrassed when I collected for the first time on my old route. Remembering who had tipped me and given me cards and presents wasn't difficult to do, but knowing how to ask them if I could return the tip or gift was awkward. But I tried.

Skip had told me that they would just say to forget it and that they'd say they were glad I'd returned. And most did, except for Mr. Long. When I told him that I'd returned and reminded him that he'd tipped me a dollar that I wanted to give back, he said he'd just expect six weeks of free delivery. I agreed. Leaving his store, I figured that six weeks at 15 cents was 90 cents, so at least he'd tipped me a dime. What a man!

My friends at school seemed OK with me for taking back my route because I'd been worried about what they'd think. I envied Mack every Sunday morning when I was delivering my route and his old one while I knew he was sleeping. Nick had quit his route, too. Attaway still delivered, and he was still leader of our class, so I thought that if he could, it'd be all right for me to continue also.

Attaway pulled a funny one at the *Democrat* the next week. We were all folding when a man stopped to buy a paper from me. Gladly, I handed him one and said that would be 5 cents. He took out his billfold and handed me a $100 bill, something I'd never seen.

"Sir, I can't make change for that." I was ready to take my paper back.

Attaway, sitting nearby folding, said, "Mister, I'll sell you a paper."

The man grinned, walked over to the leader of the eighth-grade class, and said, "What makes you think you can sell me a 5-cent paper?"

And shocking us all, Attaway reached into his billfold, took out four twenties, one ten, one five, and four ones. Then he reached into his pocket and got three quarters and two dimes and, taking the $100 bill from the man's hand, counted out the exact change.

There was deadly silence from all of us as we stopped folding to watch the event. The man grinned, tipped Attaway a dime, took his *Democrat*, and left.

We cheered, "That away, Attaway!" which was our favorite way to compliment him. I guess I learned why he was a leader.

That Friday all went well, collecting until South Seventeenth Street. When I parked my bike, I could hear laughter inside the house, and as I got closer I could see two women inside. One was my customer, whose husband was away in the war. She was in a full slip standing by an ironing board doing her ironing. I could see several beer bottles on the floor, and I was a little scared, but I asked to collect. Then I saw the other woman. She, too, was in her slip, but she had her leg propped over the arm of a stuffed chair. I could easily see her underwear.

My customer, who seemed to be drunk, told me that her friend had the 15 cents, and I could come in and get it.

I said I'd collect next week and turned to leave. She said to just open the screen door and get the 15 cents.

Reluctantly, I did. And when I put my hand out to get the 15 cents, her friend grabbed my hand and put it where it shouldn't have been. I had all kinds of scared feelings, so I pulled loose and left. The rest of that day and night my thoughts were about that event. I didn't tell anyone because I was too scared to. But I knew that part of me liked what happened.

The next week my customer apologized and blamed it on too much beer.

I'd make another $20 deposit, even after I'd spent money on fall school clothes and school books. I also paid for Linda's books when I bought mine. Hers cost only $5.50. That gave me $560 in the bank. Dad wasn't repaying me, almost like he'd forgotten he even owed me. But that was mostly all right. He'd sold the two downtown buildings to Mr. Casmedes, the owner of the White House Café. Dad said that the buildings were going to have to be renovated, and he didn't have the money to pay to fix them up, so he just sold. I thought I'd get repaid with some of the money from the sale, but I didn't.

Since D-Day last June 6, our troops had done well, the *Democrat* reported. Paris had been retaken by the Allied forces last month on August 25. But the Germans had begun using flying robot bombs which hit and killed thousands of English civilians and caused a lot of damage. We carriers talked a lot about these V-bombs, as they were called, and wondered if they could travel as far as from Germany to the U.S. I asked Mr. Snow what he thought, and he told me that the only way they could hit us would be if somehow the V-bombs could be shot from a surfaced sub. He reassured me that the chances of that happening were slim. I trusted what he said.

My cousin, Ralph Tate, had been injured going north into Italy, but he seemed to be recovering. We drove to Tishomingo to visit Ralph's parents, my Uncle Cliff and Aunt Suzy. They were glad, as was I, that he'd be OK, even though they wondered whether he'd ever be able to run hurdles for the Oklahoma A&M track team again.

The *Democrat*'s war news was encouraging. Some of my customers talked about the war ending soon, but I wasn't too sure. When I saw Mrs. Lively that day, I told her that if all the scrap metal we kids had collected were made into bombs and dropped on Hitler that my improper prayer would be answered.

"Improper prayer? What do you mean by that?" she inquired.

I explained, "Some time back my mother heard my prayer when I asked God to cause Hitler to die. She stopped me and told me that my prayer was an improper one. That's what I meant by improper, Mrs. Lively."

"Well, Mr. Johnson, you tell your mother that Mrs. Lively, who has lived a lot longer than she, knows proper prayers and improper prayers. I hope your improper prayer is answered. I think it is a proper request to God. By the way, did you sign your name on any of the scrap metal you collected?" she asked.

"Yes, as the *Democrat* encouraged, I did. You remember back in June when the paper printed the statements about autographing a bomb to be delivered to Hitler? I didn't autograph a bomb, but I did put my name on several large pieces of scrap metal. Maybe they became a bomb."

"I hope your metal goes straight down Hitler's throat and that your name is stamped right in his heart."

"Yes, ma'am, that'd be OK with me," I said, quite surprised that she used such expressions. "I'll pray another improper prayer tonight and tell God you told me to say it," I added with a big laugh.

Mrs. Lively, never livelier in my years of knowing her, waved her cane at the sky and said, "God, you listen to Mr. Johnson. He's a wise one."

She seemed to me to be the wise one. I liked the older woman, even though she always slowed me down by talking to me and getting me to do chores for her.

The Durant High School Lions were to play the Sherman Bearkats in football on Friday night in Sherman, Texas. George invited me to drive with his parents to see the game. We had dinner in a café, and that was unusual for me. I ordered, as Mom instructed me to do, whatever George ordered. He had chicken fried steak, so I did, too. It was not as good as Mom prepared.

Settling in at the game, I was interested to see how the Lions would hold up against the Texas team. It didn't take long to find out. The end of the first quarter we were down 34-0. At the end of the game, the score was 84-0. And the Bearkats even had their center playing running back, trying to hold down the score.

The Sunday *Democrat*'s story quoted the first-year Durant coach, Lynn "Bull" Marsh: "It was a tough loss. I hope I'm here long enough to avenge this. Sherman will hear from the Lions in the future." After seeing the game, I thought it would be best to never, never, never schedule them again. I didn't like to lose—never had.

A few weeks later, I invited George to ride the Frisco train with me to Madill, where Dad would meet us as he finished a vanilla run. Then we'd go to the Madill vs. Durant game. I told George that Dad would buy us dinner. As George and I were on the train, we crossed the brand new railroad bridge across the newly forming Lake Texoma.

We could begin to see how large Lake Texoma would be. The *Democrat* had stories that the total shoreline of the lake would be about 1,200 miles, as Dad had told me on our family picnic. George and I laughed about how glad we were we'd never have to walk around our new lake.

Since the train ride took just thirty minutes, in no time we were in Madill, where Dad met us at the station. We found a drive-in café, where Dad bought us hamburgers and Cokes. He said he'd had good vanilla sales that day. Then we found our way to the Wildcats' football stadium.

We beat Madill 13-0. Football, I thought, is a good sport, and I hoped I'd be a good player in high school. I liked Coach Marsh.

The week after the Madill game, the *Democrat* had a story about Sherman playing an ineligible player and forfeiting the game to

Durant. All of us carriers laughed about turning a 84-0 loss into a 1-0 win. Attaway said that you never can count the Lions out of any game, and we all responded, almost in unison, "That away, Attaway!" But the men at the Plaza Barber Shop who were the Saturday morning quarterbacks said we couldn't turn a 84-0 loss into a 1-0 win. They weren't very impressed by the Lion team.

My Cardinals lost the World Series to the Yankees. But I knew we'd win next year.

Church continued. And I was always there. Dan and I quit our Ford-Chevy game because there might not be enough cars that passed by our window to complete a bet. Gas rationing stopped our game. But Dan, in his creative way, began to fill in time by designing airplanes on paper he'd bring. I sat and watched his skillful left hand as he meticulously drew them as they appeared in his mind. *Meticulous* is a word I learned in Miss Harrison's English class. Dan challenged me to another bet, and he said there wasn't any way to know who would win.

"What kind of bet can that be?" I asked.

In his way of knowing, he replied, "P.J., you know about when a preacher is asked by another church to come and be their preacher, don't you?"

"Sure, that happens lots of times."

"And you know he always says that he has to pray and seek God's hand to lead him, don't you?"

"Yeah, but what's the bet?" I asked.

"I betcha that God's hand leads the preacher to the new church only when there's a bigger salary, a better parsonage, or some kind of better working condition that meets his needs. You want to bet?"

"Well, I can see where we'd never settle that one, but you have a point. Where in the world do you dream up this kind of stuff, Dan?"

He remained silent.

Then I asked, "Dan, do you think that preachers ever lie? I've heard Brother White tell us so many stories that just can't be true."

Dan grinned as he said, "That's what my mother calls 'speaking ministerially.'"

When we got in the Mercury after church, I asked Mom about "speaking ministerially" and if she thought that was different from not telling the truth.

She responded, "Son, men use hyperbole, so I rarely consider men's talk as literal truth."

When we got home, I had to get my dictionary to find the definition of *hyperbole*. I liked the definition: "exaggeration for effect, not meant to be taken literally." Maybe I'd be better able to understand men's talk.

Miss Harrison was the most demanding teacher I'd ever had. She was the word cop. Drill, drill, drill. "You must not ever misuse *may* and *can*," she'd say. "Now, Margaret Rose, you use them correctly."

And Rosie said, "May I please close my book?"

Miss Harrison smiled.

Then Rosie said, "I can close my book when I'm finished."

Miss Harrison smiled and asked Phyllis to use *good* and *well* correctly.

And Phyllis responded, "I am well today."

And Miss Harrison smiled.

"I did a good deed when I helped in the scrap collection."

And Miss Harrison smiled.

"Now, Mack, use the subjunctive correctly. Don't confuse *were* and *was*. Think before you answer."

And Mack, after some thought, said, "I wish I was going to the football game."

And Miss Harrison frowned. Pointing her finger at Mack, she explained again why *were* should be used in the subjunctive mood. Then she made him say his sentence again, using the correct *were*.

Drill, drill, drill—that was Miss Harrison. Next she said we'd learn to diagram sentences. We learned slowly, but I learned the system and found it easy—at least much easier than math or industrial arts. Miss Harrison nearly always came to the door to pay me when I collected on Fridays. And she was nice to tell me that I was as smart as my sister Earleen. That was a real compliment. I was really learning a lot in her class. She'd even written a nice compliment on one of my assignments that meant a lot to me.

Miss Harrison said that I had exceptional ability to comprehend and retain information, even going so far as to write that it was a special God-given gift. It was nice to read, but I never had thought of my ability to memorize poems, prepositions, all forty-eight states and their capitals, the presidents of the U.S. in order, the seventy-seven counties in Oklahoma, my customers' names and whether they'd paid (without keeping my route book), or other stuff like that as a gift. I thought that anyone could do it if they worked at it. Maybe I'd learned to keep that stuff in my head because I'd worked to memorize all my Cardinals' batting averages and other important baseball statistics. But she'd said it was a gift. Maybe if it were true, it was the same gift Earleen had, because she really had a BIG gift!

I felt especially good all the rest of the day about what Miss Harrison had written. I grinned when I thought about how my fourth-grade art teacher, Miss Wheat, had told me my picture wasn't any good. Now Miss Harrison had written that I had a God-given gift. I vowed that I'd use my gift as a way to give back something to God. I just wasn't sure what that would be.

James Davis checked out a book from the school library to read for his book report for Miss Harrison. A word he found in the book caused us all to squirm and be embarrassed. Miss Harrison took the book, lectured us all for twenty minutes on the "devil's language," and threw the book into her waste basket after tearing out the page with the word on it and then tearing it into tiny pieces. We decided that she didn't like vulgar words like some of us did.

Miss Willis' Oklahoma history class was interesting. We studied about the five civilized tribes. Those were the Cherokee, Choctaw, Creek, Chickasaw, and Seminole. It was fun to study about the Chickasaw because my Grandmother Tate was one-eighth—or something like that—Chickasaw.

The Cherokee and the Trail of Tears caused me to wonder if something like that could ever happen again. We discussed that issue, and I argued that it could, especially if we lost the war. My classmates argued against me, which was not unusual.

Miss Willis asked, "How many of you had at least one parent who was born in Indian Territory?"

Out of twenty-four in class, fourteen held up hands.

"And how many of you had both parents born in Indian Territory? Now, remember, before you answer, that Oklahoma became the forty-sixth state in 1907. Now, raise your hand if both parents were born in Indian Territory." There were six of us who raised our hands.

We studied about the "land rush" in 1889 and learned that

Guthrie became the capital overnight and remained the capital until the State Seal was stolen from Guthrie and taken to Oklahoma City.

Oklahoma was my state, and I loved it. Its history made it clear to me why it was such a great place to live, in spite of the dust bowl years in the panhandle, the poverty of a lot of its people, its tornadoes, and the way certain groups of people were treated.

Miss Casady was great, but math, once again, hit me like a brick. I had Bs on my test and was panicked that I'd make my first B ever. And then she increased the number of tests, and it seemed as if the problems were easier. My six-weeks grade was an A. She saw me in the hall and told me that she'd given more tests so I could improve my grade.

"Thanks, Miss Casady, but please don't tell the rest of the class. They'll kill me."

"I know, Paul. This is between you and me. Arrange time during study hall so you can let me help you."

And I did. Math was tough.

I deposited another $20 on November 2. That gave me $580. Still no repayment from Dad, and he never mentioned the subject.

It was election time. FDR vs. Dewey. Dad had complained bitterly about FDR's New Deal and said that he'd vote for Dewey. And Dad was against FDR's fourth term, as he said he'd also been against his third term.

"Dad, you do REA work that President Roosevelt signed into law. Isn't that reason enough to vote for him?"

"No, that's history. FDR is too tied in with foreign people. That's not good for us."

"Are you an isolationist?" I asked, trying to impress him with a new school word.

"I guess I am, in some ways. We should never have gotten into this war."

Not knowing whether to be quiet or to argue with him, I said, "We better not change horses in the middle of the war."

"Stream," he said, correcting me.

"I know it's *stream*, but I mean *war*. We're about to win, so let's keep him in office."

"You think what you want to, but you can't vote, and I'm voting for Dewey."

"I'll bet Mom votes for President Roosevelt."

"Only if she wants to walk to the voting poll. I'll keep the car gone all day."

Election day was the only time I ever pumped Mom on my bike. She was scared to death, but she said it was worth it to cancel Dad's vote.

I vowed that day that I'd always vote for Democrats.

Mom fixed a big butterscotch pie and teasingly wouldn't let Dad have any of it because he'd voted for Dewey. I got two large, delicious pieces. It went down well and continued to taste even better after FDR won again.

On my route extension, I'd counted five houses that had banners with one blue star and one with two blue stars. And when I collected, I asked about their servicemen. The mothers or wives seemed to appreciate it and would tell me more than I really wanted to know because I needed to move along. But I listened to their stories and concerns.

Christmas season once again. We were all thinking more about the war than gifts. More Allied victories were happening, but the *Democrat* reported, almost daily, our men being killed. Generals Eisenhower, MacArthur, and Patton were in the news quite a bit. Occasionally, I'd get a V-mail from my cousin, Erten, who was on a ship someplace in the Pacific. He couldn't write very well, and his spelling was poor, but I always enjoyed getting a letter from a real war-involved navy man. I'd always write him a letter.

Our Christmas was traditional. Tommie was home from college and seemed to hold the center of attention. For the first time ever, I was really glad to see her. She seemed to treat me nicely for a change, even volunteering to do some of my chores. I didn't know what she was learning at college, but whatever it was, I liked it.

She had become a member of the college debate team, and she and her debating partner, Deward Finch, the college president's son, were undefeated in four debates. I liked that. I liked competition.

Gifts were clothes, for the most part. I gave Tommie a nice decorative pillow for her bed at college.

Tommie had gotten a part-time job in the state capitol building working as a secretary. She'd get out of classes at noon, eat lunch, catch a bus to the capitol, which was a thirty-minute ride, and work until 6:00 P.M., getting back to college about 6:45. The college had a silly rule—at least I thought it was silly—that dorm room lights had to be out at 11:00 P.M. on school nights, so Dad had installed a light in Tommie's closet so she could study after 11:00 in her closet. She said that was working out fine, except that she frequently would fall asleep there. I laughed at the thought of someone asleep in a closet.

While I'd saved $40 more, I'd spent $20 for Christmas presents. But I deposited $20 and had an even $600 by January 10. I'd convinced myself that Dad would never pay me any more on his loan, and I had tried to convince myself that it was OK. We got along great.

I'd gotten all A's first semester, thanks to Miss Casady's help. No one ever knew what she'd done to help me. I just knew that Miss Casady's red hair had something to do with her need to help me. And she was a Methodist, too. Something about that combination was working for me. Miss Harrison had given only three A's in English—to Jeanne Paul, Billie Jean Parrish, and to me. I learned so much from her. Choir was an easy A, but it couldn't have been based on my ability to sing. And Oklahoma history was a good A. Perfect attendance continued. I also had never missed a single day of route delivery either. Dad had helped me when I was on crutches from my dog bite, but I went along in the car with him.

We had two snows in February. Quite unusual, but we did. Snowmen appeared on the school grounds, and snowball throwing was fun, except for a dumb thing I did. Mrs. Atkison, a woman who lived just across the street from our school, was a frequent substitute teacher. At noon one day, while we were throwing snowballs, she was coming back from her lunch at home. The guys started throwing, but none hit. She was laughing and in the spirit of it all when one I threw hit her directly in the eye.

Panic hit. My friends hollered, "Run," and they did. I just stood there for a second looking at her. She'd fallen to her knees, and her purse was on the ground. Some kind of voice inside me told me to go help her, which I did. In a few seconds she recovered, and I walked with her into the building to the principal's office. My heart was in my throat. *Would she be all right?* I wanted to know from the principal. She was, and I was greatly relieved.

But she was substituting for Miss Harrison that day, and my English class was just after lunch, so she asked me to answer every question and diagram sentences on the board. She told the class why she was doing it. The skin under her eye was already turning black and blue. I wasn't feeling very good. After school I went to my customer's business, Leonard Floral, and bought a $3 bouquet and wrote an apology on a card and asked Mrs. Leonard to deliver them to Mrs. Atkison.

Mr. Leonard asked me what I'd done to need to buy her flowers, and I told him.

"Well," he said, "she was my sweetheart once in high school, and I'd like to have hit her too after she ditched me. Tell you what I'm going to do. No charge for these flowers. They're on me," he said with a big grin as he chomped down on an unlit cigar.

I don't know what all I learned that day, but one thing was for sure: *Don't throw snowballs at teachers.*

While selling a bottle of vanilla to Mrs. Garrison in February, I got to visit with Mr. Garrison. He asked, "How is junior high? Let's see now... you're an eighth-grader, aren't you?"

"Yes, sir, 8B. In a few more months, I'll be a ninth-grader," I said boastfully.

"You're still making all A's?" he asked.

"Yes, sir. Math is difficult, but English, history, and choir are good subjects. Miss Harrison is one of the best teachers I've ever had."

"I've heard she's good, yet difficult, but you'll learn from her. And, by the way, you remember several years ago when you wanted more men teachers, don't you?"

"Yes, sir, and I still haven't had any like I'd want. You want to come teach me?" I asked kiddingly, yet half seriously.

"Probably be better than being a principal. But what I want you to know is that your ninth-grade science teacher will be Mr. J. M. O'Neal. And he's the great teacher you've been looking forward to. Not only is he a top-notch teacher, but he also likes to encourage his students to become scientists, and he has a great sense of humor in his classes. You'll like him a lot."

"I've heard good things about him from several of my ninth-grade friends. I'm looking forward to being his student." I smiled as I thought both about being a ninth-grader and finally having a good teacher who is a man.

I inquired of Mr. Garrison, "Are you enjoying your year?"

"Yes, it's fine. My wife and I are considering returning to graduate school at OU, where I'd like to complete a doctorate in higher education administration. The more I think about it, the more I'd like to become a president of a college or university."

"Ooh, don't leave Durant, Mr. Garrison. Washington Irving wouldn't be the same without you."

"Thanks, P.J., but I want new challenges."

"Well, if you become a college president, I'll consider being a student at your college."

"I thought you were going to Bethany-Peniel."

"Probably will. Just hope the preachers are better around the college than they are here. I'm tired of church."

With that I left, feeling good for having had him as my principal for five years.

By March I'd deposited $40 more and had $640. Soon the grass and weeds would be green, and I could earn more. My lawn mower was fine but no longer great. I hoped the war would soon be over so I could get not only a new mower, but also lots of things we'd gone without, especially chewing gum. A guy without Double Bubble just isn't complete, I had thought many times. Some kind of gum named Orbit was on the shelves, but chewing it wasn't too good. All of us kids tried to like it. I'd buy mine at Mrs. Smith's grocery store on my route. She also liked it when I'd take time to buy a Coke and peanuts. She'd grin when I'd open my box of peanuts, and there would be a nickel or a dime inside. That was the way the peanut company would try to get me to buy its peanuts. It worked. And then those redskin peanuts went into my Coke, and I had a real treat. Mrs. Smith was interesting to talk with. She always talked about her son and my friend, Billy Wayne. I could tell she was really proud of him.

I had become friends with most of my new customers, and I was glad I'd decided to keep my route for another year.

My neighborhood was changing for the better because kids around my age were moving in. Dwain Hiberd, Marlene and Barbara Howard, Robert Glafcke, and Billy and Buddy Tomme had all moved within a block of my house. Dwain sometimes went with me to deliver my route. Glafcke began to help me enjoy popular music. Marlene was good to me, even though she liked Nick and Glafcke more. Buddy and I got along well. He seemed to like Rosie Newman a lot. And I was glad my personal route was improving a bit, too.

CHAPTER 20
Understanding Dad

On Saturday, March 24, Dad asked me to ride around with him in the Mercury for a while.

"What's up, Dad?"

"I just want to ride and talk a bit. Can you spare me some time?"

"Sure, let's go."

So we were back into the old reliable Mercury, where we'd spent many, many hours together, so many that it seemed like it was our second home. We just drove around a while, and Dad didn't seem to have much to talk bout. Finally, he turned west onto Main Street and parked in front of the Durant National Bank.

"Where're we going, Dad?"

"Let's just sit here and talk," he said with a tone of voice that seemed serious.

I didn't know what to think, so I decided it'd be best to be quiet and listen.

"Son, in another month you'll be fourteen. Do you remember several years ago when you and I drove around and I showed you the Johnsons' property and I told you what your mother and I planned to do about building our house?"

"Sure do, Dad, just like it was yesterday. And you told me you wanted me to get jobs, make money, and not rely on your money."

"And you've done a great job by helping me out. And especially when you loaned me the money to have this Mercury overhauled. I know I haven't repaid all of my loan, and it's continually on my mind to do it, but one expense seems to follow another, and I can't get enough money ahead to pay you," he quietly said as he looked out the car window away from me.

"Dad, that's OK. I guess I'm just happy that the money was there. You don't have to pay me back another dime. I have plenty of money."

"Thanks, Son. I guess it's tough on me knowing that I've never been very successful making money, but our family has never wanted for anything. We've gotten by well, lived in a nice house, had a car, and have always dressed OK. And I'm so very proud of you three kids. I guess that you kids make my life successful, even if I don't have much money."

"Dad, money has always been something that concerns you more than it does anyone else in the family—well, maybe I am concerned about my money—but I have made enough. And after I quit my route, I'll probably get a Saturday job at a grocery store or find work that I can do that fits my school and football schedule. And Tommie is paying her way through college. So quit worrying so much about money, Dad."

"That's easy to say, but hard to do, Son. I've thought about it for so long that it's just always there. I think you're old enough now to try to understand a little bit more about why I'm so concerned—and maybe unsuccessful. So bear with me and try to understand me. Are you ready for my personal history lesson?"

"I guess so, Dad," I said, not knowing what to expect.

"I've really had some tough times in my life with what I call tragedies. Maybe they wouldn't be tragedies to others, but to me they've just knocked the wind out of my sails. There have been so many deaths of Johnsons that it keeps me blue quite a bit of the time. My mother and father's first child, a girl named Willie Lee, was born in 1878 and died seven weeks later. Of course, I wasn't born yet, but my mother always told sad stories about her death. And my brother Chester died in 1905, when he was twenty-four, and I was six. Dad died in 1912, when I was thirteen. Next, my brother Barney died in 1915, when I was sixteen, and then Weaver in 1927, when I was twenty-eight. Those were tough losses for me. And then I married the woman in Oklahoma City and our baby died shortly after being born. Soon after that we got divorced. In

1922, your mother and I got married, and Billy Lee, your brother, was born in 1924, but he just lived for a little over a month. Then my mother died in 1938. You remember that, don't you?"

"Yes, sir, she was a fine granny to me."

"And then I helped your mom with her sadness about the death of her two parents. So it's been a tough time for me. Since I didn't finish high school, I've always thought others might look down on me a bit. So I guess I'm trying to tell you that I've had a lot of bad luck in my life, even if you don't believe in luck."

He continued, "And to make things worse, the great depression wiped out nearly all the Johnson wealth. You remember I showed you the worthless stock certificates, don't you?"

"Yes, I remember them, even though I haven't thought about that in a long time."

"So I ask you to try to understand me a little bit more. I try as best I can, but good money and I just don't seem to ever get together."

I sat there on the front seat of the Mercury, fiddling with the frayed seat cover, just wondering what to say to Dad. I noticed that for the second time in my life I was seeing tears roll down his cheeks. Maybe there was luck, and his was bad, but I still didn't want to believe in luck.

Gathering my courage, I said, "Dad, thanks for telling me your history. I guess I just didn't ever think about all those tragedies the way you've told me about them. I know how changed Mrs. Gooding has been since Bruce was killed in the war. And I remember being so sad when my dog died. Maybe that helps me understand how you, too, could have changed. But I want you to know that you're a great dad, and I wouldn't trade you for any other dad in the whole world."

"Even for a millionaire dad?" he joked.

"Well you've got me between a rock and a hard place," I teased back.

And with that, things got easier between us while we sat. But he had more to tell me.

"I'd like to strike a deal with you. Since you say you now have plenty of money, I'll agree to let you drive the Mercury quite a bit when you get sixteen and get your driver's license in place of my repaying the loan to you. And I'll buy the gasoline as long as you stay behaved in the car. If anyone, and I mean anyone, ever tells me that you're abusing the car or disobeying the law of the road, you and the car will forever be through with each other. Understand?"

"Yes, sir, and I promise I won't be reckless."

"Then it's a deal, is it?"

"How much do I get the car, Dad?" trying to bargain a bit more.

"We'll determine that later. But you'll be able to drive around town and drag Main Street and show off to the girls," he said with a big laugh.

"Oh, Dad, leave girls out of this," I said, knowing I was blushing once again.

"Oh, there'll come a time when you'll find them pretty, and you'll want a girlfriend."

"I hope so, but I don't want to talk about it now."

"Well, is it a deal, or not?"

"Deal."

"Shake on it, Son." And we did. It was another new experience to shake hands with Dad, and it felt warm and good. I felt very close to him and tried my best to understand him. I recalled that early in my days with route 7 that I'd heard the coins jingle in my pocket, and how I liked the sound. It made me think I could make a fist when I had some money. The same feeling came over me while I was shaking Dad's hand. It, too, made me feel like I could make a fist— a fist of young manhood.

"I've shared a lot with you today, Son, and I'll ask you to keep it between you and me. So don't tell your mother, sisters, friends, or anyone, at least in my lifetime."

"I'll do that, Dad. I vow I'll never tell them."

"And there's another thing I need to get your help on. Your mother sometimes fears that you'll drop out of high school, or something worse. And that'd just crush her. I guess she thinks that if I didn't finish, maybe you won't either. She wants you to be a college graduate and successful, just like I want you to do, too. So you may want to talk with her and convince her that you'll always stay in school. Will you agree to talk with her?"

"Do you really think it's necessary, Dad? It seems clear that I'm a good student and that I like school very much. There's no way I'd ever quit."

"I know that, but your mother would like to hear it from you.

It's important to her that you attend the Nazarene college that Tommie is attending. So, if you're willing, tell her that you'll go to Bethany-Peniel like Tommie is."

"That may be OK, Dad. But why is it important to you that I stay in a Nazarene group since you don't even go to church?"

"That's another long story, Son. But I'll make it short. I don't believe that God has ever given me any breaks, or good luck, so I'm angry at God and churches—all churches. But you'll have to decide for yourself about God and religion and churches. I just want to stay away from those as much as I can. But your mother has her opinions, and I think that she and you should get along. So please tell her what I've suggested about school and college."

"Dad, I'll talk to Mom; that's easy to do. What's hard to do is sit here and hear you say that you don't think God has given you any breaks. I don't know much about God, but I think I make my own breaks. And I get tired of hearing Brother White preach the way he does, and I don't believe half of what he says, but I'm not angry at churches, just disappointed about feeling trapped in order to please Mom. But I'll talk with her."

"I don't ask that you understand me, just love me and accept all of me you can because I'm your dad. Maybe someday you can understand why I feel so blue much of the time. I'll try my best."

With that said, he started the engine, backed out and headed west on Main, turned north on Fourth, and soon parked in front of our house. He told me to go talk to Mom, and then waved and grinned at me as he drove off.

Inside, I found Mom fixing some food for the next day's Sunday dinner. She was humming one of her favorite hymns, "What a Friend We Have in Jesus."

"Mom, I'd like to tell you some of my thoughts about school and church if you're willing to listen."

"Only if they are thoughts that meet my approval. If not, I'd rather not hear them."

"Oh, I think you'll like them." And I went ahead. "Mom, I really do like school, and I'm going to try to graduate as one of the top students in my high school class. So you never have to worry about me ever quitting."

"That's good to hear. And I approve of those plans."

"I plan to try to be a good football player. I don't know how good I can be, but I'm going to try. Unless I'm a good enough player to get a college football scholarship, I'll probably plan to go to Bethany-Peniel College, like Tommie is doing. But I still don't think I'll ever be a minister, and you'll just have to accept that."

"Son, I guess I've come to grips with that decision, but I still hope that you'll not ever turn a deaf ear to God's voice. He works in ways which sometimes we don't understand." And then Mom, in her special way, said, "Son, I know you'll make good grades and be successful, probably even at football. Somewhere in the Tate and Johnson bloodline is a success story waiting to be written in a bigger way than we've known up to now. The Johnsons were very successful financially until death and the depression wiped them out. And the Tates have a history of politics and education. So I imagine that business, politics, or education will be your future, especially now that you've decided against the ministry. So keep those three in mind."

"Mom, that's good advice. I've had fun learning, and I've worked hard to earn money. I like both learning and earning money. If I choose to be a teacher or a businessman, I'll vow to you to do my best to make Dad and you proud."

Then Mom chuckled in a way that I wasn't accustomed to and said, "I remember a game that was used by parents with their very young children as a way to help them know what a child would be when he grew up. While it was only a game, it was somewhat serious. And we played it with you. We lined up a Bible, a dollar, and a school book a few feet away from you and asked you to get one and bring it to us. You brought the school book. Since I wanted you to get the Bible, we did it again, and I moved the Bible closer, but you still brought the school book. I'll never forget my disappointment, but since I trained to be a teacher, I was satisfied with the school book. Maybe God wants you to be a great teacher."

"Mom, I'll try to be good at anything that I decide to do—I've always done that—and I'm satisfied that I can make mostly good decisions about my life."

"Yes, you do work hard. And you help out a great deal, and I love you for being a good son. I just will always pray that you stay committed to God."

"I'll go to church, Mom. Well, except I won't when I'm on the high school football team and there's a revival and a game the same night. Football will be first."

"You'll probably get hurt playing football, Son."

"Maybe so, but I have to play."

"Can you keep your good grades and play?"

"Sure, why not? I've always been busy doing several jobs and kept good grades."

And then I decided I'd try to clinch the argument. "Mom, since I inherited your intelligence, what else could I do but be an A student?"

She blushed, and I knew I'd won. With a few words of encouragement from her, our talk was over.

It was a satisfying morning, and I thought that I had grown up a great deal by a new closeness to Dad and a workable agreement with Mom. And I was farther along my route.

CHAPTER 21
The Ending and the Beginning

April was just around the corner. Only two more months of school and I'd finish being an eighth-grader. I was feeling much better about myself as a student, not very good about my singing and math skills, but loving history and English.

I was looking forward to August, too, so that I could quit my route. Frequently, I reminded Skip that he'd need to find my replacement by mid-August so I'd have time to teach him the route and the collection process. Skip said he was evaluating two or three subs and would make a choice in plenty of time.

And then Dad and Mom got a wonderful phone call from Tommie in Norman, Oklahoma. She and her partner, Deward Finch, had just won the national debate championship.

Dad just about went out of his mind, he was so happy. And Mom cried and praised God. Linda and I just watched them because we'd never seen them this happy. I was pleased, too, but I really didn't think it was as big a deal as winning a football championship.

Dad called Mr. "Slew" Hewett, the father of Tommie's debate partner in high school. Then he called the debate coach at Southeastern, Mr. Houston, whom Dad didn't even know. And Miss McKinney, our neighbor who taught at the college, came by to congratulate Mom and Dad.

Then Dad went to Leonard's Floral and ordered a bouquet of flowers to be sent to Tommie in Bethany. That was a first, Dad buying flowers. So I just had to ask, "Dad, if I win a championship, what'll you send me?"

He grinned as he said, "Son, the only championship you'll ever win is for the most newspapers delivered by one carrier during the war."

That struck me as odd that he said that, but it got me to thinking. Other than for the two weeks I'd quit my route, I'd delivered the *Democrat* for all of World War II and even before.

That afternoon as I was folding my newspapers, I thought that my two hands had folded all the news that the *Democrat* had printed about the war. So, I thought, even though I hadn't been old enough to be drafted, I'd helped in a small way by keeping my customers up-to-date with war news. That thought caused me to feel patriotic.

Thursday, April 12, 1945, was a cloudy, rainy day in Durant. School went all right. And I got to the *Democrat* to do my usual preparation of papers to be mailed. And then I got my route papers and folded them. Since it was raining, I got my paper sack under my extra-sized raincoat in such a way that I could reach in and get a paper to throw. Just as I was walking out the door, I heard a loud voice say, "Don't let any newsboys go. The president is dead, and we've got to rerun the front page."

Skip was nearby. "Skip," I asked, "which president?"

And Skip just about broke a young boy's heart when he said, "P.J., President Roosevelt just died in Georgia. You'll need to wait until we run an extra."

"You mean, my president? How did he die?"

"I'm not sure yet. But no one killed him. It was a natural death, I think."

And that's all I knew until I got the new edition of the *Democrat* with its very large headlines, "FDR DEAD," followed by some information.

I threw all my folded newspapers away and, as I'd been told, folded the new edition rapidly. Skip wanted all the carriers to get the papers delivered as quickly as possible because the customers would want the story. Already people were coming inside where we were folding and asking to buy the *Democrat*.

The sky outside was about as scary looking as I'd ever seen. Tornado season in Oklahoma keeps a person jittery, especially under the threat of the dark—almost black—sky that I saw when I was about to go outside to get my bike and deliver my route.

Again, "Stop the newsboys," a voice called out. Skip stopped two other carriers and me as we were leaving. We went back inside only to learn that a town about fifty miles away—Antlers, Oklahoma—had been hit by a tornado.

A second special edition would have to be published. Mr. Price, the press operator, was busier than I'd ever seen. He was giving orders left and right. "Not every day a newspaper has to do two special runs," he was saying as he moved from one place to the next.

They delayed us carriers until enough news had come in to print the Antlers story. The article estimated that between 75-100 people had been killed, that 300-400 homes had been destroyed, and many, many other persons had been injured. The downtown part of Antlers had almost been demolished.

So I got my third edition of the April 12, 1945, *Democrat* somewhere around 5:45. It was raining extremely hard, but much to my surprise, as it was to Skip and the other carriers, people were flocking in to buy the paper. I saw about thirty of my customers arrive within fifteen minutes, so I gave them their copies.

The weather was so bad that Skip wouldn't let the carriers leave, yet people kept coming to get a paper. I thought it was strange, in a way, because they could get the news on the radio, but still they wanted the *Democrat*.

That day was the only day that I didn't deliver my route, yet all my papers were either given to a route customer or sold.

I called home to tell Mom that I was safe and what I was doing. She seemed relieved. Skip let us all go home about 6:45 P.M. when the weather cleared a bit.

And as I rode the five blocks home, it began to sink in on me. My president was dead. And people nearby were dead. I hurt.

Mom had saved me leftovers, but I wasn't hungry. I sat with Mom and Dad listening to the news. The announcer said that Vice President Harry Truman had already been sworn in as president. There was a lot more, but I could hardly listen. I went to bed about 9:00 P.M. and said the most proper prayer I could think of.

The next day we students were still stunned. All the talk was either about the president's death or about Antlers. All teachers helped us understand what the death meant to our nation, especially in wartime. The radio stations, other than for news about the events of war, the death of FDR, and the new President Truman, all played sad music.

That afternoon, Friday, April 13, was collection time. Not a single customer complained about not getting a paper Thursday—not even Mr. Long. It took me an extra long time to collect because most customers kept me longer to talk about FDR's death.

Mom reminded me that President Hoover had been in office when I was born, but I'd really had just Roosevelt as my president. I did like it that my new President Truman was from Missouri. That'd make him a Cardinal fan. Well, I thought, he might be a St. Louis Browns' fan, but I quickly changed that thought. Any person who becomes president from Missouri has to root for a winner. So he had to be a Cardinal fan.

The *Democrat* printed many, many stories about President Roosevelt, his funeral, and the new President Truman. A word that I saw printed and heard talked about was *mourn*. And I guess we kids did our share.

Life went on. War news was encouraging, and then the news came that Hitler had apparently killed himself on April 30. My improper prayer had finally been answered. The Nazis were ready for surrender. And V-E Day arrived when President Truman announced that the Germans had surrendered unconditionally on May 7, even though the *Democrat* didn't print it until May 8 in a very special edition. It was one of my better days as a carrier to deliver such great news.

We had a victory party at school. Even Mr. Hall led a few victory cheers for the good ole USA. But then he reminded us how much more our troops had to do to defeat Japan.

A wonderful thing happened as I stopped by Mrs. Smith's grocery to hand her the *Democrat* and to buy a Coke and peanuts. She asked me if I liked Double Bubble.

"Mrs. Smith, you know I do. Haven't seen any since shortly after the war began. Teachers seem to think that the only good thing about the war is that we kids can't blow bubbles. Be glad when it's back on your shelf again."

"Look here, P.J.," she said as she leaned over and pulled out a box of Fleer's Double Bubble from underneath her counter. "I just got this today from my salesman. Billy Wayne hasn't seen it yet, and I don't care if he does. I'm like your teachers. His blowing bubbles just about drives me wild. So, P.J., do you want to buy the whole box?"

"You've got to be kidding me, Mrs. Smith. Take the lid off and let me see the gum with my own eyes."

And she did. One hundred of the most beautifully wrapped pieces of Double Bubble the world had ever seen! I picked out three pieces just to hold them gently and sacredly.

"Mrs. Smith, you mean you'd really sell the whole box to me?"

"Yes, for $1. A penny a piece."

Fortunately, I had $1.27 with me. I counted out a dollar's worth of change, got the box of gum, put in it my paper bag, and sprinted in race-style fashion around the rest of my route. The only thing I'd promised Mrs. Smith was not to tell a person, especially her son Billy Wayne, where I got the gum.

For several days I was the most popular eighth-grader with my friends, and I would have been the least popular student with my teachers if they'd known who gave everyone Double Bubble.

Soon school was out, and I would be a member of a class which had a name rather than a number. Even though *freshman* sounded awful, it was better than *seventh* or *eighth* grades. Now I'd have a real identity.

After school was out, I made another deposit, which gave me a total of $800. And, if I worked hard, I'd have $1,000 by the end of the summer. I had begun keeping my bank balance to myself, never discussing it with Dad or Mom. Occasionally, Mom would ask if I were paying my tithe, and I'd tell her I was.

I knew that I was ready to play football next fall. We had several good athletes in our class, as well as in the seventh grade, and we all talked about winning state in our senior year. We even had talked about our lineup to win state, but we knew the coach would have that decision to make. Someone had printed in large letters who would be on our team and the position played.

Quarterbacks: Ely and England
Halfbacks: Tomme and Wylie
Center: Smith
Guards: Attaway, Davis, Westbrook, Paul
Tackles: Johnson, Mills, Atherton, Robinson
Ends: McElreath, Hurst, Herron, Hughes, Tidwell

So we looked forward to our senior team, the team we hoped would win it all in '48. Someone put our team names on a handmade poster in the Lion's Den, a small "Coke and hamburger" store next to the junior high school and across from the high school. Mr. and Mrs. McQueen, the owners, let it hang there.

We kicked a lot of footballs and caught a lot of passes that summer, dreaming about the big games that were ahead.

August 6 came with another extra large headline: "ATOMIC BOMB DROPPED ON HIROSHIMA." The article discussed the very destructive results. We carriers knew the war was about over.

Then on August 9, we dropped the bomb on Nagasaki, leaving that city in ruins and killing many people. The *Democrat* covered the news well. On August 15, an article told about the Japanese accepting surrender, and on that day I began training a sixth-grader for my route. His name was Thomas. A decent kid, but he seemed so young to take on such a responsible job. I really didn't know whether he could meet my standard or not. While delivering, he missed seven porches and had to park his bike and go place the paper on the porch. And he met Miss Woodward and Mrs. Lively.

That Friday, when I collected with Thomas, I introduced him to them and told them he'd be their news carrier on September 1. I'd see them next Friday for my last collection. I got a small "thank you note" printed to give to my customers and inserted it into Thursday's *Democrat* before my last collection day.

And they once again showed me their thanks on that last collection Friday. It was really, really tough to quit.

And the war was over the first week of September! Durant danced in the streets! Durant celebrated! Durant's cars honked! I decorated my old bike with red, white, and blue streamers and paraded around up and down Main Street, waving an American flag. And there was Mr. Snow, marching in his World War I uniform, guided by his children. He seemed very happy.

I'd grown up during the war, and I'd been a kid, too, but war did something to me. I never wanted another one.

I went to Truby studio a few days later to pick up the picture I had made to give to Skip. I liked it. There was a fourteen-year-old freckled-faced, big-eared, redheaded young kid with his arms extended slightly with his palms up. I printed a caption with my very best penmanship, which said, "AROUND THESE HANDS WAS FOLDED

· 224 ·

THE *Durant Daily Democrat* WITH ALL THE NEWS PUBLISHED BY THE BEST NEWSPAPER IN THE WORLD OF WORLD WAR II. THANKS, SKIP."

I let Tommie look at my picture and the words I'd written. She laughed.

"What's so funny?" I demanded, feeling a bit hurt.

"This is too maudlin," she responded.

"What's that mean?"

"As I've told you a thousand times, look it up for yourself."

"OK, I will, but how do you spell it?"

"M-A-U-D-L-I-N," she said with emphasis on each letter.

Getting my dictionary, I found it. I guess she meant all of my stuff was too sentimental. Well, that's the way I meant it to be. Maudlin or not, I was going to give it to Skip.

And on the first Saturday of September, I bought a 5x7-inch frame to put the picture in and took it by the *Democrat* and gave it to Skip. He got up from his squeaky chair and gave me a hug. That was the first hug I'd ever had from a man. In many ways, Skip had been like a dad to me. And we went to the Durant Drug Store, where I bought him a Malt-O-Plenty.

I told him that if I ever became a millionaire, I was going to build a statue of him and put it in front of the *Democrat* building, right on the Third Street sidewalk. He laughed and thanked me.

As we departed, I thought I'd also build a statue of Mr. Garrison and put it on the lawn of Washington Irving High School.

My paper route was over. Another route was just beginning. P.J. looked forward to it.

Epilogue

The downtown area of Durant, Oklahoma, has changed dramatically from the downtown of my youth. While I understand the multiple necessities for these changes, nevertheless, viewing the area which seemed vital to my youth almost breaks my heart and pierces my soul. The vestiges of a busy retail family of stores with its community of voices and cacophony of business activity are missing. The town—all of it—helped me to become better than I might have been otherwise. And the *Durant Daily Democrat* and the many other purchasers of my youthful services helped mold me into a productive adult.

It is probable that the giant supermarkets, busy drive-in banks, large shopping centers, and quick-order restaurants may—and I emphasize MAY—offer today's youth a quality of life that by their perceptions fulfills the same, or similar, needs that my downtown provided me. But I still highly value the downtown of my youth as part of my extended family which helped to initiate me, inculcated into me many good values, and modeled many adequate roles of men (and women) for me to follow.

The expansion of Durant has obliterated route 7. The beautiful old houses on West Main and the fragile, yet comfortable, houses south toward the Frisco railroad are about ninety-eight percent razed. In their place stand monuments to air-conditioned quick service, especially huge automobile sales areas, restaurants, businesses, and new bypassing U.S. Highways 69 and 75, accompanied by motels and filling stations.

What takes the place of community? Where does the inculcation of values into today's youth occur? Family, church, school, athletics, boys and girls groups—yes! And more are needed. I have no answers to suggest here. Perhaps that's another book.

WHATEVER HAPPENED TO ... AND MORE:

- Harrell Garrison received his doctorate and served for many years as the president of Northeastern Oklahoma State University in Tahlequah.
- Mr. Frank V. (Skip) Bunn retired from the *Democrat* in 1982, but maintained a desk there and worked until his death in 1997 at age ninety-four. There is a city park named in his honor. The headline of an article in the *Democrat*, July 16, 1993, stated, "'Skip' Had Positive Impact on Young Lives." I had not maintained any contact with him and had written this entire book before "rediscovering" Skip's local heroic status. My experience with him as a youth was validated once again.
- Mack McElreath married Steveanna Harrison (Stevie in the book), and they live in Duncan, Oklahoma, where they own and manage a successful Mexican restaurant, El Palacio.
- George Boyet lives in Napa, California, with his wife, Mary Ellen. George is retired after teaching many years at Napa Junior College. Mary Ellen, whom George met in Napa, is a retired high school teacher of French. They are world travelers.
- John Shaw lives in Austin, Texas. He is a retired executive of IBM. His wife, Sally, is an attorney.
- Our Durant High School class of '49 football team won all of our home football games at Paul Laird Field, but we did not win the state championship. Just wait until our next lifetime!
- The Johnson family made it in various ways, some good, some sad. Tommie Earleen graduated from Bethany-Peniel College (now Southern Nazarene University) summa cum laude and married Milton Parrish, a Nazarene minister and a church district superintendent. Milton was a member of the D-Day invasion troops, and he remained a chaplain in the U.S. Army

Reserve until his retirement. Their daughter, Mrs. Gary (Debbie) Clark, lives with her husband in Oklahoma City.
- Linda graduated from Bethany-Peniel College also. She lives near Oklahoma City.
- The old maroon '39 Mercury got a new sibling in 1950—a new two-tone brown Mercury. Dad kept the old one to carry his electrical supplies to jobs. Dad drove to Bethany in the new Mercury in my sophomore year after I'd broken my foot again. I was on crutches, and he wanted to make certain that I'd be able to continue my "route." While there he gave me a $20 bill and a twenty-minute lecture on frugality. That event helped me to "close the books" on the mostly unpaid loan I'd made to him.
- Dad discontinued making TRI-PURE vanilla in the late '50s. I still have on my hearth the five-gallon jug, which had held hundreds of gallons of that wonderful "muddy water," as his customers called it. Occasionally, I take the old cork out of the jug and revisit the wonderful fragrance of my "vanilla youth."
- We have a beautiful magnolia tree in our backyard in Commerce, Texas, which we bought from Foote Nursery on route 7.
- Mom died from cancer in 1955; Dad from cancer in 1968.
- The *Durant Daily Democrat* is now located at North Second and Beech. It was purchased in 1988 by Community Newspapers Holding, Inc., of Birmingham, Alabama, which owns many other newspapers. The owners of the *Democrat* of my youth, the Storys, sold the newspaper to Bob and Dick Peterson. Later owners were the Donrey Media Group and the Stephens Group.
- The *Democrat* now has about twenty-four carriers with an average route of 250 customers. The monthly subscription fee for the six-day-a-week *Democrat* is $7, and the average monthly salary for each carrier is around $600. Nearly all carriers deliver from a car or truck. The average size of the paper is fourteen pages, with daily circulation ranging between 6,500 and 7,000. Can the reader imagine what P.J. would have done with $600 a month as a young carrier!

And now for P.J. I made it, too. I received the B.A. degree in 1953 from Bethany-Peniel College (now Southern Nazarene University) magna cum laude. In August 1954, I earned the Ed.M. in Guidance from the University of Oklahoma. Having served in the U.S. Army until August 1956, I returned to OU to begin my doctorate in Guidance. While there, through a tennis-playing friend, I was reintroduced to Norma Hewett, a younger sister of my high school tennis doubles partner. They are in the book. Norma had attended Wellesley College for two years but returned to OU so she could receive a public school teaching certificate.

We married in 1957 and lived two years in Salina, Kansas, where Norma taught in the third grade and I at Kansas Wesleyan University.

Returning to OU to finish my doctorate, we not only got my degree, but also were excited over the birth of our first daughter, Amy.

In August 1961, I received my doctorate and moved to Commerce, Texas, where I was employed by East Texas State University (now Texas A&M—Commerce). (An aside: This is the alma mater of my Highway 82 man—Sam Rayburn.) Our younger daughter, Ellie, was born in 1962. We have lived in Commerce since, except for a one-year absence (1966-67) to assist in the opening and managing of the Job Corps Center for Women in Guthrie, Oklahoma. The center is still open to both women and men.

I retired in 1995 after thirty-five years of teaching in a university setting. Norma received the master's degree and doctoral degree from East Texas State University (now Texas A&M—Commerce). She taught both at the university and in the sixth grade in Greenville, Texas, and retired in 1996. I now have the status of professor emeritus.

I was privileged to conduct, along with Dr. Patricia (Pat) Love, ten years of workshops in Texas to provide continuing education to licensed professional counselors. Literally thousands of persons attended our workshops. As a licensed professional counselor, I also maintained a small private practice.

Amy and Ellie graduated from the University of Texas at Austin, both Phi Beta Kappa. Amy received the J.D. from Harvard Law School, clerked for one year for the U.S. district judge of the Eastern District of Texas, William Wayne Justice, served three years as Governor Ann Richards' appointee as public insurance counsel, and is presently an environmental attorney. She is married to Michael Savage, M.D., and they have a daughter, Rachel. Ellie worked in a prison system setting, received her master's degree in counseling from Arizona State University, worked as a therapist for the Lutheran Family Service Center in San Antonio, and later received her Ph.D. in psychology from the University of Oregon. She did a pre-doctoral internship at the Veterans Administration Hospital in Seattle, Washington, and a post-doctoral internship in Brownsville, Texas. She is married to José Domínguez, M.S., who is a systems analyst at the University of Oregon. They have two daughters, Emily and Allison.

All in all, my route has continued to be productive and enjoyable.

And Coach Marsh, the one who lost to the Sherman, Texas, Bearkats 84-0 in his first year as coach, finally got satisfaction when his basketball team defeated the Bearkats 105-18 in 1946. And his team didn't have to forfeit for playing an ineligible player!

Finally, even though I've already lived a "long life," I expect to live many more years provided that if one "honors his father and mother, his days will be long upon the earth," because to the best of my recall, I did "honor" them both.

About the Author

PAUL JOHNSON was born and reared in Durant, Oklahoma, graduating from Durant High School in 1949. He holds a B.A. degree from Bethany-Peniel College (now Southern Nazarene University) and Ed.M. and Ed.D. degrees from the University of Oklahoma. After two years in the U.S. Army, he married Norma Hewett in 1957. In 1961 they moved to Commerce, Texas, where he taught for thirty-three years in the Department of Counseling at East Texas State University (now Texas A&M-Commerce). He now holds the title of professor emeritus at the university. Among many activities and pleasures of his life, he enjoys golf, politics, and spending time with his wife, his daughters Amy and Ellie and their husbands, and three granddaughters.